Fridtjof Siebert

Hard Real-Time Garbage Collection
in Modern Object Oriented Programming Languages

Dr. Fridtjof Siebert
aicas GmbH
Haid-und-Neu-Straße 18
76131 Karlsruhe, Germany
siebert@aicas.com
http://www.aicas.com

ISBN 3-8311-3893-1

Die Deutsche Bibliothek – CIP-Einheitsaufnahme
Ein Titelsatz dieser Publikation ist bei
Der Deutschen Bibliothek erhältlich.

Fridtjof Siebert: Hard Real-Time Garbage Collection in Modern
Object Oriented Programming Languages, Dissertation Universität Karlsruhe.
Books on Demand Ausgabe Mai 2002
Verleger: aicas GmbH, Karlsruhe
Herstellung: Books on Demand GmbH
Umschlaggestaltung: Fridtjof Siebert
Satz: Reprofertige Vorlagen vom Autor

Zur Erlangung des akademischen Grades eines Doktors der Ingenieurwissenschaften von der Fakultät für Informatik der Universität Karlsruhe genehmigte Dissertation von Fridtjof Siebert aus Stuttgart.
Tag der mündlichen Prüfung: 9. Juli 2001
Erster Gutachter: Prof. Dr. Walter Tichy
Zweite Gutachter: Prof. Dr. Jochen Liedtke
und Prof. Dr. Gerhard Goos

Abstract

Modern object oriented programming languages such as Java or Eiffel use automatic garbage collection. This feature provides safe memory management that protects the user from hard to debug programming errors and difficult to maintain programs on the one hand and secure execution of untrusted code on the other hand. A typical garbage collector consists of four phases: 1. Root scanning: all objects that are referenced by root references are marked; 2. Mark: all objects reachable from marked objects are marked as well; 3. Sweep: all objects that are not marked are known not to be reachable and their memory is freed; and 4. Compact: Allocated objects are moved such that free memory becomes a contiguous range.

Even though a significant amount of research in the area of automatic memory management was carried out in the last decades, current implementations do not provide useful or provable real-time guarantees. Thus, garbage collection cannot be used in a wide range of real-time applications. The main difficulties are four aspects of the garbage collector: Support for multiple threads, root scanning, fragmentation of the heap and deciding when to run the garbage collector. This dissertation presents techniques that solve these difficulties. A garbage collector using these techniques has been implemented and is used in a new implementation of a Java virtual machine and a static compiler for Java. This implementation guarantees a worst-case execution time of a few thousand (Power-PC-) machine instructions for an allocation of a small object (32 bytes), while the system uses up to 70% of the available memory. The implementation offers a run-time performance that is comparable to traditional, non-real-time Java implementations.

To be able to support several threads, so called *synchronization points* are used. All activities of the garbage collector occur only at these points and it is convenient to restrict scheduling of threads to these points as well. The compiler automatically inserts synchronization points into the code such that an upper bound on the thread preemption delay can be given.

During root scanning, all objects that are referenced by local variables or processor registers are marked. This marking typically requires suspending the examined thread, which leads to delays that are hard to predict. In a hard real-time system, all delays must be predictable. The solution proposed in this dissertation is to ensure that copies of all root references are stored on the heap whenever a synchronization point is reached. In between synchronization points, root references do not need to be stored on the heap. The compiler automatically generates code to store the root references. The data structures that are used to store these copies are all reachable from a single root object. Consequently, all stored root refernces are reachable from this single root object and the root scanning phase is reduced to marking this object. Marking the copied root references becomes part of the garbage collector's mark phase. It is shown in this thesis that the overhead for saving copies of root references is limited and does not prevent an efficient implementation.

Allocation and deallocation of objects of different sizes in a system with dynamic memory management can cause fragmentation. Fragmented memory is unused memory in small non-contiguous ranges that cannot be used to satisfy larger allocation requests. Fragmentation can cause severe loss of memory utilisation that is hard to predict. Current implementations often use compaction to fight fragmentation. Compaction causes difficulties when short real-time guarantees are required for the tasks of moving arbitrarily large objects and adjusting arbitrarily many references to an object that has been moved by the memory management system. Since moving objects around seems to inherently contradict the predictability requirements of real-time systems, the compaction approach has been dropped. Instead, an object model based on non-movable blocks of a fixed size is used. Objects and arrays are constructed from several blocks that need not be contiguous in memory. The surprising result is that this object model permits an efficient runtime performance.

The decision when to run the garbage collector in a real-time system must ensure that the runtime spent for garbage collection is predictable and limited, while it also must guarantee that sufficient memory will be recycled such that all allocation requests can be satisfied. Current implementations typically use a separate thread for the garbage collector.

This thread can perform garbage collection work during processor idle time. However, this approach makes predictions on the overhead and efficiency of the garbage collector extremely hard. The solution presented here does not use a separate thread for garbage collection. Instead, the garbage collector is activated within an application thread whenever this thread allocates memory. The amount of garbage collection work performed is determined dynamically as a function of the size of the free memory. It is shown that this work is sufficient to recycle enough memory. A reasonable upper bound for this work can be given.

The presented techniques solve problems that so far prevented the use of modern object oriented programming languages in real-time systems.

Zusammenfassung

Hart echtzeitfähige Speicherbereinigung in modernen objektorientierten Programmiersprachen

Moderne objektorientierte Programmiersprachen wie Java oder Eiffel benutzen automatische Speicherbereinigung (Garbage Collection). Dies ermöglicht eine sichere Speicherverwaltung, die einerseits den Benutzer vor Programmierfehlern und schwer wartbaren Programmen schützt, und andererseits eine sichere Ausführung von nicht vertrauenswürdigem Code erlaubt.

Ein typischer Speicherbereiniger besteht aus vier Phasen: 1. Wurzelidentifikation (Root Scanning): Alle von Wurzelzeigern erreichbaren Objekte werden markiert; 2. Markierung: Alle von markierten Objekten erreichbaren Objekte werden markiert; 3. Sammlung (Sweep): Alle nicht markierten Objekte sind unerreichbar und werden freigegeben; und 4. Kompaktierung: Allozierte Objekte werden so verschoben, dass der freie Speicher ein zusammenhängender Bereich wird.

Obwohl sich in den letzten Jahrzehnten sehr viel Forschung mit automatischer Speicherbereinigung beschäftigt hat, geben derzeitige Implementierungen keine nützlichen oder beweisbaren Echtzeitgarantien. Speicherbereinigung kann in vielen Echtzeitanwendungen nicht eingesetzt werden. Die Probleme liegen dabei vor allem an vier Aspekten des Speicherbereinigers: Die Unterstützung mehrerer Fäden (Threads), die Wurzelidentifikation, die Bekämpfung der Speicherfragmentierung und die Entscheidung, wann der Speicherbereiniger aktiviert wird. In dieser Dissertationen werden neue Techniken vorgestellt, die diese Probleme lösen. Ein Speicherbereiniger und darauf aufbauend eine virtuelle Maschine und ein statischer Compiler für Java wurden implementiert. Die Implementierung garantiert für eine Allokation eines kleinen Objektes (32 Bytes) eine Ausführungszeit von wenigen tausend (PowerPC-) Maschineninstruktionen während das System 70% des Arbeitsspeichers ausnutzt. Die Implementierung bietet eine Laufzeitperformance, die vergleichbar ist mit der herkömmlicher, nicht echtzeitfähiger Java-Implementierungen.

Um mehrere Fäden zu unterstütztn werden Synchronisationspunkte verwendet. Alle Aktivitäten des Speicherbereinigers sind auf diese Punkte beschränkt. Es ist sinnvoll, auch das Scheduling von Fäden auf diese Punkte zu beschränken. Um das Scheduling innerhalb einer beschränkten Zeit zu erlauben, stellt der Compiler sicher, dass Synchronisationspunkte häufig genug in den Code eingefügt werden.

Während der Wurzelidentifikation werden alle Objekte markiert, die von Referenzen in lokalen Variablen oder Prozessorregistern erreichbar sind. Dies erfordert typischerweise das Anhalten des untersuchten Fadens, und führt damit zu schlecht voraussagbaren Unterbrechungen. Die in dieser Dissertation vorgeschlagene Lösung ist es, vom Compiler sicherzustellen, dass alle Wurzelzeiger bei Erreichen eines Synchronisationspunktes auch auf der Halde gespeichert sind. Die Datenstrukturen, die für diese Speicherung benötigt werden, sind alle von einem einzigen Wurzelobjekt aus erreichbar. Dadurch wird die Wurzelidentifikationsphase auf das Markieren dieses einen Objektes reduziert, das Markieren der gespeicherten Wurzelzeiger verlagert sich in die Markierungsphase. Es wird in dieser Arbeit gezeigt, dass der Aufwand für das Speichern der Wurzelzeiger begrenzt ist und einer effizienten Implementierung nicht im Weg steht.

Allokation und Deallokation von Objekten unterschiedlicher Größen in einem System mit dynamischer Speicherverwaltung verursacht Fragmentierung. Fragmentierung ist das Problem, dass kleinere, nicht zusammenhängende freie Speicherbereiche für gröflere Allokationen nicht genutzt werden können. Dies kann zu erheblichem, schlecht vorhersagbaren Verlust an Speicherausnutzung führen. Bisherige Implementierungen verwenden häufig Kompaktierung des Speichers, um Fragmentierung zu bekämpfen. Dies verursacht jedoch Probleme, wenn kurze Echtzeitgarantien für das Verschieben von beliebig groflen Objekten und das Anpassen von beliebig vielen Referenzen auf ein verschobenes Objekt benötigt werden. Da das Verschieben von Objekten den Anforderungen an Vorhersagbarkeit offenbar völlig widerspricht, wurde die Idee der Kompaktierung verworfen. Stattdessen wird ein Objektmodell basierend auf nicht verschiebbaren Blöcken fester Gröfle verwendet. Objekte und Felder werden aus mehreren, möglicherweise nicht aufeinanderfolgenden Blöcken zusammengesetzt. Das überraschende Ergebnis ist, dass dieses Objektmodell eine effiziente Ausführung erlaubt.

Die Entscheidung, wann der Speicherbereiniger in einem Echtzeissystem aktiviert wird, muss sicherstellen, dass der Aufwand für den Speicherbereiniger vorhersagbar und beschränkt ist, während andererseits garantiert werden muss, dass ausreichend Speicher vom Bereiniger zurückgewonnen wird, damit alle Allokationen bedient werden können. Bisherige Implementierungen benutzen typischerweise einen separaten Faden für den Speicherbereiniger. Dieser Faden kann ansonsten ungenutzte Rechenzeit für die Speicherbereinigung nutzen. Vorhersagen über den Aufwand und die Effektivität sind damit jedoch nur äußerst schwer möglich. Die hier vorgestellte Lösung benutzt keinen separaten Faden, sondern aktiviert den Bereiniger bei jeder Allokation. Die Menge an Speicherbereinigungsarbeit bei einer Allokation wird dynamisch als Funktion der Gröfle des freien Speichers bestimmt. Es wird gezeigt, dass für jede Applikation mit beschränktem Speicherbedarf diese Arbeit ausreichend ist, um genügend Speicher zurückzugewinnen, und dass eine obere Schranke für diese Arbeit angegeben werden kann.

Die vorgestellten Techniken lösen die Probleme, die bisher den Einsatz moderner, objektorientierter Programmiersprachen in Echtzeitsystemen verhindert haben.

Contents

Wir sprechen von den komplexen Abläufen im Hirn, im Gemüt, im endokrinologischen Bereich – zum Erfassen der intimsten Zusammenhänge haben wir einzig diese vage Sammelvokabel: Komplexität. Nichtssagender geht es kaum. Solche Wörter sind uns nur im Weg.

Sie haben geradezu inhibitorische Wirkung. Sie hemmen den Geist darin, seiner Technik auf die Schliche zu kommen. Man unterschätze nicht die „Botenstoffe" der Sprache. Es gibt geisthemmende und geiststimulierende Begriffe.
–Botho Strauß

1. Introduction

1.1 Motivation

Modern object oriented programming languages such as Java [AG98], Eiffel [Meyer92], etc. rely on the concept of automatic garbage collection to provide safe memory management. Garbage collection protects the user from hard to debug programming errors and difficult to maintain programs on the one hand and provides secure execution of untrusted code on the other hand. C-style explicit memory allocation and reclamation techniques are a major obstacle for object oriented programming [Meyer88].

Even though a lot of research in the area of automatic memory management has been carried out in recent decades, current implementations of garbage collectors still fail to give useful or proven real-time guarantees on their runtime performance. While modern programming languages are to a growing extent applied for the development of systems that require real-time guarantees, such as embedded systems used for controlling or monitoring of technical devices, garbage collection is not applicable in these systems. Standards for real-time programming using the Java language that are currently being defined sacrifice automatic memory management and security to make this language suitable for real-time systems [RTJEG00, JCons00]. The resulting crippled Java language lacks an important part of the benefits of modern object oriented programming languages. Some of the benefits that come with the use of Java in non-real-time systems are hence not available for the development of real-time systems.

1.2 Garbage Collection Basics

The most widely used algorithms for garbage collection in object oriented languages such as Java are based on the mark-and-sweep or mark-sweep-compact algorithms [McCarthy60, Edwards]. Garbage collection with these algorithms is a cyclic process. A single garbage collection cycle consists of several phases illustrated in **Figure 1.1**. These phases are

Root Scanning

All objects on the heap that are referenced by root variables are marked. Root variables are all variables that are not stored in the heap itself, i.e., variables on the runtime stacks of all threads, within processor registers or in global variables that are stored outside of the garbage collected heap.

Mark

During the mark phase, all objects on the heap that are reachable from marked objects will be marked as well. This phase continues until no new objects can be marked, i.e., until all objects that are reachable from root references are marked.

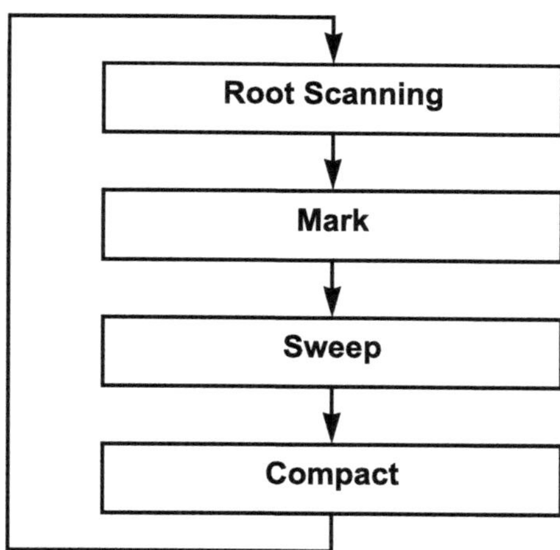

Figure 1.1: Phases of a typical *mark-sweep-compact* garbage collection cycle.

Sweep

After the mark phase, all allocated objects that have not been marked are known to be unreachable. These objects are garbage; their memory can be reused. Thus, during the sweep phase, the heap is traversed and all unmarked objects are added to free memory.

Compact

Identifying unused objects and freeing their memory is unfortunately not sufficient. After the sweep phase free memory will in general be non-contiguous. This fragmentation of memory makes small ranges of free memory unavailable for allocations of larger objects and can eventually lead to severe loss of memory utilization. The common solution to this problem is the use of an additional compaction phase during which all allocated memory that survived the sweep phase is moved such that free memory forms a single contiguous range.

In an incremental garbage collector, these four phases must be executed in small increments of garbage collection work while the application continues its execution and modifies the heap. For the garbage collector to be hard real-time, the amount of work to be done in these increments must be predictable and it must be guaranteed that the garbage collector recycles sufficient memory to satisfy the application's allocation requests.

1.3 Definitions of Basic Terms

For brevity, this dissertation uses vocabulary that is established in the memory management and real-time communities without giving explicit definitions of all the terms that are used.

A comprehensive glossary of memory management terms that was originally collected by Harlequin is now maintained by Xanalysis software tools. It is available online [Xanalys01]. A good reference for terms used to describe real-time systems is Jane Liu's book [Liu00].

1.4 Contributions of this Work

The contribution of this work is the development of missing techniques that make garbage collection practical and efficient for modern object oriented programming languages for real-time applications with tight timing constraints. The main contributions are as follows.

1.4.1 Synchronization of Threads and Garbage Collection

To be able to support several threads, so called synchronization points are used. All activities of the garbage collector occur only at these points. It is convenient to restrict scheduling of threads to these points as well. The compiler automatically inserts synchronization points into the code such that an upper bound on the thread preemption delay can be given.

1.4.2 Root Scanning

During root scanning, all objects that are referenced by local variables or processor registers are marked. Marking typically requires suspending the examined thread, which leads to delays that are hard to predict. The solution proposed here is to ensure that copies of all root references are stored on the heap whenever a synchronization point is reached. In between synchronization points, root references do not need to be stored on the heap. The compiler automatically generates code to store the root references and to remove the stored references of roots that are deleted. The data structures that are used to store the copied references are all reachable from a single root object. Consequently, all stored root refernces are reachable from this single root object and the root scanning phase is reduced to marking of this object. Marking of the copied root references becomes part of the garbage collector's mark phase. To avoid inconsistencies when storing roots while marking is going on, write barrier code ensures correct marking of stored roots. It is shown that the overhead for saving copies of root references is limited and does not prevent an efficient implementation.

1.4.3 Non-Fragmenting Object Model

Allocation and deallocation of objects of different sizes in a system with dynamic memory management can cause fragmentation. Fragmented memory is unused memory in small, non-contiguous ranges that cannot be used to satisfy larger allocation requests. Fragmentation can cause severe loss of memory utilisation that is hard to predict. Current implementations often use compaction to fight fragmentation. This compaction causes difficulties when short real-time guarantees are required for the tasks of moving arbitrarily large objects and adjusting arbitrarily many references to an object that has been moved by the memory management system. Since moving objects around seems to inherently contradict the predictability requirements of real-time systems, the compaction approach has been dropped. Instead, an object model based on non-movable blocks of a fixed size is used. Objects and arrays are constructed from several blocks that need not be contiguous in memory. The surprising result is that this object model permits an efficient runtime performance.

1.4.4 When to Run the Garbage Collector

The decision when to run the garbage collector in a real-time system has to ensure that the runtime spent for garbage collection is predictable and limited, while it also must guarantee that sufficient memory will be recycled such that all allocation requests can be satisfied. Current implementations typically use a separate thread for the garbage collector. This thread can perform garbage collection work during processor idle time. This approach, however, makes predictions on the overhead and efficiency of the garbage collector, as required in a real-time system, extremely hard. The solution presented here does not use a separate thread for garbage collection. Instead, the garbage collector is activated within an application thread whenever this thread allocates memory. The amount of garbage collection work performed is determined dynamically as a function of the size of the free memory. It is shown that this work is sufficient to recycle enough memory. A reasonable upper bound for this work can be given. This upper bound will be determined in number of machine instructions on the Power-PC processor.

1.5 Structure of this Dissertation

Following this introduction, this dissertation starts with a description of the problem in chapter 2, *Problem Statement.* An overview of the state of the art and related work is then given in chapter 3, *State of the Art and Related Work.*

Chapter 4 gives an overview of the approach that will be presented in the subsequent chapters. The following three chapters describe techniques that have been developed for the solution: chapter 5, *Threads and Synchronization,* presents basic synchronization between threads and garbage collection work, chapter 6, *Root Scanning,* presents a technique for performing root scanning incrementally, and chapter 7, *Fragmentation,* presents an object model that avoids fragmentation and hence avoids the need for compaction. Following the presentation of these techniques, their integration into a new garbage collector implementation is described in chapter 8, *GC Algorithm, Write Barrier and Heap*

Layout. The activation of this garbage collector that ensures worst-case execution times for the collector is then described in chapter 9, *Garbage Collector Activation.*

The following chapter 10, *Deterministic Execution of Java's Primitive Operations,* focusses on the real-time aspects of the complete Java implementation, including those that are not directly affected by the garbage collector. Finally, the implementation is analysed in chapter 11, *Evaluation of the Implementation*, and an example for the determination of worst-case execution times in real-time critical systems is presented.

Some chapters are partly based on previous publications. The affected chapters and the corresponding earlier publications are: *5. Threads and Synchronization* [Siebert99.1], *6. Root Scanning* [Siebert01], *7. Fragmentation* [Siebert00], *8. GC Algorithm, Write Barrier and Heap Layout* [Siebert99.2], *9. When to Run the Garbage Collector* [Siebert97, Siebert98] and *10. Deterministic Execution of Java's Primitive Operations* [SW01]. Techniques used in the developed Java implementation and compiler were previously published as well [WdFD+98].

Chapters 4, 5, 6, 8 and 9 are addressing different and partly unrelated aspects of the presented technology and implementation. To facilitate the quick comprehension of the different techniques, these chapters are written such that reading the complete thesis is not required to understanding one of these chapters. Unfortunately, readers of the complete thesis will find some redundant information due to this fact. I apologize for this and recommend skipping the few redundant paragraphs.

Appendix A lists tables of the numerical values that are illustrated graphically in the figures throughout this text.

It would be so nice to forget about memory.
–Bertrand Meyer

2. Problem Statement

Subject of this thesis is the development of techniques for hard real-time garbage collection in the context of the implementation of modern object oriented programming languages such as Java. A proof shall be given for a hard upper bound for the worst-case execution time of an allocation of an object that is in the order of a few thousand machine instructions while the application uses 70% of the available memory for reachable objects.

The efficiency of the approach shall be examined by implementation of a virtual machine, runtime environment, standard classes and a static compiler for the execution of Java in bytecode format.

2.1 Definition of Hard Real-Time Implementation of a Programming Language

A hard real-time implementation of a programming language is an implementation that enables static determination of worst-case execution times (WCET) for the language's primitive operations in a given application. This means that the WCET can be determined before the application is actually executed by the user, possibly with the help of tools that analyse the application's resource requirements.

A simple way to guarantee a WCET on an operation is to cause some kind of exceptional situation in case the deadline given by the WCET is not met. E.g., one might imagine a system that guarantees a WCET of 0.5 milliseconds for the allocation of an object. In case the allocation can not be performed within this limited execution time, an exception such as *OutOfMemoryError* or *TimeOutException* is thrown. Such a system is of little use since the user has no guarantee that the operations actually execute in the desired way within their guaranteed WCET. This motivates the second requirement for a hard real-time implementation of a programming language: Any primitive operation must be executed successfully within its WCET bound.

Real-time systems typically perform several different periodic or sporadic tasks with different frequencies, execution times and real-time deadlines [Liu00]. Different scheduling techniques such as earliest-deadline-first or rate-monotonic scheduling are used for timely execution of the tasks. An important requirement of the scheduling algorithm in most of these systems is that tasks must be able to preempt running tasks in bounded time. For the language implementation, this requirement means that thread preemption times must be bounded by a worst-case preemption time (WCPT). The WCPT gives an upper bound for the time that is required for a high priority thread to become active (e.g., as a result of an external event) while a lower priority thread is running.

Finally, practical real-time systems are often manufactured in large quantities and the cost of a single unit is an important parameter. To reduce costs, the cheapest (slowest, smallest) hardware should be used. For some applications, simpler technology is preferred to improve the reliability in hostile environments. Consequently, WCET and WCPT should be short and the systems memory requirements should be low enabling the use of cheap and robust hardware.

In summary, the following four requirements for the hard real-time implementation of a programming language have been identified:

1. Statically determinable worst-case execution times (WCET) for primitive operations;
2. Successful execution of primitive operations within WCET bound;
3. Bounded worst-case thread preemption time (WCPT); and
4. WCET and WCPT must be small, i.e., in the order of a few thousand machine instructions, and the systems memory overhead must be low, i.e., the percentage of memory that is actually used by the application must be a significant fraction (50% to 100%) of the total memory.

2.2 Requirements for a Hard Real-Time Garbage Collector

In the context of automatic memory management, the relevant primitive operations are

1. Memory read accesses for objects and arrays
2. Memory write accesses for objects and arrays
3. Allocation of objects and arrays

The hard real-time implementation of a garbage collected memory management system must ensure worst-case execution times for these operations, it must guarantee the successful execution of these operations (including the allocation!), and it must enable thread preemption within bounded time. For the implementation to be useful in real systems, the worst-case execution times and thread preemption times must be small and the overall memory overhead of the systems must be low.

2.3 Difficulties

There are a number of difficulties that arise for the implementation of a hard real-time garbage collector as just defined. These difficulties include

- the garbage collector must guarantee detecting and recycling garbage memory;
- object and array access code and any additional read or write barrier code (see [Pirinen98]) that may be required by the implementation must provide short worst-case execution times;
- the garbage collector must give guarantees on its performance – a test that the system 'works' is not sufficient;
- the garbage collector must be exact, i.e., it must not use any conservative pointer identification techniques that may prevent it from recycling unreachable memory;
- the garbage collector must guarantee that allocation does not fail due to memory fragmentation;
- the garbage collector must never prevent preemptive scheduling of another thread for more than a short and bounded time; and

- the garbage collector must catch up with the application and recycle memory quickly enough to satisfy all allocation requests.

Furthermore, there are a number of other difficulties that arise in the real-time implementation of a modern object oriented programming language such as Java. Guarantees on the worst-case execution times of primitive operations are required. The primitive operations that cause difficulties include

- dynamic method invocation in the context of single and multiple inheritance (class extension and interface implementation in Java parlance);
- type checking; and
- thread synchronization (monitors).

The aim of this dissertation is to provide solutions to these difficulties and to permit the use of modern object oriented programming languages such as Java in the domain or real-time and safety-critical applications.

2.4 Limitations

For the memory management technique presented in this work, only minimal limitations for the application domain are to be made. The limitations that could not be avoided are

- the target system must either be a single processor system;
- or, if it is a multi processor system, several threads that modify the same garbage collected heap can never run concurrently on different processors; and
- an upper bound for the amount of reachable memory used by the application is known.

Limiting the technique to a single processor clearly reduces its application domain. Future research might lead to a relaxation of this limitation. However, on a single processor, any number of threads may still execute in the usual, interleaved of 'quasi-parallel' fashion.

Requiring an upper bound for the memory used by the application instead is a requirement that cannot be relaxed on any finite system. Requiring bounded memory for real-time systems is common practice, traditional real-time system even use static allocation to avoid any unpredictability due to dynamic memory allocation. The presented technique enables dynamic allocation and garbage collection as long as an upper bound for the amount of memory used by the application is known.

3. State of the Art and Related Work

A significant amount of work was carried out in the area of automatic memory management. This chapter can only give a short overview of the publications relevant to real-time systems and techniques that are used or similar to those presented in this thesis. A more detailed discussion of related work that concentrates on certain aspects of the algorithms appears in the following chapers.

3.1 Overview on Garbage Collection Techniques

For a general overview on garbage collection techniques, the book written by Jones and Lins is a good start [JL96]. Wilson compiled a comprehensive survey of garbage collection techniques for single processor machines [Wilson92, Wilson94].

Bengtsson and Magnusson give a short overview of 'real-time' garbage collection techniques (copying, mark-and-sweep, generational), comparing the efficiency for different heap configurations [BM90]. A good survey of non-garbage collected dynamic storage allocation techniques is given by Wilson et. al. [WJNB95].

3.2 Early Work on Real-Time Garbage Collection

The first garbage collectors where developed in the early days of LISP programming. A short description of the automatic memory reclamation process is given in a publication by John McCarthy [McCarthy60], even though it was not referred to as garbage collection.

The difficulties of garbage collection in real-time systems were discovered soon and solutions for real-time garbage collections were developed: D. G. Bobrow described a system that allows incremental garbage collection using a write barrier that notifies the collector of changes in the memory graph made by the application in 1968 [Bobrow68]. The garbage collector runs as a separate thread. Read and write barriers are used to enable accessing of objects that may be moved by the collector and to inform the collector about changes made to the heap. No solution for root scanning is given and it can be expected that the approach causes a significant runtime overhead.

Donald E. Knuth's classic *The Art of Computer Programming* [Knuth73] credits M. Minsky on how real-time garbage collection may work, but leaves the remainder of the solution as an exercise for the reader.

3.3 Incremental and Concurrent Mark-and-Sweep Garbage Collectors

An emphasis of previous research was to enable that a garbage collector runs concurrently with the main application program (the mutator) or performs its work in small increments. Widely applied is the three-colour marking described by Dijkstra et. al. [DLMSS78]. The algorithm uses two phases: *mark* and *sweep*. The first phase marks all reachable memory, while the second phase adds the remaining unmarked memory to the free list. The algorithm permits concurrent execution of the garbage collector and the application program. A write barrier ensures consistency of the system. The write barrier is special code executed whenever a reference value is written into the heap. It informs the collector about the change of the memory graph.

Dijkstra introduced three different colours, *white*, *grey* and *black* to describe the marking state of an allocated object. The colours have the following meanings

white The object has not been found to be reachable yet.

grey The object has been found to be reachable, but objects directly referred to by this object may still be *white*.

black The object has been found to be reachable and no objects directly referred to by this object are *white*.

The mutator and the mark phase of the garbage collector have to ensure the invariant that no *black* object contains a direct reference to a *white* object.

At the beginning of the garbage collection cycle all objects are *white*. Then, all objects that are directly referenced from a root references are marked *grey* in an atomic operation before the mark phase starts. The invariant trivially holds at the beginning of the mark phase since there are no *black* objects.

The *mark* phase of the collector takes a *grey* object *o* at a time and shades all *white* objects reachable from this *grey* object. Then it shades the object *o* itself *black*. The invariant remains valid since no objects referenced from *o* are *white*.

The write barrier has to shade objects whenever a reference assignment violates the invariant. This is the case in an assignment of the form

```
a.f = b;
```

if the object referred to by *a* is *black* and the object referred to by *b* is *white*. To keep the invariant intact, the object referred to by *b* is shaded *grey* in case its colour is *white* using the following write barrier code.

```
if (colour(b)==white) {
   colour(b) = grey;
}
a.f = b;
```

To make the write barrier more efficient, the colour of *a* is not checked by the write barrier. *b* will consequently be shaded *grey* in some cases where this is not necessary to keep the invariant valid (whenever *a* is *white* or *grey*, the colour of *b* does not need to be changed from *white* to *grey*). The result is a more efficient write barrier.

The *mark* phase ends as soon as there are no *grey* objects left; all objects are either *white* or *black*. The invariant then ensures that all reachable objects are *black* since all root objects were shaded *grey* at the beginning of the cycle, no object's colour was changed to white, and there are no *grey* objects left. Hence, all *white* objects are known to be unreachable from root references.

During the sweep phase, these *white* objects are then added to free memory and the colour of *black* objects is reverted to *white* for the next cycle to start with all objects being *white*.

Dijkstra extends this algorithm to avoid the need for fine-grain synchronization between the garbage collector thread and the mutator thread. The algorithm without this synchronization, however, does not permit the use of several concurrent mutator threads.

Queinnec et. al. suggest running the mark and sweep phases concurrently (mark-during-sweep), so that two threads or processors are performing garbage collection and the overall performance of the system is improved [QBQ89]. Wallace and Runciman [WR93] combine this approach with a small stack for marked objects in their incremental collector that is supposed to be used in embedded real-time systems. Unfortunately, the quadratic worst-case execution time of their implementation disqualifies it for many applications. Huelsbergen and Winterbottom further improve mark-during-sweep by avoiding fine-grain synchronization [HW98].

A promising extension of Dijkstra's mark-and-sweep garbage collection algorithm for multiprocessor systems is presented by Doligez and Gonthier [DG94]. Unlike Dijkstra's algorithm, this algorithm permits several concurrent application threads. A more complex write barrier and a sophisticated synchronization mechanism at the beginning of a GC cycle enable parallel garbage collection without fine-grain synchronization. When a reference is written to the heap, the write barrier requires marking of the overwritten reference value or the new value depending on the state of the concurrent garbage collector thread. The garbage collector uses a three phase synchronization mechanism at the beginning of a collection cycle. All application threads need to react to the collector's synchronization requests regularly (e.g. by executing special code inserted into the control flow by a compiler). The first two phases of the synchronization ensure termination of all memory related operations, while the third one requires all application threads to mark the root references local to the thread, such as references on the thread's runtime stack.

The approach is interesting since it avoids the need of fine-grain synchronization for systems with multiple mutators and multiple processors. Only at the start of a garbage collection cycle, the described synchronization process is required. During the cycle the collector and the application threads do not interfere with one another.

Unfortunately, the infrequent synchronization of all threads that is required by the approach for root scanning causes bad worst-case execution and thread preemption times, and the collector does not give guarantees on actually recycling sufficient memory. Additionally, the approach fails to remove fragmentation, but this could be fixed using the object model that will be presented in chapter 7.

Domani et. al. have recently extended the algorithm by Doligez and Gonthier with Java-specific features and implemented it for Java [DKP00, DKLS+00]. The algorithm was extended to support finalization, weak references and (String-) intern tables as required by Java. Support for conservative scanning of thread stacks for root references was added since accurate information on where to find references is not available in their implementation. Enhancements were made to support multiprocessor architectures with out-of-order memory accesses. The performance was measured and compared to a stop-the-world mark-sweep collector using a multithreaded benchmark on a multiprocessor system. The concurrent collector performs better if more than three application threads are used. Response times are reported to be short and evenly distributed for their implementation. Measured maximum response times were 100ms for 7 threads or less and 540ms for more threads.

Conservative stack scanning, memory fragmentation, unpredictable synchronization and lack of progress guarantees by the collector make this approach not applicable to hard real-time systems.

Dubé, Feeley and Serrano present a real-time garbage collector [DFS96]. The approach uses a mark-compact scheme that incrementally moves objects.

All references use an additional indirection through a handle. This permits updating of references of moved objects. A special read- and write barrier is used to access large objects that are moved incrementally to avoid long pauses. For small objects, no read barrier is needed since these objects can be moved atomically without too long a pause. For small objects, only a write barrier is needed to inform the collector of changes in the memory graph.

In this approach, the garbage collection work is performed whenever an allocation occurs. The amount of garbage collection work is the product of the size of the object that is allocated and a constant value called *ratio*. This *ratio* is calculated off-line as a function of the maximum amount of reachable memory in the system. The calcuation takes into account the work that needs to be performed in the mark and compaction phases of the collector. The *ratio* is selected such that the amount of memory allocated at the beginning of a garbage collection cycle never exceeds a certain bound and that every garbage collection cycle terminates before the system's free memory is exhausted. This calculation is similar to the static garbage collection progress that will be presented in this chapter 9.

The algorithm was implemented within a rudimentary Scheme interpreter. Some basic runtime measurements were made using a Fibonacci function written in Scheme and comparing the results to a non-real-time Cheney-style garbage collector [Cheney70] (see section 3.4 below). The real-time garbage collector causes a slowdown of a factor 3 in this simple test.

An important drawback of the algorithm is a limitation on the number of root references, which makes the approach impractical for languages that store references in runtime stacks of arbitrary sizes. Also, the extreme slowdown even in an interpreted environment will make this approach impractical for many applications.

3.4 Two-Space Copying Garbage Collectors

Baker's copying real-time collector [Baker78] is the first GC to provide real-time guarantees on allocation (CONS operations in LISP) coupling garbage collection work and allocation and using knowledge of the memory requirements of the system to control the amount of garbage collection work. The algorithm is based on the ideas of Fenichel and Yochelson [FY69] and the improvement by Cheney [Cheney70]: The heap is divided into two semi-spaces: *from-space* and *to-space*. During collection, all live objects from *from-space* are evacuated into *to-space*. When all objects reside in *to-space*, the role of both spaces is swapped (the 'flip') and the next collection cycle begins. Drawbacks of the approach are high memory demand for the two semi-spaces (*from-space* and *to-space*) and bad runtime overhead due to the use of read barriers. Baker also proposes generalizing the mechanism for objects of arbitrary sizes (such as arrays) by incrementally copying them.

Brooks improves Baker's algorithm by introducing a forwarding pointer in all objects that either points to the object itself (if it resides in *to-space* or has not been moved yet), or to the *to-space* copy of an object in *from-space* that has been moved to *to-space* [Brooks84]. All accesses to the object are performed through the forwarding pointer, avoiding different treatment of *from-* and *to-space* objects and improving total runtime performance of the system at a cost in memory overhead.

Baker later proposed a simplification of his original algorithm that avoids moving objects [Baker91]. He calls this new algorithm the 'treadmill'. It uses a circular double linked list of all objects, different regions of this list correspond to *from-space*, *to-space* and free memory. Unfortunately, this algorithm has difficulties when dealing with objects of different sizes. Fragmentation can cause serious worst-case memory loss (the number of different allocation sizes used times the maximum amount of memory used).

Wilson and Johnstone [WJ93] have further improved Baker's algorithm avoiding the overhead caused by a read barrier used in the original approach and using segregated storage to manage different sized chunks of memory. They provide no good solution for fragmentation in their approach either. Limiting the allocation size to powers of two reduces the worst case loss due to fragmentation at a high cost of internal fragmentation (padding of chunks to the next power of two), while worst-case fragmentation can still be large.

Nettles and O'Toole [NT93] avoid the overhead due to the read barrier in Baker's copying collector by a replication scheme and change logs that record changes made to an object residing in *from-space*. Their implementation achieves GC pause times in the order of tens to hundreds of milliseconds, which is sufficient for most systems using an interactive user interface, but not for real-time control systems.

Blelloch and Cheng describe a multiprocessor real-time extension of Baker's original two-space copying collector [BC99]. Large arrays are copied incrementally, so that the collection work is split up into several small chunks, and a replication scheme similar to the Nettles and O'Toole implementation is used to avoid the read barrier. The biggest drawback of the approach is root scanning at the beginning of a GC cycle and flipping of the two semi-spaces at the end of a cycle. For these operations all processors are interrupted and need to mark all the objects referenced from their registers or change the references from *from-space* to *to-space*, respectively. In a system that stores local values on the processor stack, all references stored on the stack would have to be treated just as references stored in processor registers causing a long pause time (linear in the size of the stack) for these operations. Since updating of the references is required, it would be difficult to apply an incremental scanning technique such as that presented in chapter 6 to avoid this pause.

3.5 Conservative Garbage Collectors

Conservative garbage collectors are used when no information on the exact whereabouts of references is available (e.g., when garbage collecting the heap of a C or C++ program), or the overhead of maintaining exact information up-to-date appears to be prohibitively high (as for references stored in local variables on the stack or in processor registers). In a conservative garbage collector, references are identified by looking at the values of data stored in memory that may contain references. Any bit pattern that is a valid object reference is considered a reference, even though it may as well be any other data like a floating point number that happens to be a valid reference.

A good example of an incremental conservative collector is the Boehm-Demers-Shenker collector [BDS91]. It uses virtual memory hardware to enable the garbage collector to run concurrently with the applications and it gives short average pause times.

Joel F. Barlett describes how a partly conservative garbage collector that does not have exact information on the references in registers and stacks can compact the heap by moving only those objects that are known not to be referenced by a pointer in a register or on the stack that was identified conservatively [Barlett88].

Hennessey [Hennes93] proposes a conservative 'real-time' garbage collector based on Baker's treadmill algorithm [Baker91]. The implementation provides poor maximum pause times of 8-30ms due to atomic root scanning, does not fight fragmentation and cannot give guarantees on its effectiveness due to conservative scanning.

Hirzel and Diwan have conducted experiments to measure the effect of different levels of accuracy of pointer identification on the effectiveness of garbage collection [HD00]. Their approach used two runs of a set of test applications. The first run was used to identify the locations that hold references, the second run then used this information to collect statistics. An important result is that the hardware platform has an important impact on the effectiveness of conservative pointer identification. On a Alpha/UNIX, a 64-bit machine, conservative scanning was effectively reclaiming unused objects, the number of falsely identified references was very low. Instead, on 32-bit machines such as SPARC, type accuracy can be important and can avoid larger numbers of pointer mis-identifications.

All conservative approaches have in common that they cannot give guarantees on their performance: A value that is misidentified as a reference may keep the collector from recycling or moving some object. Since this object itself may reference an arbitrarily large data structure, the collector may fail to detect an arbitrarily large amount of garbage memory, resulting in unpredictable system failure. Such a system can give no guarantees on its performance, not to mention real-time guarantees [Wentw90]. Worse, such a system is vulnerable to attacks that exploit knowledge about the conservative garbage collector implementation that can cause system failure due to low memory!

3.6 Hardware-Supported Garbage Collectors

Since pure software solutions to the real-time garbage collection problem have posed severe difficulties, many hardware-supported approaches were proposed. The first one was presented by Guy L. Steele Jr. [Steele75], who proposes a two-processor system. One processor executes a LISP-application, while another processor is responsible for garbage collection without interrupting the execution of the application. Steele defines a synchronization method between the GC and the application processors that allows parallel relocation of objects, describes a mechanism for concurrent access to the free list by both processors and uses write- and read barriers to ensure correctness. For an efficient implementation, Steele suggests the design of specialized processors. An unsolved issue in such a system is to guarantee sufficient progress of the garbage collecting processor in the case that the application allocates memory faster than it can be recycled. I do not know of any implementation of this approach.

Nilsen and Gao also present hardware supported real-time garbage collection. Their approach goes a step further than Steele's by proposing an independent memory module that is connected to the system's memory bus. This module gives an abstract view of a garbage collected heap and an encapsulation of garbage collection related features such as read or write barriers. The garbage collected module can be treated similar to normal memory. The system proposed by Nilsen is based on Baker's two-space copying algorithm [Baker78].

Appel, Ellis and Li [AEL88] propose using virtual memory hardware to implement read- and write barriers and implement a real-time collector based on Baker's algorithm [Baker78]. This approach is not appropriate for many embedded real-time system since virtual memory hardware is often not present in such systems and the worst-case execution times of memory accesses are likely to be unacceptably high due to the traps each memory access may cause.

A novel approach to garbage collection that uses *on-chip multithreading* in new processor architectures has been presented by Heil and Smith [HS00]. So-called service threads are used to perform garbage collection work and write barrier code. The hardware profiling features of these architectures perform the required write barrier code for store-instructions. The collector runs as a separate thread on the same processor using a concurrent non-copying generational garbage collection algorithm (see next section). The performance of this system was analysed using simulation. The largest pause time that was observed was 53,000 clock cycles, the average runtime overhead of the garbage collector was only 0.6%.

3.7 Generational and Age Based Collectors

Many so-called generational garbage collector implementations are based on the heuristic that old objects tend to live longer than younger ones. This idea was first presented by Lieberman and Hewitt [LH83]: Generational collectors restrict frequent collections to a subset of the total heap that contains the youngest objects (the youngest generation) to reduce the average pause times and total garbage collection overhead. A major problem of this approach in a system that requires real-time guarantees is that it is based on heuristics that may not hold for the actual application. The original generational heuristic together with the experience that references tend to link young objects with old objects more often than old objects with young objects do not hold for all applications. Worse, the heuristics were developed for LISP systems and there is little research on whether they also hold for modern object oriented systems. For the application of generational garbage collection in a hard real-time system, a quantitative measure needs to be found to determine the degree to which a given application behaves as expected by the heuristics.

Sharma and Soffa presented a parallel implementation of a generational collector that is capable of concurrently running several collectors [SS91].

A 'real-time' implementation of a generational collector was presented by Engelstad and Vandendorpe [EV91]. Collection work is coupled with allocation and based on heuristics that control the amount of collection work so that the system is less likely to run out of memory. However, the scheme doesn't seem to give any guarantee that enough collection work will be performed for the system not to run out of memory. The authors have measured that this implementation bounds garbage collection pause times to 0.5-10ms, which is just enough to use it for interaction with humans, but not for most technical applications of real-time controllers. Even if one considers the higher processor speeds that are available today, one can expect that this approach will not perform significantly better on todays hardware taking the larger memory sizes into account that are used in today's systems.

A 'quasi real-time' generational collector was presented in [DL93] for Concurrent Caml Light, a multi-threaded implementation of ML. A crucial prerequisite for this implementation is the notion of mutable and immutable objects in ML. The latter can be duplicated, so that each mutator (thread) can have its own private young generation heap that holds copies of these objects. Other objects are allocated in a shared heap, the old generation. Each thread performs the garbage collection of its own private young generation. A separate thread is responsible for collecting the shared heap using an extension of the Dijkstra et. al. algorithm [DLMSS78]. This approach ensures an upper bound for the pause times of private collections, but it cannot guarantee sufficient progress of the collection of the shared heap, requiring unpredictable stopping of threads to wait for the termination of this collection or extension of the address space whenever the garbage collector does not catch up with the allocation speed of the application.

The mature object space algorithm (the train algorithm) described by Richard L. Hudson and J. Eliot B. Moss attacks the difficulties that arise in a generational collector when collecting the old generation, which usually requires a long disruptive garbage collection pause [HM92]. The space of the old generation is split up into many small 'cars' that are collected one car at a time. Cars are grouped into trains in a way that all objects in a large cyclic structure eventually end up in the same train and can be recycled as soon as there are no references left to the whole train. The biggest problem of the train algorithm is the quadratic time that detection of garbage may take in the worst case.

Recent research indicates that the heuristic that generational collection is based upon may be improved [SMcKM99]. The basic idea of this *age-based* garbage collection is first to sort objects by their age measured in allocation time. Then the collection should be limited to the subrange of the allocated memory that has the highest object 'mortality'. To find this subrange, the collector starts collecting the oldest region of the heap. After each cycle, this region is moved toward the younger objects immediately next to the survivors of the collection of the current region. This way, the collected region slides down towards younger objects until it remains relatively stable at an area of high mortality (i.e., low survival rate). Simulation has shown that this approach can significantly reduce the cost of copying in a generational collector. The problems of this approach are that cyclic structures that extend over the collected region cannot be recycled and that tracking inter-generational pointers is more complex compared to a generational collector that only distinguishes between 'young' and 'old' objects.

3.8 Root Scanning

Root scanning is the task of finding all references to objects on the heap that are present outside of the heap itself in local or static variables or in processor registers. Little work has been published in the area of root scanning for real-time garbage collection.

Christopher presented an interesting approach that is based on reference counting and that avoids the need of scanning root references that are stored outside of the heap [Christop84]. The idea is that all objects with a reference count higher than the number of references from other heap objects to this object must be reachable from a root reference outside the heap. All the objects reachable from such a root reference are then used as the initially marked set in the marking phase of the garbage collector. The disadvantage is the high runtime overhead that is required to keep the reference counts accurate: any assignment between local reference variables needs to ensure that the reference counts are adjusted correctly.

Shaham, Kolodner and Sagiv have analysed the time objects are in use by different Java applications and compared this time with the time these objects are reachable and hence retained by the garbage collector [SKS00]. They found a potential in the range from 23% to 74% of memory savings for the applications they analysed. The savings are possible if objects are reclaimed after their last use and not retained until they become unreachable. A large fraction of these objects are retained due to references on the stacks. Many of these objects can be reclaimed early if root scanning takes the lifetime of local variables on the stack into account, which is done by the root scanning mechanism that will be presented in chapter 6.

3.9 Scheduling Garbage Collection

Some research has also been done in the area of scheduling garbage collection in a real-time system:

In the system proposed by Roger Henriksson [Henrik97, Henrik98], real-time guarantees for memory management of some high-priority processes can be given as long as low-priority processes that are interleaved with the garbage collection process obtain sufficient CPU time. This time has to be sufficient so that the system can perform enough recycling work to satisfy the allocations performed in the high-priority processes. Henriksson bases his collector on Baker's algorithm [Baker78] and reserves enough space in the target *to-space* so that high-priority processes can allocate their objects even right before a flip of *from-* and *to-space*.

Kim et. al. [KCKS99] describe a way to schedule a garbage collection task in a system with periodic and sporadic real-time tasks using the sporadic server approach. The scheduling requires knowledge on the allocation behaviour (amount of allocation within one period) of all real-time tasks to ensure schedulability of the garbage collector.

3.10 Restricting GC Activity to GC-Points

Several papers proposed restricting GC work to certain points during the execution, such as [Agesen98], [SUN99.2] or [AFGHS00]. This restriction reduces the need for accurate information on root pointers and write barriers outside of these *GC-points*. A specialized compiler or interpreter inserts *GC-points* in the code. It has been shown that, for a specific architecture, it is even feasible to reduce the granularity of these *GC-points* to single machine instructions by providing detailed information on the whereabouts of references without causing too much overhead [SLC99].

Arnold et. al. go even further in the Jalapeño JVM and restrict thread switches to certain points in the code [AFGHS00]. They refer to these points as *yield points*. These *yield points* are inserted automatically by the compiler at method prologues and on loop back edges to support quasi-preemptive thread scheduling. A special bit within the processors is used to check for the need to call the scheduler. This bit is set periodically using a timer-interrupt mechanism. The publication does not describe the effects these *yield points* have on the garbage collector implementation. A similar approach and its effects on the garbage collector will be presented in chapter 5.

3.11 Empirical Studies

Johnstone analysed the actual fragmentation of the heap during the execution of different real applications using different allocation strategies [Johnstone97, Johnstone98]. The result is that, in contrast to 'random'-simulations, the fragmentation caused by real programs tends to be low in practice if a good allocation placement strategy is employed. Johnstone implements a non-compacting real-time garbage collector expecting that fragmentation will not be an issue. Unfortunately, the fragmentation analysis is not done with garbage collected systems, so that it is hard to generalize the results to the delayed memory reclamation process caused by a garbage collector. Furthermore, empirical results on fragmentation are of no help in hard real-time or safety-critical systems that need to give guarantees on their effectiveness and efficiency.

Dieckmann [Dieckm99] analysed the memory usage of the Java programs in the SPECjvm98 benchmark. One of her results is that the generational heuristic that young objects die young holds for the tested programs, but that it is less pronounced compared to other programming languages such as SML/NJ or Smalltalk. Most of the tested programs allocate normal Java objects and arrays in similar numbers, while the fraction of live memory used for arrays varies significantly between 25% and 100%. Another result of the analysis is that reference values typically occupy less than 50% of the heap data. Most of the heap is used for non-reference data such as *int* or *char* values. The average sizes of Java objects allocated varies between 12 and 23 bytes, while the average sizes of arrays differ strongly, but the average sizes are below 100 bytes in most cases. The average size of objects and arrays together is fairly small: between 17 and 30 bytes in the analysed programs.

3.12 Live Memory Analysis

Persson presented a method for predicting the maximum amount of live memory in object oriented languages [Persson99]. The amount of memory used is predicted by a static analysis of the program and its data structures. Annotation of the source code by the user is needed to bound the size of recursive data structures. The resulting maximum amount of live memory can be used to configure the heap size in a real-time garbage collector that needs a bound on the percentage of the heap that is used for live memory, as all real-time garbage collection algorithms that guarantee that the system does not run out of memory do.

In contrast to this approach for live memory analysis, the approach proposed in chapter 11 makes use of automatic runtime analysis of an application and manual memory analysis if the automatic analysis is not sufficient.

3.13 Real-Time Garbage Collection for Java

Alex Garthwaite and Scott Nettles published the first paper presenting incremental garbage collection for Java [GN97]. A write barrier was added and a backpointer from every object to its handle was introduced to enable incremental compaction. Unfortunately, little information on the performance or possible real-time guarantees of their implementation is available from this publication.

Harris proposed a novel static analysis of Java programs that permits automatic detection of garbage after scanning a part of the heap by exploiting knowledge of the class structure of the application and the type information of fields [Harris99]. He defines a may-refer-to relation between classes, and the garbage collector can recycle unmarked objects as soon as all objects of classes that may refer to the unmarked object's class have been scanned.

Nilsen identified the potential of Java for real-time systems programming and listed the important requirements for a real-time extension of Java [Nilsen96]: Determination of worst-case and actual execution times of functions, task priorities for rate monotonic analysis [LL73], static cyclic schedules and real-time garbage collection based on allocation rates [NG95].

Two competing specifications for real-time extensions for Java are being defined: the Real-Time Java Experts Group defines additional APIs for real-time features [RTJEG00], while the J-Consortium specifies a Real-Time-Core [JCons00] which is a separate runtime environment and programming language that resembles standard Java, but that cannot be mixed directly with normal Java code. Well defined interfaces enable the interaction of the Real-Time-Core code, which is supposed to contain time critical functionality, with non-real-time standard Java code.

3.14 Building Objects out of Blocks

The idea to build data structures out of uniform blocks all the same size is at least as old as the first Lisp systems. Its application to object oriented programming language is fairly new.

The architecture developed in the Mushroom project uses a two-level addressing scheme [WW93]. An address consists of an *object identifier* and an offset selecting a word in the object. The offset is limited to eight bits. Larger objects are constructed in software from smaller object similar to a filesystem that presents the illusion of a file as a contiguous stream of bytes which is in reality implemented as separate blocks on the disk. Unlike the block model presented in chapter 7, the motivation for the block structure in the Mushroom project is the limitation of the offset to eight bits, not the need to avoid fragmentation.

Rounce [Rounce91] described an architecture that uses a tree structure of blocks of equal size to represent lists. This representation is similar to the array structure proposed in chapter 7.

4. Overview of the Approach

Before the next chapters will describe the techniques developed in this dissertation in more detail, this chapter gives a short overview of the overall approach.

The garbage collector is based on Dijkstra's incremental mark-and-sweep algorithm. The difficulties that need to be overcome first before this algorithm can be used in a real-time environment are the root scanning phase and memory fragmentation. Then, the algorithm needs to be implemented such that it can operate in small incremental steps. Finally, the garbage collection work has to be performed such that sufficient memory is recycled while worst case execution times for allocation can be guaranteed.

4.1 Use of Synchronization Points

An important prerequisite of the approach is the introduction of synchronization points that will be described in chapter 5. The execution of garbage collection code is restricted to these points, such that a consistent view of the heap needs to be established by application code only at these points. Additionally, thread switching is also restricted to synchronization points such that heap operations in different application threads that lie in between synchronization points are automatically atomic. This atomicity of short code sequences is important for the implementation of the write barrier shown below.

4.2 Root Scanning

The root scanning phase of the garbage collector is practically eliminated completely. The implementation ensures that all locally used references are copied into dedicated data structures on the heap at a synchronization point. These data structures are all reachable from a single global root pointer.

During root scanning the garbage collector needs only mark this single global root pointer. To ensure the consistency between garbage collector and mutator, write-barrier code is executed when local references are copied to the heap.

4.3 Fragmentation

The approach does not move objects to compact the heap. To deal with fragmentation, the heap is treated as an array of blocks of a single fixed size. Objects occupy at least one block, larger objects are constructed out of a graph of several blocks. These blocks may be non-contiguous in memory, so fragmented memory can still be used for allocation.

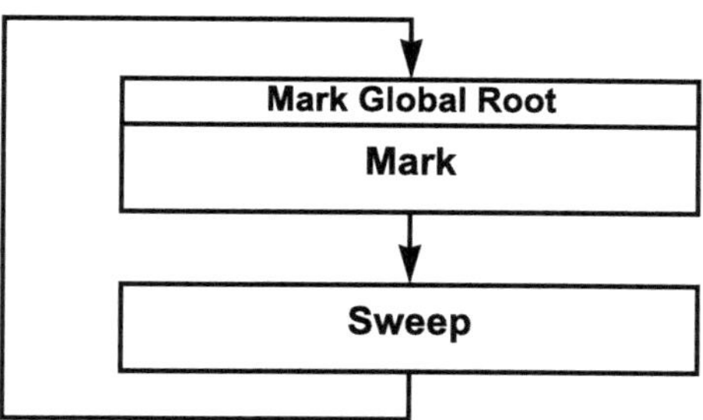

Figure 4.1: Phases of the garbage collection cycle:
The mark phase starts with marking of the global root pointer
and then incrementally marks all reachable blocks.
The sweep phase then adds all unmarked blocks to the free list.

The root scanning of all copied local references is done incrementally during the mark phase. There is no need for a compaction phase.

4.4 Garbage Collection Algorithm

With the reduced root scanning phase and the lack of a compaction phase, the garbage collection cycle of the mark-and-sweep collector consists of the mark and sweep phases only as shown in **Figure 4.1**. The mark phase is preceded by the marking of the global root pointer.

The garbage collector does not know about the structure of objects. It works on single fixed size blocks. A bit-vector is used to mark the position of reference words within blocks. The incremental steps of the mark and sweep phases perform work on a single block for each step.

4.5 Garbage Collector Invariant

Each block has an associated colour as in Dijkstra's algorithm. These colours are

white The block has not been found to be reachable yet.

grey The block has been found to be reachable, but the objects referred to by this object may still be *white*.

black The block has been found to be reachable. It was examined by the mark phase and all objects directly referred to by this object are either *grey* or *black*. This means that this block must have been reachable at the beginning of the current garbage collection cycle.

The garbage collector and the application threads have to ensure that the Invariant

INV No *black* object refers directly to a *white* object

holds during the collector's mark phase. The invariant ensures that each sequence of references that starts from a black block and ends with a *white* block has at least one intermediate *grey* block.

This invariant is invalidated whenever a reference to a *white* block is stored in a *black* block. Additional write barrier code needs to be executed to ensure that the invariant remains true even for these reference stores. The write barrier code for the assignment $b.f = r$ is illustrated in **Listing 4.1**.

```
if (gc_mode != SWEEP) {
  if ((r != null) && (colour(r) == white)) {
    colour(r) = grey;
  }
}
b.f = r;
```

Listing 4.1: Write barrier code for the store operation *b.f* = *r*. The object referenced by *r* is marked *grey* if it is *white*.

At the beginning of a garbage collection cycle, all blocks are *white*. The root scanning at the beginning of the mark phase marks the global root block *grey*.

One incremental step of the mark phase takes a *grey* block *b* from a global list of all *grey* blocks (s.b.) and marks all *white* blocks that are referenced by *b* *grey*. Then it marks *b* *black*. The mark phase finishes as soon as there are no grey blocks left.

Since the global root block was marked *grey* at the beginning of the mark phase, the colour of no block is set to *white* during the mark phase, and there are no *grey* blocks left after this phase, the global root block is *black*. Thus, the invariant ensures that all reachable blocks are *black* at the end of the mark phase. All *white* blocks are unreachable.

The sweep phase now traverses all blocks and frees the memory of *white* blocks, while it reverts the colour of *black* blocks to *white*.

4.6 Using a Linked List for Grey Blocks

For the efficient implementation of the mark phase, *grey* blocks must be found in constant time in each incremental step of this phase. To enable constant time retrieval of *grey* blocks, all *grey* blocks are stored in a linked list. One machine word of memory is reserved for the colour of each block. This word is used as a link reference for the list of *grey* blocks. The colours *white* and *black* are encoded using special values that are not valid references.

When a linked list of *grey* blocks is used, the write barrier code has to add a block to the *grey* list to mark it *grey*. The code for the assignment *b.f* = *r* using this list is illustrated in **Listing 4.2**.

```
if (gc_mode != SWEEP) {
  if ((r != null) && (colour(r) == white)) {
    colour(r) = grey_list;
    grey_list = r;
  }
}
b.f = r;
```

Listing 4.2: Write barrier code for the store operation *b.f = r*. A linked list *grey_list* of *grey* blocks is used.

4.7 Performing Garbage Collection

Garbage collection is performed in short code sequences that treat a single block at a time during the mark and sweep phases. The total number of blocks that need to be marked or swept is bounded by the amount of allocated memory.

Garbage collection work is performed at allocation time only. Chapter 9 presents a method to determine the number of blocks that need to be marked or swept at the allocation of one block of memory. This method guarantees that the garbage collector recycles sufficient memory to satisfy all allocation requests by the application. An upper bound for the execution time of an allocation can be given for applications with bounded memory requirements.

4.8 Overview of the Java Implementation

To show the performance of the presented garbage collection approach in real applications, its behaviour when applied to Java programs was analysed. To do this, it was not sufficient to just implement the garbage collection technique. Due to the significant impact of the presented techniques on all aspects of a language implementation, it was required to develop a complete Java implementation from scratch. Re-using an existing implementation and adopting it to use a modified garbage collector was rejected regarding the significant changes that would have been required, not to mention legal intellectual property issues.

4.8.1 JamaicaVM

The resulting Java implementation is called *JamaicaVM*. It started as a full Java virtual machine implementation that was capable of interpreting Java bytecode with Java's features like exceptions, threads, dynamic class loading, reflection, etc.

For running real applications such as those in the SPECjvm98 benchmark suite [SPEC98], an implemention of Java standard libraries, notably the packages *java.lang, java.lang.reflect, java.io* and *java.util*, was added.

The Java Native Interface *JNI* [SUN97] was implemented in the JamaicaVM to enable the use of native code (code written in programming languages like C). In addition to this, a simpler and more efficient second interface for native code, the *Jamaica Binary Interface*, was implemented for the native code used in the standard libraries.

4.8.2 Builder Utility

Time-critical applications often occur in embedded systems. These systems typically have limited ressources (memory and CPU-power), they often have no file-system or network connection and usually they lack a standard user interface (screen, keyboard, mouse). For executing Java applications in these systems, the JamaicaVM has been extended by a *builder* utility that constructs a single executable file out of a set of Java applications and the Jamaica virtual machine. The executable file can then be stored in ROM or Flash memory and executed on systems that do not have a file-system. Nevertheless, the Java application created by the builder are full Java applications, in particular they still support dynamic class loading.

To cope with the tight ressource restrictions in embedded systems, the builder has been extended by features that reduce the memory demand of Java applications:

Classfile compaction

A more compact format is used to store Java class files in ROM/Flash.

Smart Linking

Smart linking is the process of detecting and eliminating unused methods and fields in a program. The builder includes an optional smart linking facility. However, this optimisation is not applicable to programs that use dynamic class loading since the smart linking process cannot predict what methods or fields will be accessed by classes that are loaded dynamically.

Execution out of ROM/Flash

Java bytecodes are not copied into RAM when classes are loaded. To save RAM, the classfile data is accessed directly in its compact ROM format.

4.8.3 Static Compiler

Java implementations typically use sophisticated *just-in-time* compilation techniques to enhance the runtime performace of Java applications. Since just-in-time compilation causes significant variations in the execution time of a method, this technique is not suitable for real-time systems. Nevertheless, a compilation technique is needed to obtain reasonable performance. In JamaicaVM, a static compiler was implemented that compiles the methods of a Java application given in bytecode format into C source code, that can then be compiled into executable machine code for the target system. The compiler has been included in the builder utility such that compilation becomes a seamless part of the build process.

The compiler generates code that takes into account the special needs of the garbage collector. It knows about the object model that is based on fixed size blocks, it generates synchronization points that allow thread switching, it generates code to save local references to the heap and it generates write-barrier code when references are modified.

To achieve better performance, the compiler performs standard optimizations including common subexpression removal, dead code elimination, loop invariant optimization similar to those described in [WdFD+98]. Special optimizations eliminate redundant runtime checks such as null-pointer or array bounds checks.

Java bytecode is very compact compared to the machine code generated after compilation. To find a good trade-off between execution time and code size, the compiler can be controlled by profiling data to compile only a given percentage of the methods most executed frequently.

Der Täter ist dem Tun nur hinzugedichtet – das Tun ist alles.
–Nietzsche

5. Threads and Synchronization

One of the biggest problems for a real-time garbage collector is the support for multiple application threads. In this chapter, a mechanism for synchronization between threads and the activities of the garbage collector will be presented. It will also be shown how this mechanism can be used to maintain exact information on root references and how it can be used to optimize write barrier code. Finally, some of the aspects and implications of this mechanism for a Java implementation will be discussed.

This chapter is based on a previous presentation at the Real-Time Systems Symposium 1999 in Phoenix [Siebert99.1].

5.1 Introduction

The difficulties caused by synchronization between the garbage collector (GC) and several mutator threads have so far made an implementation of an exact, incremental, hard real-time garbage collector for such widely used languages as Java [AG98] impossible. Because of the lack of reliable GC, Java cannot be used in a wide area of real-time applications.

Multi-threaded systems complicate garbage collection significantly, but threads are also a required prerequisite for serious system development. The implementation is further complicated when incremental and exact garbage collection [Wilson98] is required: The garbage collector activity is intertwined with the execution of the main program (the mutator) and communication between GC and the mutator-threads is required.

For incremental scanning of the memory-graph to be correct, most garbage collection algorithms rely on a write barrier to inform the collector about changes made by the mutator [Pirinen98]. The write barrier code typically requires writing a word or a bit conditionally to indicate the change of the graph, in addition to the actual memory write required for an assignment.

Write barrier code often must not be preempted by GC activity. On standard hardware, it cannot be implemented using a single atomic instruction. Additional locking code is required to ensure atomicity.

There exist few garbage collectors that do not require this locking. One is presented by Huelsbergen and Winterbottom [HW98], but this algorithm is limited to a single mutator thread and not applicable to multiple mutator threads. Another one is the multi-processor garbage collector by Doligez and Gonthier [DG94]: This approach uses a significantly more complex write barrier that marks both references, the assigned and the deleted one, and it uses a complex synchronization of all threads at the beginning of each garbage collection cycle. This approach is nevertheless similar to the mechanism proposed here as it requires insertion of synchronization points, but with the difference that scheduling is not restricted to these points.

Another difficulty that arises in multi-threaded systems is scanning values on the stacks for root pointers. Current implementations often use conservative scanning techniques [Barlett88] that do not require exact information on the location of references. This conservatism makes it impossible for the implementation to give guarantees on the amount of memory that will be recycled and the effectiveness of defragmentation. Even worse, the system becomes vulnerable to denial-of-service attacks that exploit knowledge about the conservative implementation of the garbage collector [BLT98]. These deficits make such an implementation unusable for security relevant domains and for applications that require guarantees on allocation requests or real-time deadlines.

To achieve small pause times in an incremental garbage collector it is required to incrementally scan the stacks of the involved threads for root pointers. This incremental scanning requires not only exact information on the references in the stacks of all threads, but also information on the changes made to the stack-frames between incremental root scanning steps.

5.2 Synchronization Points

All the difficulties described above are complicated by the use of system-level (native) threads that impose no restrictions on when thread switches may occur. If garbage collection work is required, there is little information available on the state of threads. It is possible to obtain more accurate information by determining the program counter of a thread that is not running and using it to obtain information on the thread's state. This would, however, be rather complicated and highly platform dependent.

The solution proposed here is to restrict garbage collection activities to certain *synchronization points*. These *synchronization points* are automatically inserted in the code by a compiler or virtual machine. At such a synchronization point, a test of a global variable indicates if a thread switch is required, and some code is executed if this is the case.

Garbage collection activity is only performed when all threads are stopped at a synchronization point. Consequently, no garbage collection activity may occur in between two synchronization points. A consistent state of the data structures related to garbage collection in between synchronization points is not required.

In addition to the synchronization between the garbage collector and the application threads, concurrent execution of several threads must not corrupt any of the global data structures used for memory management. The write barrier code can be problematic here if it must be implemented as an atomic operation. In the presented system, the write barrier needs to add objects to a global list; it has to be implemented atomically.

The required atomicity of write barrier code introduces an additional need for synchronization between the application threads of the garbage collected system. Thread switches between application threads must not occur during the execution of write barrier code.

To avoid the overhead of this additional synchronization, the synchronization points that were introduced for the garbage collector can be used. All thread switches between garbage collected threads are restricted to synchronization points as well. With this restriction, there will never be more than a single garbage collected thread running on the system[1].

[1] provided it is a single-processor system. Parallel systems are not considered here.

Limiting thread switches to synchronization points has some important consequences. The most obvious one is that only one processor on a multi-processor systems can be used by all garbage collected threads. If the other processor can not be used for different tasks, this mechanism makes sense only on uniprocessor systems. Since all code sequences that lie in between synchronization points are atomic no additional synchronization code is required for any sequence of operations that needs atomic execution if it does not contain a synchronization point.

The runtime overhead of synchronization points has to be kept minimal. As much code as possible should be executed conditionally, reducing the overhead as long as synchronization is not required. **Figure 5.1** shows the required code for a synchronization point as pseudo-C code. The thread scheduler sets the flag *threadswitch_required* whenever a different thread than the currently running one should become active.

```
if (threadswitch_required == true) {
    ... store information on thread's state ...
    ... allow thread switch ...
}
```

Figure 5.1: Basic synchronization point code.

These synchronization points have to be inserted frequently enough so that preemption of threads is possible with a minimal delay. Limiting the thread preemption time is required in real-time applications where high priority tasks have to be able to preempt lower priority tasks within a fixed delay. A compiler or virtual machine implementation such as TurboJ [WdFD++98] or JDK [SUN_JDK] can generate code in a way that guarantees frequent execution of synchronization points. This code must be generated within all loops, at (potentially recursive) calls and within long sequences of linear code (i.e. linear control-flow paths including forward branches). For a given platform it is possible to guarantee an upper bound for the length of the time interval between two synchronization points.

This synchronization technique is a software approach to a similar mechanism implemented in hardware for the scheduling of processes on transputer processors [Inmos93]. In a transputer, certain instructions such as jumps are so-called descheduling points and scheduling of other processes can only take place at these instructions.

In software, synchronization points can be realized using system-level (native) threads and a global semaphore [Dijkstra65] acquired by a mutator thread to execute. To allow a thread switch at a synchronization point, this semaphore will be released and directly reacquired to enable a different mutator thread or the GC to take over the processor, as in

```
V(global_thread_semaphore);
P(global_thread_semaphore);
```

When synchronization points are used, the restrictions imposed on the mutator by the garbage collector are relaxed significantly for the code between two synchronization points. There are three main aspects:

1. Invariants do not need to hold

The invariants required by the garbage collector do not have to hold in between two synchronization points. A typical GC invariant [Pirinen98] is

No black object refers directly to a white object.

It is sufficient to restore the invariant by the time the next synchronization point is reached. Compared to more fine-grain synchronization techniques, optimizing compilers gain freedom to modify all the code in between synchronization points. Even code modifying the heap, such as the marking within a write barrier or allocation of an object, can profit from optimizations such as redundancy elimination [KR94] or instruction scheduling [HKHW96]. The invariant can be destroyed temporarily by these optimization, as long as they are restored at the next synchronization point.

2. No locks required

No locks are required to modify the memory graph or global data used for memory management. Especially write barrier code and allocation of objects can be performed without the need for locks on the accessed data structures since all threads are halted at synchronization points and are guaranteed not to modify these data structures at the same time.

3. No exact reference information required

Even for exact garbage collection, information on local reference variables is not required in between two synchronization points, since garbage collection cannot take place. The root scanning phase of the garbage collector requires exact information on local references. Any local variable or register that is used to hold a reference and that has a lifespan that lies completely within two synchronization points hence does not need to be added to the root set.

5.3 The Garbage Collector

To run the garbage collector, we have a choice between two possibilities: Either, we have the garbage collector running as a separate thread parallel to the mutators, or we intertwine garbage collector and mutator activity doing garbage collector increments within the mutator threads. Since the amount of garbage collection work that is required can be expressed as a function of the amount of allocation that is going on (see chapter 9), the latter solution seems to be preferable. Doing incremental garbage collection within the mutator threads also allows a fair accounting for garbage collection work: when increments of the collection work are performed at allocations, the threads performing allocations have to provide the CPU-time for the garbage collector activity required to satisfy the allocation requests.

The garbage collector code itself can contain synchronization points, so that thread switches can be allowed even while the garbage collector is scanning memory. A simple approach would be to add synchronization points after scanning of each object in an incremental mark-and-sweep garbage collector. The term *scanning* is used here to refer to either *marking* or *sweeping* of an object, depending on the current phase of the garbage collection cycle. If a low priority thread performs a garbage collection increment that consists of scanning several objects, high priority threads can still preempt this process after scanning of each of these objects. If the time required to scan one object is bounded, the preemption time will also be bounded.

5.4 Root Scanning

One of the biggest problems for a real-time garbage collector is scanning of root pointers. Root pointers are reference values that are stored locally on the stack or in registers of a mutator thread. Whenever the garbage collector scans the root pointers, exact information on their whereabouts is required. Fortunately, this can happen only if a thread switch is actually required. **Figure 5.2** illustrates how this information can be provided conditionally at a synchronization point. Since the set of life variables is statically determinable, the recording of this set can be performed storing a single reference to a structure describing this set in the current frame. It is executed only in the case that synchronization is actually required, so the average runtime cost is minimal.

```
if (threadswitch_required == true) {

    cur_frame.roots = set of life locals/registers
                      that hold references;

    ... allow thread switch ...

}
```

Figure 5.2: Recording the set of life variables as roots for the garbage collector in the current stack frame (*cur_frame*) at a synchronization point.

5.5 Call Points

Unfortunately, it is not sufficient to have root information on the routine that is currently being executed, but the same information is also required for all methods that are currently active, so that the list of active stack frames can be traversed and scanned. It is consequently required that the mutator threads store information on the caller's root pointers on calls.

Figure 5.3 illustrates the code that would be required to perform a call in a system not using constant-time root scanning as shown in the next chapter. The code registers the root set of the caller and performs the actual call. The garbage collector traverses the list of stack-frames during root scanning. If the single frames are not linked anyway, the size of a stack frame can be stored with the root information. This link or size will permit finding the address of the following frame without executing additional code at runtime.

```
cur_frame.roots = set of life locals/registers
                  that hold references;

Result = CallMethod(arguments)
```

Figure 5.3: Code for root scanning and synchronization at a call point.

5.6 Example

As noted above, the use of synchronization points as described allows for several optimizations that are not possible when system-level (native) threads are used directly in a garbage collected system. **Figure 5.4** illustrates a small Java method to insert an element at the head of a non-empty doubly-linked list.

```
class Node {
  Node next, prev;
}
class List {
  Node head;
  void insertHead(Node node) {
    node.next = head;
    head.prev = node;
    head      = node;
  }
  ...
}
```

Figure 5.4: Java method *List.insertHead.*

In this example, a write barrier that marks the newly assigned reference is used. **Figure 5.5** shows pseudo-C code that is needed to implement this method using a traditional incremental collector and system-level (native) threads.

```
void insertHead(List this, Node node) {
  atomic{ node.next = this.head; markGrey(this.head); }
  atomic{ head.prev = node;      markGrey(node);      }
  atomic{ head      = node;      markGrey(node);      }
}
```

Figure 5.5: *List.insertHead* using system-level (native) threads. The write barrier code in this example marks the assigned reference *grey.*

Using synchronization points and the optimizations that become possible by their usage, the code will look like the one presented in **Figure 5.6**. Here, no atomic instructions are required, the code is automatically atomic since it is not interrupted by synchronization points. Because it is a short leaf method, no code for a synchronization point is required within the method. And finally, the garbage collector marking can profit from compiler optimizations (like common subexpression removal) that can easily detect that the second marking of the object referenced by *node* is not necessary.

```
void inserthead(List this, Node node) {
    node.next = this.head; markGrey(this.head);
    head.prev = node;      markGrey(node);
    this.head = node;      /* node already marked */
}
```

Figure 5.6: *List.insertHead* using synchronization points. The second marking of *node* becomes redundant and can be removed.

5.7 Optimizing Synchronization Point Overhead

Several simple optimizations can be used to reduce the runtime and code-size overhead caused by the introduction of synchronization points. Some of them are presented here:

Loops that have a known number of iterations (e.g., for-loops with constant bounds and constant increments of the index variable) do not necessarily need the synchronization point code. The compiler can determine the execution time of the loop. In case the loop finishes quickly enough, no synchronization point is needed within its body, the loop can instead be treated as if it was a linear stretch of code.

The same holds for calls to leaf-methods: If the call target is known to the compiler and the execution time is known as well, the compiler may decide that synchronization is not needed for a call. This condition is likely to hold for a call to the method presented in **Figure 5.4**. An optimizing compiler can omit additional code at a call to this method. This optimization can be extended to non-recursive methods (those that only call leaf methods or other non-recursive methods): There is no need for a synchronization point if the compiler can determine the time needed to execute the call and the time is small enough.

Small loops that need a synchronization point within their body may suffer more significantly from the additional code that has to be executed on every iteration. A compiler can reduce the overhead in this case by unrolling the loop a few times. The unrolled loop still requires only a single synchronization point, reducing the overhead to 50% by unrolling once, to 33% by unrolling twice, etc.

A compiler that has full control over the machine code that is being generated may assign a register to the flag *threadswitch_required.* The thread scheduler will have to indicate the need for synchronization by directly setting this register. This approach will avoid the need for a memory access and significantly reduce the overhead by synchronization points. However, the number of registers available for computations will be reduced by one causing more spill code in systems with high register pressure.

A trade-off can be found between the overhead introduced by synchronization points and the speed of preemption required by the application. Allowing the compiler to generate longer stretches of code without a synchronization point can amortize the overhead due to synchronization, while requiring a check for synchronization frequently, e.g., every 100 machine cycles, will enable quick preemption at an additional cost in code size and runtime performance.

5.8 Implications for a Java Implementation

This section presents three implications that arise when synchronization points are applied to a Java [LY96] implementation that do not have a direct relation to garbage collection: The efficient implementation of Java monitors, difficulties that arise by the presence of native code and the object layout.

5.8.1 Java monitor implementation

Due to the frequent use of monitors, their implementation has an important impact on the overall performance of a Java implementation. David F. Bacon et. al. have shown that an efficient monitor implementation can speed up typical Java applications by an average factor of 1.22 [BKMS98].

In a system that limits thread switches to synchronization points, the implementation of a Java monitor at the virtual machine or compiler level is simplified significantly. Since the code between synchronization points is automatically atomic, no locking mechanism is required to request or change a monitor's state. Special hardware support as provided by atomic test-and-set, compare-and-swap or load-locked and store-conditional operations is not needed, simplifying portability.

In case of contention, the threads waiting for a monitor to become available have to save their current state and allow a thread switch in the way a thread switch is allowed at a synchronization point.

In the case that a synchronized Java method or statement does not contain a synchronization point, it is not even necessary to enter or exit the monitor. It is sufficient to test if the monitor is available, and wait for it to become available if this is not the case. Since other threads can become active only at synchronization points, no other thread can possibly request this monitor before it would be released by the current thread, so no code for entering or exiting it is required here.

A highly efficient monitor implementation for Java is presented by Yang et. al. [YLPM+99], with a reported performance increase of a factor of 21. But the presented mechanism does not work with system-level (native) threads, it requires user-level threads with explicit triggering of thread scheduling. With the automatic creation of synchronization points, this scheme can be used without explicit scheduling by the Java program, as if the system would use system-level (native) threads.

5.8.2 Dealing with native code

A particular problem arises with the presence of native code, as it may be used in Java using the Java Native Interface Specification [JNI97]. Since a compiler or virtual machine has no influence on the native code, it cannot be guaranteed that code for synchronization points is being executed sufficiently often. Native code that waits for some I/O event or that tries to obtain a monitor may force the whole system to wait for the event or cause a deadlock.

For Java, the JNI interface has been designed to disallow any direct accesses to the Java memory within native code. Any accesses have to be performed through calls to routines of the JNI interface. These access calls permit to run native code in a system-level (native) thread that is not synchronized with other Java threads or the garbage collector. To perform the call from Java code to native code, we have to record the current state of the root set and allow other Java-threads to become active while the native code is running. The global semaphore has to be released before the execution of native code starts. When the native code returns, a running Java-thread has to be stopped at a synchronization point before normal execution can continue. The global semaphore has to be reacquired. **Figure 5.7** illustrates the code.

```
...store information on thread's state...

// allow thread switches:
V(global_thread_semaphore);

// execute the native code while other java threads
// are allowed to run
Native_Call();

// disallow thread switches
P(global_thread_semaphore);
```

Figure 5.7: pseudo-C code to call native method from Java code

5.8.3 Field packing

Current Java implementations use an object layout that allocates at least one machine word of memory for every field, even though several smaller values like byte or char types could be stored within a single word. One reason for this is that on modern RISC architectures such as Alpha [Sites92], no atomic operations to write sub-word values are present. To write a byte, the word containing the byte must first be loaded, the new value must be inserted at the correct position and the modified word must be written back to memory.

Without any further synchronization and with the presence of system-level (native) threads, this is incompatible with Java's concurrency model since a concurrent write of a different field, that happens to be stored in the same word, may have no effect.

Again, the presence of synchronization points removes these problems since the sequence of instructions to write sub-word data automatically becomes atomic. The denser object model that becomes possible will reduce memory demand and at the same time increase locality.

5.9 Experimental Results

To analyse the performance overhead due to the use of synchronization points the static Java compiler of the Jamaica Virtual Machine (see chapter 4, *Overview of the Approach*) was used. This compiler generates synchronization points in all method prologues, before back-branches in loops and in long linear stretches of code. For the experiments, this code was disabled and the runtime performance was compared with the performance achieved with synchronization points enabled.

For the code with synchronization points three different frequencies of synchronization points were analysed. The frequencies are measured by the number of intermediate instructions of the compiler that can be executed by the longest stretch of code in between two synchronization points. Most of these intermediate instructions correspond to one or two machine instructions on a RISC processor, while a few instructions are more complex and require a short linear sequence of a few machine instructions (e.g., interface calls, type checks, etc.). The analysed frequencies are 10, 100 and 1000 intermediate instructions. It would be better to know the exact number of machine instructions and cycles in between two synchronization points. This was unfortunately not possible in this analysis since *C* code was used as intermediate representation and no detailed information on the resulting machine code was available at the time the synchronization points are generated in the code. A compiler that generated machine code directly would have the required information to determine the number of machine instructions and cycles between two synchronization points.

The analysed applications are the tests from the SPECjvm98 [SPEC98] benchmark suite. Only one test from the benchmark suite, *_200_check*, is not included in the data since it is not intended for performance measurements but to check the correctness of the implementation.

For execution, the test programs were compiled and smart linked using the Jamaica Builder. The programs were then executed on a single processor (333 MHz, UltraSPRACE-IIi) SUN Ultra 5/10 machine with 256MB of RAM running SunOS 5.7.

Figure 5.8 illustrates the runtime performance of the benchmarks, while **Figure 5.9** shows the code size of the *'strip'*ped binary files as compiled for SUN/SPARC. *'strip'* is a Unix command that removes unneeded symbol information from binary files.

The average runtime overhead of synchronization points compared to the version without synchronization points is 4.8% for a frequency of 1000. It varies between –2% and +9% for the different tests, the presence of synchronization points in one case even improved the runtime performance (*_209_db*). This improved performance is probably due to a bad optimization decision done by the *C*-compiler when compiling this test without synchronization points.

For the frequency 100, the average overhead is 6.7%, it ranges from -1% to +10%. With the highest frequency 10, the code generated for one test

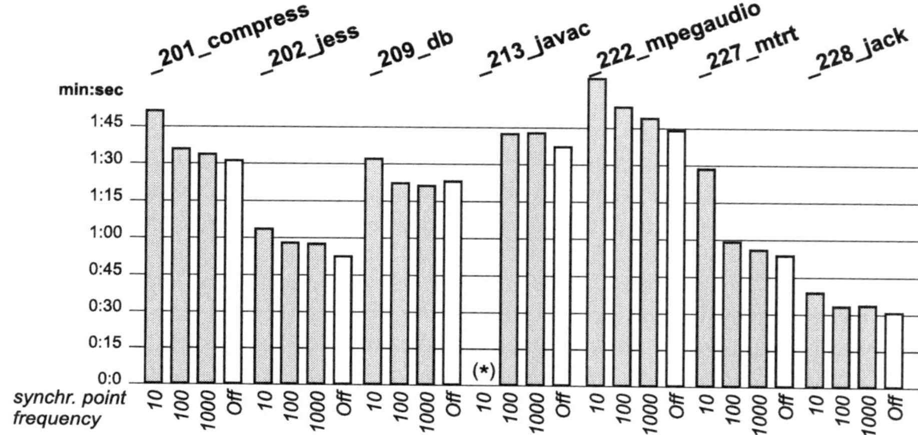

Figure 5.8: Runtime performance for SPECjvm98 benchmarks with different frequencies of synchronization points. The frequencies are measured in number of intermediate instructions between two points.

(*) High frequencies in this test caused some methods to become too large to be handled by the C-compiler (gcc)

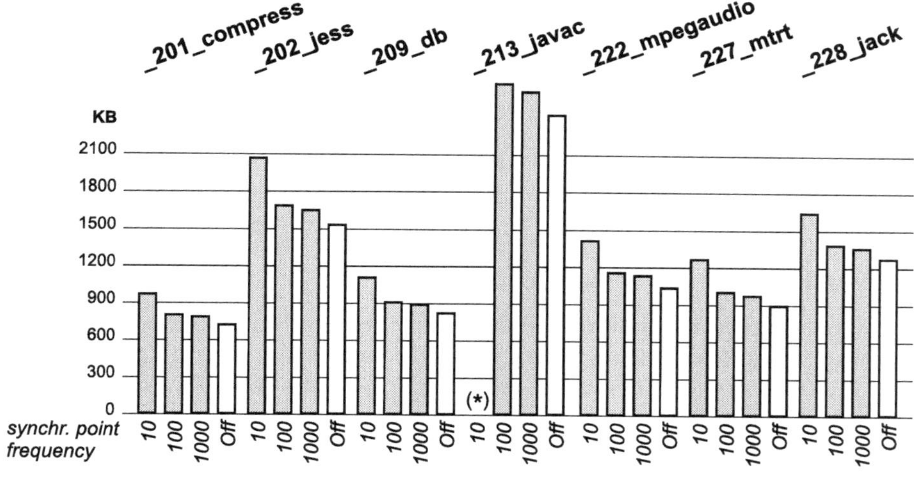

Figure 5.9: File size of executable binary file for SPECjvm98 benchmarks with different frequencies of synchronization points. The frequencies are measured in number of intermediate instructions between two points.

(*) High frequencies in this test caused some methods to become too large to be handled by the C-compiler (gcc)

(*_213_javac*) was too large to be handled by the *C* compiler. The remaining tests saw an average overhead of 24.23% that varied from 11% to 46%.

The runtime overhead is low for all test when the lower frequencies 1000 and 100 are used. It can, however, become significant for the high frequency of 10 intermediate instructions.

The average code size overhead is 8% for a frequency of 1000. For higherr frequencies, the overhead becomes more important: 10% (frequency 100) and 35% (frequency 10). The code size overhead does not vary as heavily as the runtime performance between the different benchmark programs.

It can be expected that more intelligent placement of the synchronization points can reduce the runtime and code size overhead. A program-wide control-flow analysis may be used to detect redundant synchronization points within loops or in method prologues.

5.10 Application to Multi-Processor Systems

The presented approach is not directly applicable to multi-processor systems, only a single garbage collected thread can run at any time. The application to multi-processor systems is left for future research here.

A possible approach is to allow concurrent execution of several threads as long as no garbage collection activity is required. Only if the garbage collector requires a consistent view of the heap, all threads have to execute until they reach the next synchronization point.

One important requirement for such a technique to work is that code executed in the mutator threads, e.g., write barrier code, either does not need to be atomic or uses of exteremely efficient synchronization mechanisms.

5.11 Summary

A new mechanism to synchronize mutator threads and garbage collection on single processor systems has been presented. It has been shown that this mechanism enables one to provide information for exact incremental garbage collection that is hard to achieve when system-level (native) threads are used directly. Furthermore, the presented mechanism enables efficient code by avoiding the need for explicit atomic code sequences and by enabling write barrier code to profit from standard optimizations such that the compiler may even remove write barrier code completely for some writes.

Several optimizations have been presented that can reduce the introduced overhead. The trade-off, that can be made between this overhead and the delay for preemption, has been analysed.

Finally, ways to handle three specific problems and applications when using the presented mechanism in an implementation of Java have been presented: monitors, native code and field packing.

6. Root Scanning

Root scanning is the task of identifying references to heap objects that are stored outside of the heap itself, in global and local variables and on the execution stack. Root scanning is particularly difficult if it is done within an incremental deterministic garbage collector that needs to be exact and give hard timing guarantees. In this chapter, a method that permits exact root scanning is presented. The basic idea is to ensure that copies of all root references exist on the heap whenever the garbage collector becomes active. This approach reduces the root scanning phase of the garbage collection cycle to an efficient constant-time operation. A Java virtual machine and a static Java bytecode compiler that use this technique have been implemented and analysed using the SPECjvm98 benchmark suite. This Java implementation has deterministic memory management as needed in real-time systems that is difficult to achieve with traditional methods to perform root scanning and unparalleled by current implementations.

This chapter is based on an earlier presentation at the International Conference on Compiler Construction 2001 in Genova [Siebert01].

6.1 Introduction

With the rising popularity of modern object oriented programming languages such as Java, garbage collection has finally been accepted as a means for memory management, even though it typically brings a high degree of indeterminism to the execution environment. Nevertheless, Java is more and more promoted as a development tool even for real-time critical systems that require deterministic execution [JCons00, RT-JEG00].

The indeterminism of garbage collection has two separate aspects: the garbage collector causes pauses that are hard to predict while the automatic detection of free memory makes predictions on the memory demand of an application difficult.

To avoid long unpredictable pauses caused by the collector, incremental or concurrent garbage collection techniques are employed [DLMSS78, Baker78, DG94, DFS96]. A garbage collection cycle can be performed in small increments while the main application executes. Each collection cycle starts with the root scanning phase, during which all references outside of the heap are detected and the referenced objects on the heap are marked (e.g. by setting a variable associated to the object to a value that indicates the object is reachable). These references include references on the local stacks of all threads, in processor registers and in global variables outside of the heap. After the root scanning phase, the collector continues by recursively marking objects referenced by objects that have already been marked.

The root scanning of the stack of one thread typically requires suspending the corresponding thread during the time the references are scanned. This suspension can cause pause times that are too long for time-critical real-time applications that require short response times.

In addition to these pause times, there is often not enough information available on where references are located and which references are live. Conservative techniques can be employed in this case. Conservative root scanning treats all bit patterns that happen to represent legal object addresses on the heap as if they were actual pointers to heap objects. This technique usually works well since it is unlikely that a random integer or floating point value on the stack is a legal object address, but it makes the memory management completely unpredictable. Another difficulty in this approach are dangling references that refer to objects on the heap, but that represent dead variables that are no longer used by the application and hence cause memory leaks.

A deterministic garbage collector that can be used in safety-critical systems requires exact information on the roots. Additionally, an incremental garbage collector that is to be employed in hard real-time systems has to guarantee that the pause times for root scanning are bounded and short.

6.2 Related Work

Little work has been published in the area of root scanning for real-time garbage collection, but several papers describe mechanisms for conservative and exact root scanning.

The application of conservative root scanning in a *mostly copying* compacting garbage collector has been presented by Barlett [Barlett88]. This collector refrains from moving an object and changing its address if the object may be referenced from a conservatively identified root reference.

Boehm presents a practical implementation of a conservative garbage collector for C using conservative root scanning [Boehm88] and describes methods that reduce the likelihood for pointer misidentification during conservative root scanning [Boehm93]. Heap addresses that are found to be referenced by misidentified pointers are *blacklisted.* The referenced memory is not used for any allocation, the blacklisted areas are lost. Since it is likely that the same address is misidentified repeatedly, this blacklisting avoids larger memory leaks through references stored in the blacklisted areas.

Goldberg [Goldberg91] describes a method for tag-free collection based on an idea by Appel [Appel89]. Appel's approach uses the return address stored in a function's activation frame to determine the function to which the activation frame belongs. When this function is known, the types of the variables within the activation frame can be determined. Goldberg uses the fact that in a single-threaded environment, root scanning occurs only at calls or memory allocations. Additional information can be associated with each call point that describes a function's frame at this point, taking into account the lifespan of local variables. On some architectures, this technique can be implemented without direct runtime cost. Goldberg also proposes an extension of his approach for multi-threaded environments: If garbage collection is needed, all running threads should be stopped at the next allocation or procedure call.

Diwan et. al. [DMH92] propose the use of tables generated by an optimizing compiler that describe live pointers and values derived from pointers. These tables enable the garbage collector not only to find references and derived pointers, but also to update the references to compact the heap. For multi-threaded environments, an approach similar to Goldberg's is suggested: when GC is triggered, suspended threads are resumed such that they reach their next *GC-point*. The compiler ensures that the time needed to reach the next *GC-point* is bounded.

Agesen et. al. [ADEM98] compare exact root scanning with the conservative approach that is typically used in Java implementations. The average reduction in heap size they achieved when using exact root scanning is 11% for a suite of 19 benchmarks they analysed, while the effect was more dramatic on a few tests.

Stichnoth et. al [SLC99] show that it is feasible to avoid the need for *GC-points* and instead provide exact information on live root references for every machine instruction generated by a compiler. They use sophisticated tables to map the instruction address to the corresponding live root reference information.. This exact information avoids the need to resume suspended threads when garbage collection is triggered. *GC maps* are needed to hold the exact information. The space required for theses maps is about 20% of the size of the generated code.

A compact format for live pointer information has been presented by Tarditi [Tarditi00]. The techniques used by Tarditi are assigning numbers to call sites and to use these numbers to index arrays, two-level tables or sparse arrays and runtime dissambly of the executable code at potential return addresses.

The disadvantage of all these approaches is that they do not avoid the pause time due to root scanning. Dubé, Feeley and Serrano propose to put a tight bound on the size of the root set such that the root scanning time is limited [DFS96]. Since this will not be practical for all systems, they suggest to scan roots incrementally, which would require the use of a write barrier for all assignments to root references and impose a high runtime cost.

6.3 The Garbage Collector

The technique for root scanning presented here is largely independent of the actual garbage collection algorithm. The explanation is therefore limited to the description of the mechanisms relevant for root scanning. An incremental mark and sweep collector has been implemented, but the technique may also be applied to different incremental garbage collection techniques that have been presented in earlier publications [DLMSS78, Baker78, DG94, DFS96]. For compacting techniques, additional difficulties will arise when updating root references. The use of handles would be a solution here.

6.4 Synchronization Points

An important prerequisite for the root scanning technique presented in the next section is to restrict garbage collection activity and thread switches to certain points during the execution of the application. The idea has been presented in chapter 5 and similar mechanisms have been employed earlier [Agesen98]. When synchronization points are used, garbage collection and thread switching at arbitrary points during the execution is prohibited. Instead, garbage collection and thread scheduling can occur only at synchronization points. These points are inserted automatically into the code by a compiler or a virtual machine. The implementation must insert the code required at a synchronization point frequently enough to ensure short thread preemption delays. Since garbage collection activity is restricted to synchronization points, root scanning occurs only at these points. A concurrently running thread may cause garbage collection activity only if all other threads are suspended at synchronization points.

A possible implementation of a synchronization point is shown in **Listing 6.1**. A global semaphore is used to ensure that only one thread is running at any time even when preemptable system-level threads are used. This semaphore is released and reacquired to enable a different thread to become active. The code is executed conditionally to avoid the overhead of the semaphore whenever a thread switch is not needed. The thread scheduler has to set the global flag *threadswitch_required* whenever a thread switch is needed.

```
...
if (threadswitch_required == true) {
    ...
    /* allow thread switch */
    V(global_semaphore);
    P(global_semaphore);
    ...
}
...
```

Listing 6.1: Code for conditional synchronization point

The use of synchronization points has several important effects on the implementation:

1. The invariants required by an incremental garbage collector do not have to hold in between two synchronization points. It is sufficient to re-

store the invariant by the time the next synchronization point is reached. An optimizing compiler can consequently modify the code in between synchronization points even in a way that temporarily invalidates the invariants. E.g., the compiler may have write barrier code take part in instruction scheduling.

2. Between two synchronization points, no locks are required to modify the memory graph or global data used for memory management. In the context of automatic memory management, write barrier code and allocation of objects can be performed without the need for explicit synchronization for accessing global data structures. Since all other threads are suspended at synchronization points and are guaranteed not to modify this data at the same time, the accesses are atomic.

3. Exact reference information is required only at synchronization points since garbage collector activity can only take place at these points.

6.5 Constant Time Root Scanning

The idea presented here is to ensure that all root references that exist outside of the garbage collected heap have to be present on the heap as well whenever the garbage collector may become active. I.e., the compiler has to generate additional code to store references that are used locally on the program stack or in processor registers to a separate *root array* on the heap. Each thread in such a system has its own private root array on the heap for this purpose.

All references that have a lifespan during which garbage collection may become active need to be copied to the root array. Additionally, whenever such a reference has been stored but is not used anymore, the copy on the heap has to be removed from the root array to ensure that the referenced object can be reclaimed when it becomes garbage.

To ensure that the garbage collector is able to find all root references that have been copied to the root arrays, it is sufficient to have a single *global root pointer* that refers to a list of all root arrays.

The root scanning phase at the beginning of a garbage collection cycle can be reduced to marking a single object: the object referenced by the global root pointer. Since all root arrays and all references stored in the root arrays are reachable from this global root pointer, the garbage collector will eventually traverse all root arrays and all the objects reachable from the root variables that have been copied to these arrays.

Since all live references have been stored in the root arrays, all local references will be found by the garbage collector.

The effect of this approach is that the root scanning phase becomes part of the garbage collector's mark phase: While the collector incrementally traverses the objects on the heap to find all reachable memory it incrementally traverses all root references that have been stored in the root arrays.

To maintain the incremental garbage collector's invariant, it is important to use the write barrier code when local references are stored into root arrays.

Another minor problem are root references in global (static) variables. A simple solution is to store all static variables on the heap in a way that they are also reachable from the global root pointer. If this is not possible, a solution could be to always keep two copies of all static variables, one copy at the original location and another one in a structure on the heap that is reachable from the global root pointer.

6.6 Saving References in Root Arrays

Saving local references in root arrays on the heap is performance critical for the implementation: Operations on processor registers and local variables in the stack frame are frequent. Storing these references in the root arrays and executing the write barrier typically requires several memory accesses and conditional branches. To achieve good performance the number of references that are saved to the heap must be as small as possible.

The garbage collector may become active at any synchronization point. From the perspective of a single method, the collector can as well become active at any call, since the called method may contain synchronization points. It is therefore necessary to save all local references whose lifespan contains a synchronization point or a call point. For simplicity of terms, synchronization points and call points will both be referred to as *GC-points* in the following text.

It is not clear when the best time to save a reference would be. There are two obvious possibilities:

1. *Late saving*: All references that remain live after a GC-point are saved directly before the GC-point. The entry of the root array that was used to save the reference will then be cleared right after the GC-point.

2. *Early saving*: Any reference with a lifespan that stretches over one or several GC-points is saved at its definition. The saved reference is cleared at the end of the lifespan, after the last use of the reference. Note that a lifespan may have several definitions and several ends, so code to save or clear the reference will have to be inserted at all definitions and ends, respectively.

It is not obvious which of these two strategies will cause less overhead. *Early saving* may cause too many references to be saved, since the GC-points within the lifespan may never be reached, e.g., if they are executed within a conditional statement. *Late saving* may avoid this problem, but it may save and release the same reference unnecessarily often if the reference's lifespan contains several GC-points that are actually reached during execution.

A third possibility analysed here is a mixture between early and *late saving*, which can be done as follows:

3. *Mixed*: Since synchronization points that use a conditional statement like the one shown in **Listing 6.1** are executed only when a thread

```
...
ref<1> := ...;
...
ref<n> := ...;
...
if (threadswitch_required == true) {
    Save_To_Root_Array(ref<1>);
    ...
    Save_To_Root_Array(ref<n>);

    /* allow thread switch */
    V(global_semaphore);
    P(global_semaphore);

    Clear_From_Root_Array(ref<1>);
    ...
    Clear_From_Root_Array(ref<n>);
}
...
use(ref<1>);
...
use(ref<n>);
...
```

Listing 6.2: Conditionally saving live references *ref*<*1*> to *ref*<*n*> at a synchronization point switch is actually needed, it makes sense to use *late saving* for lifespans that only contain synchronization points but no call points. In this case, the saving of references in the root array before the thread switch and the clearing of the entries in the root array when execution of the current thread resumes can be done conditionally within the synchronization point, as shown in **Listing 6.2**. Whenever a lifespan of a variable contains call points, *early saving* is used since it is likely that one of the call points is actually executed and requires saving of the variable's value.

6.7 The Jamaica Virtual Machine

Jamaica is a new implementation of a Java virtual machine and a static Java compiler that provides deterministic hard real-time garbage collection (see section 4.8). Root scanning is done as just described: The compiler generates additional code to save live references that survive GC-points into root arrays on the heap. There is only a single global root pointer, and the garbage collector's root scanning phase is reduced to marking the single object that is referenced by this global root pointer.

6.8 Write Barrier in Jamaica

The purpose of a write barrier is to ensure that all reachable objects are found by the incremental garbage collector even though the memory graph is changed by the application while it is traversed by the collector. Three colours are typically used to represent the state of objects during a garbage collection cycle: *white*, *grey* and *black*. *White* objects have not been reached by the traversal yet. *Grey* objects are known to be reachable from root references, but the objects that are directly referenced by *grey* objects have not been marked yet, i.e., they may still be *white*. The incremental garbage collector scans *grey* objects and marks all *white* objects that are reachable from the *grey* object *grey*. The scanned object is then marked *black*.

The write barrier has to ensure the invariant that no *black* object refers to a *white* object (alternative invariants and write barriers have been presented by Pirinen [Pirinen98]). One way to ensure the invariant is to mark a *white* object *grey* whenever a reference to the *white* object is stored. The marking is typically done using a few mark-bits that represent the colour of an object. The write barrier code then sets these bits to the value that represents *grey* whenever a reference to a *white* object is written into a heap object. Card marking has been proposed [WM89] as an alternative for generational garbage collectors. The heap is divided into cards of size 2^k words, and every card has an associated bit that is set whenever a reference is stored in a cell of the associated card. This technique allows the use of efficient write barriers [Hölzle93].

Using mark bits is efficient, but mark bits have the disadvantage that finding a *grey* object takes time linear in the size of the heap (the mark bits of all objects need to be tested), and a complete garbage collection cycle may require time quadratic in the size of the heap. This is clearly not acceptable for deterministically efficient garbage collection. For the collection cycle to be guaranteed to finish in linear time, finding a *grey* object has to be a constant-time operation. A means to achieve this is to use a linear list of all *grey* objects. Marking a *white* object *grey* then involves adding the object to the list of *grey* objects.

Listing 6.3 illustrates the write barrier code that is needed by Jamaica to store a reference in an object. Nothing needs to be done if a null reference is to be stored. For non-*null* references, the colour of the referenced object needs to be checked. If it is *white*, the object needs to be marked *grey*, i.e. added to the list of *grey* objects. One word per object is reserved for the colour value. The colours *white* and *black* are encoded using special values that are invalid object addresses. Any other value represents *grey* objects. These objects form a linked list with the last element marked with a special value *last_grey* that is no valid object address either.

The write barrier code from **Listing 6.3** needs to be executed whenever a reference is saved in the root array. **Listing 6.4** illustrates the code required to save a reference in the root array and to release it later. The index *ref_index* that is used to store a root reference can be assigned to each stored value in a similar way as an index in the activation frame is assigned to local variables that are not held in registers. Parallel to the runtime stack, the root array stores activation frames for all methods that need to save references.

6.9 Analysis Using the SPECjvm98 Benchmark Suite

As has been shown above, the best time to save root references is not obvious. To find a good approach, the tests from the SPECjvm98 [SPEC98] benchmark suite have been analysed using *late saving*, *early saving* and *mixed*. Only one test from the benchmark suite, _200_check, is not included in the data since it is not intended for performance measurements but to check the correctness of the implementation.

```
...
if (ref != null) {
   Object **colour = adr_of_colour(ref);
   if ((*colour)==white) {
      (*colour) = greyList;
      greyList = ref;
   }
}
obj->f = ref;
...
```

Listing 6.3: Write barrier code required in Jamaica when storing a reference *ref* in the field *f* of object *obj*.

For execution, the test programs were compiled and smart linked using the Jamaica builder. The programs were then executed on a single processor (333 MHz UltraSPARC-IIi) SUN Ultra 5/10 machine with 256MB of RAM running SunOS 5.7.

In addition to the performance of Jamaica, the performance using SUN's JDK 1.1.8, 1.2 and 1.2.2 [SUN_JDK] and their just-in-time compilers has been measured as well. However, these values are given for informative reasons only. A direct comparison of the garbage collector implementation is not possible due to a number of fundamental differences in the implementations (deterministic real-time vs. non-deterministic garbage collection, static vs. just-in-time compilation, etc.).

```
...
/* save ref in root array: */
if (ref != null) {
   Object **colour = adr_of_colour(ref);
   if ((*colour)==white) {
      (*colour) = greyList;
      greyList = ref;
   }
}
root_array[ref_index] = ref;
...
/* clear ref in root array: */
root_array[ref_index] = ref;
...
```

Listing 6.4: Required code to store an object in the root array at *ref_index* and to clear the entry.

6.9.1 When to Save References

First, the implementation was instrumented to count the number of references that are saved during the execution of all seven tests using the three different strategies. The results are presented in **Figure 6.1**.

Late saving of references requires the largest number of references to be saved. In one test, _213_javac, *late saving* even led to intermediate C code that contained routines that were too large to be handled by the C-compiler on our system (gcc 2.95.2). The large code overhead makes this approach impractical for some applications.

Compared to the other strategies, *late saving* causes a significantly larger number of references to be saved for all but one test. Since multi-threading does not play an important role in most of the tests (the only exception being _227_mtrt), the large number for *late saving* indicates that many lifespans that contain a GC-point cause several call points to be executed. Execution of several call points may also occur if the only GC-point in a lifespan is a call point that lies within a loop, while the lifespan extends over this loop and the single call point is executed several times at runtime.

Early saving also causes a high number of references to be saved. Obviously, many references are saved that do not need to be saved and that are handled better by the *mixed* strategy. The reason for this high number are synchronization points that lie within the lifespan, but that only infrequently cause thread switches.

In all cases, the lowest number of references were saved using the *mixed* saving heuristic. Compared to *late* and *early saving*, the difference is often a dramatic reduction of a factor between two and four.

6.9.2 Runtime Performance

The runtime performance of the tests was analysed next. For these measurements, the tests were recompiled without the instrumentation that was used in the previous section to count the number of saved root references. The results of the performance measurements are shown in **Figure 6.2**. For the analysis, the heap size was set to 32MB for all tests but _201_compress; since it required more memory to execute it was run with a heap of 64MB. The runtime shown is the real time, it was measured for three runs of each test. The values shown are the times from the fastest of these three runs.

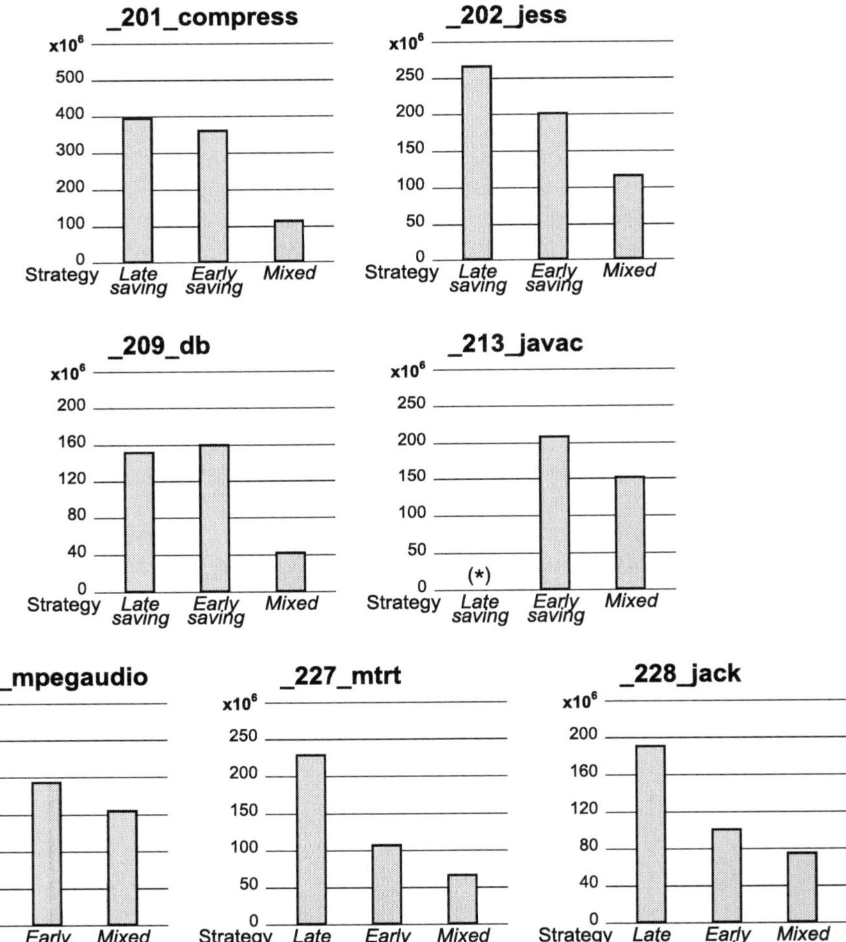

Figure 6.1: Number of references saved in root arrays using *late saving*, *early saving* or *mixed* strategies.

(*) Late saving in this test caused some methods to become too large to be handled by the C-compiler (gcc)

In addition to the performance of Jamaica, the performance of SUN's JDK 1.1.8, 1.2 and 1.2.2 [SUN_JDK] and their just-in-time compilers has been measured as well.

The runtime performance decreases with the number of references saved, hence the runtime performance of the *mixed* strategy is best in all cases.

Compared to Sun's implementation, the performance of the *mixed* strategy is similar to that of JDK 1.1.8 or 1.2, while the performance of JDK 1.2.2 was improved significantly. One can expect that better optimization in the compiler implementation and direct generation of machine code will improve the performance of Jamaica as well.

6.9.3 Runtime Overhead of Root Saving

With the number of saved variables from **Figure 6.1** and the measured runtime performance shown in **Figure 6.2** the runtime overhead of root scanning can be estimated. For this, it is assumed that the cost to save the root references is linear in the number of references saved. This assumption holds if cache and instruction scheduling effects are ignored and the likelihood for a reference value to be null or the referenced object to be marked *white* is the same for the the three strategies *late*, *early* and *mixed saving*.

With these assumptions, linear regression analysis can be used to determine the execution time if no references needed to be saved. **Table 6.1** presents the results of this analysis. The table shows the estimated execution time with no references saved. Using this execution time, the fraction of total runtime required for root saving using the three strategies has been calculated.

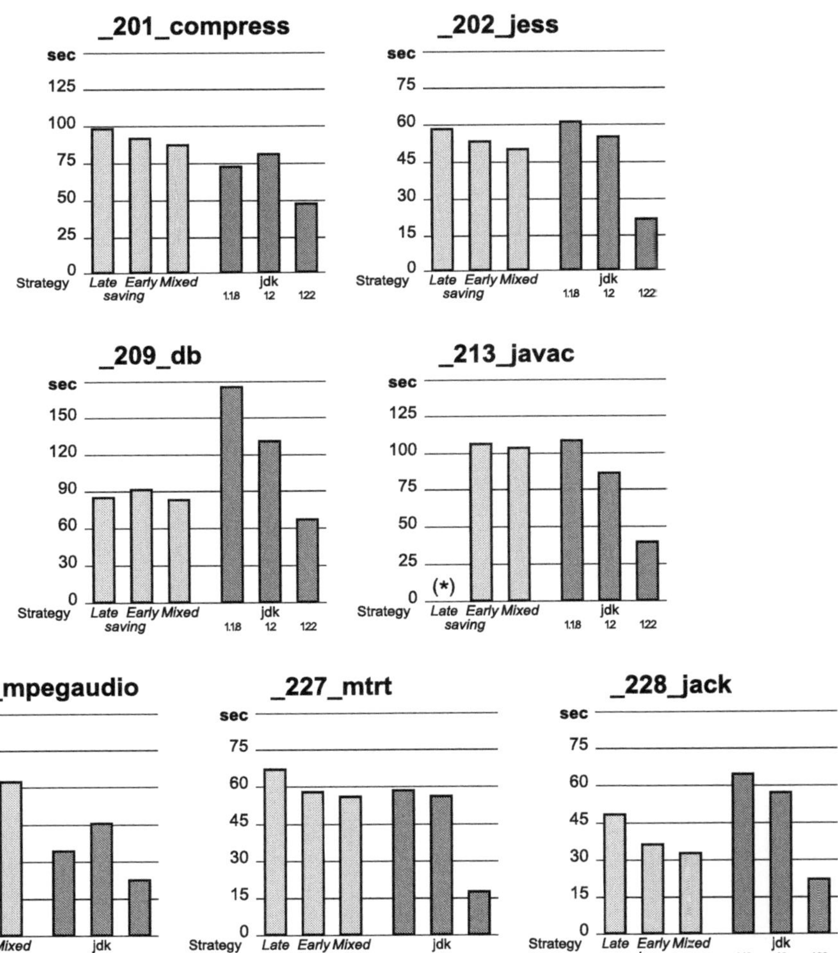

Figure 6.2: Runtime performance of the SPECjvm98 benchmarks using Jamaica with *late saving*, *early saving* or *mixed* strategies and JDK 1.1.8, 1.2 and 1.2.2

(*) Late saving in this test caused some methods to become too large to be handled by the C-compiler (gcc)

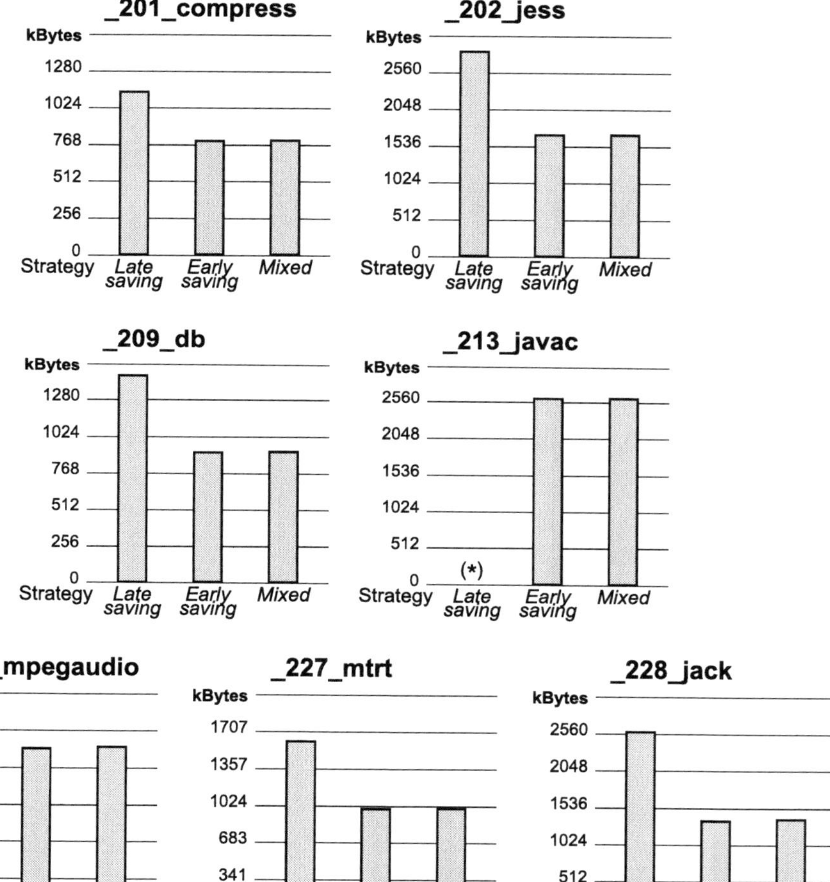

Figure 6.3: File size of executable binary file for application using *late saving*, *early saving* or *mixed* strategies when compiled for SPARC/Solaris.

(*) Late saving in this test caused some methods to become too large to be handled by the C-compiler (gcc)

Benchmark	estimated runtime w/o root saving	root saving overhead late	early	mixed
_201_compress	79.7s	19.6%	13.9%	9.6%
_202_jess	43.9s	25.4%	18.5%	13.3%
_209_db	80.2s	6.6%	13.2%	3.3%
_213_javac	97.2s	-	9.2%	6.9%
_222_mpegaudio	94.4s	13.9%	12.1%	9.9%
_227_mtrt	51.3s	24.0%	12.1%	9.1%
_228_jack	23.0s	53.0%	37.6%	30.8%
Average percentage		**23.7%**	**16.6%**	**11.8%**

Table 6.1: Extrapolated runtime without root saving overhead and percentage of runtime overhead for *late*, *early* and *mixed* saving strategies.

The estimated overhead for root saving ranges from 3.3% up to 30.8% of the total execution time when the *mixed* strategy is used, with an average of 11.8%. The average overheads for *late* and *early saving* are significantly higher: 23.7% and 16.6%. There is only one test in which *late saving* has a lower overhead than *early saving*, _209_db. *Mixed* has the lowest overhead for all the tests.

The average overhead is fairly high, but one can expect that additional optimizations can help to reduce it further. Program-wide analysis can be employed to avoid multiple saving of the same reference in the caller and the callee method. Saving of a local variable of a method is redundant whenever the program-wide analysis can show that the variable's value has been saved at all call sites that invoke this method. Points-to analysis [RMR01, Anders94] can also help to avoid saving references.

A more efficient implementation of the write barrier code that needs to be executed to save a reference will be possible if the implementation generates machine code directly. A global register could then be used to always hold the head of the *grey* list and another global register may be used to determine the colour entry associated with each object (the current implementation uses a global environment structure that need to be read explicitly). As illustrated in **Listing 6.5** and **Listing 6.6**, the use of global registers can avoid half of the memory accesses in the write barrier code.

The reason for the extremely high overhead in _228_jack should also be analysed and the responsible code should be optimized if possible.

```
        cmpwi  0,rRef,#0              #
        bc     12,2,label             # if (rRef != null) {
        lwz    rCB,cb(rEnv)           #    cb   = rEnv->colourBase;
        srwi   rColR,rRef,#3          #    colR = rRef >> 3;
        lwzx   rCol,rColR,rCB         #    col  = (*(cb+colR));
        cmpwi  0,rCol,#0              #
        bc     4,2,label              #    if (col != white) {
        lwz    rGrey,grey(rEnv)       #      rGrey = rEnv->greyList;
        stwx   rGrey,rColR,rCB        #      (*(cb+colR)) = rGrey;
        stw    rRef,grey(rEnv)        #      rEnv->greyList = rRef;
                                      #    }
    label:                            # }
        stw    rRef,offset(rObj)      # rObj[offset] = rRef;
```

Listing 6.5: PowerPC machine code for *Write-Barrier* from Listing 6.3. *rRef, rObj, rCol, rColR, rCB, rEnv and rGrey* are processor registers. The reference *rRef* is stored at *offset* in object *rObj*. *rEnv* refers to the system environment, which contains the grey list at offset *grey*. *rColR, rCol, rCB* and *rGrey* are rused for temporal values.

```
        cmpwi  0,rRef,#0              #
        bc     12,2,label             # if (rRef != null) {
        srwi   rColR,rRef,#3          #    colR = rRef >> 3;
        lwzx   rCol,rColR,rCB         #    col  = (*(cb+colR));
        cmpwi  0,rCol,#0              #
        bc     4,2,label              #    if (col != white) {
        stwx   rGrey,rColR,rCB        #      (*(cb+colR)) = rGrey;
        mv     rGrey,rRef             #      rGrey = rRef;
                                      #    }
    label:                            # }
        stw    rRef,offset(rObj)      # rObj[offset] = rRef;
```

Listing 6.6: PowerPC machine code from Listing 6.5 using using *rCB* and *rGrey* as global registers for the colour base and the grey list. Three of six memory accesses can be avoided.

6.9.4 Memory Footprint

Another important impact of the root saving code is on the code size, which is an important factor for many applications in embedded systems with limited resources. The sizes of the executable binary files generated for the tests from the SPECjvm98 benchmark suite are presented in **Figure 6.3**. The figures are the sizes of the *'strip'*ped binary files compiled for SPARC/Solaris that were used for the performance measurements in **Figure 6.2**. *'strip'* is a Unix command that removes unnecessary symbol information from binary files.

The code size cost of *late saving* is significant, the binary files are 35% to 86% larger compared to early and *mixed* saving. The smallest binary files are achieved using *early saving*, while the file sizes for *mixed* are between 0.2% and 1.7% larger than those for *early saving*.

Additional memory overhead is caused by the root arrays themselves. This memory cannot be larger than the size of the runtime stacks.

6.10 Conclusions

A new technique to do exact root scanning in an incremental, deterministic garbage collected environment has been presented. The technique allows to avoid the pause times due to root scanning. The root scanning phase of the garbage collection cycle is reduced to a cheap constant-time operation.

Different strategies to implement the technique have been implemented in a Java environment and analysed. The performance was compared to current implementations that use non-deterministic garbage collection. It has been shown that the overhead of the technique is limited and results in performance comparable to current techniques. A deterministic and efficient implementations of the root scanning phase in a real-time garbage collector is possible.

Together with the techniques described in the following chapters, garbage collected languages become applicable to new application domains such as safety-critical controls with hard real-time deadlines.

Gegen jeden, der es unternimmt, diese Ordnung zu beseitigen, haben alle Deutschen das Recht zum Widerstand, wenn andere Abhilfe nicht möglich ist.
–Grundgesetz für die Bundesrepublik Deutschland, Artikel 20.(4)

7. Fragmentation

Fragmentation can cause serious loss of memory in systems that are using dynamic memory management. Any useful memory management system must therefore provide means to bound fragmentation. Today's garbage collector implementations often do this by moving objects in a way that free memory is non-fragmented. Here, an object model that is based on fixed size blocks will be presented as an alternative. The model eliminates external fragmentation without the need to move objects, avoiding the complications introduced by moving collectors. A Java virtual machine and a static Java bytecode compiler that use this object model have been implemented and their runtime and memory performance is analysed using the SPECjvm98 benchmark suite. This Java implementation permits deterministic memory management as needed in real-time systems that is difficult to achieve with moving collectors and unparalleled by current Java implementations.

This chapter is based on an earlier presentation at the International Conference on Compilers, Architecture and Syntheses for Embedded Systems 2000 in San Jose [Siebert00].

7.1 Introduction

Allocation and deallocation of objects of different sizes in a system with dynamic memory management can cause memory fragmentation. Fragmented memory is unused memory that cannot be used by the memory management system to satisfy an allocation request. The reason is that fragmented memory may have several unused ranges that are not contiguous. Thus, allocation requests longer than the longest free memory segment cannot be satisfied.

One generally distinguishes between two kinds of fragmentation: *internal* and *external*. Internal fragmentation is memory lost due to the allocator's policy of object alignment and padding of the requested size to a bigger size (to simplify the memory management implementation or respect the processor's data alignment requirements). External fragmentation is memory lost because free memory is non-contiguous in a way that an allocation request cannot be satisfied even though the total amount of free memory would be sufficient for the request.

The amount of memory lost due to external fragmentation can be extremely high. A few objects can prevent large amounts of memory from being used to satisfy large allocation requests. If no measure against fragmentation is taken, the typical worst-case memory requirement is the maximum amount of live data times the number of allocation sizes [WJ93]. However, it has been shown that actual applications typically cause a relatively low average loss due to fragmentation [Johnstone97]. This empirical observation is nevertheless of little help for safety-critical systems that have to give performance guarantees. Furthermore, systems that do not work to reduce fragmentation are vulnerable by attacks exploiting knowledge of the memory management system to deliberately cause memory loss due to fragmentation [BLT98].

7.2 Moving Collectors

A common means to fight external fragmentation is to let the garbage collector move objects in a way that free memory is contiguous. Examples are compacting mark and sweep collectors such as the one used in Sun's Java Development Kit [SUN_JDK], or two-space copying collectors that were first proposed by Fenichel and Yochelson [FY69] and later enhanced for real-time systems by Baker [Baker78].

To avoid the need to update all references to an object that has moved, so called handles are used and all accesses to the heap are performed via a handle. Since all accesses to objects have to be performed via the handle, the use of handles essentially doubles the number of memory accesses, imposing a heavy runtime cost. An alternative for handles are forwarding pointers as proposed by Brooks [Brooks84]: Here, each object contains an additional reference that either points to the object itself or to the new location of a moved object. Again, accesses have to be performed through the forwarding pointer. The use of handles or forwarding pointers can be avoided in a blocking garbage collector, where all references can be adjusted while the application is halted. They cannot be avoided in an incremental implementation where they are needed to adjust all references to a moved object to refer to its new address within restricted time.

Changing object addresses significantly complicates optimizing compilers since address computations for fields or array elements that are performed in compiled code can become invalid by garbage collector activity. Any direct reference to an object that may move has to be known to the collector so that it can either update that reference to the new object location or avoid moving the referenced object, as in a conservative moving garbage collector [Barlett88].

Moving large objects (like big arrays) causes long pauses that are not acceptable in hard real-time systems. Dubé et. al. have proposed to move large objects incrementally to enable short GC pause times at a higher cost for accessing large objects [DFS96].

7.3 Fixed Size Blocks

A different strategy to avoid external fragmentation is to divide the heap into blocks of equal size. Small allocation requests can be satisfied by allocating a single block, while larger ones require a possibly noncontiguous set of several blocks. Blocks never move, and any free block is available for any allocation request.

For this strategy to be useful, building larger objects out of several blocks and accessing objects and arrays built this way must be completely transparent to the user. The compiler or virtual machine implementation has to take care for correct handling of decomposition and accessing of objects.

Important questions are what size should be used for these blocks and how larger objects should be built out of several blocks. The next sections present structures for objects and arrays. A Java virtual machine [LY96] and a static Java compiler have been implemented and the performance of the SPECjvm98 benchmark suite was analysed using this implementation. It should be easy to apply similar schemes to implementations of other programming languages.

7.3.1 Building Objects out of Blocks

Java objects consist of a set of instance fields and a fixed number of words for virtual method table, type information, etc.

Instance fields are inherited through class extension. The subclass can add new fields to the set of inherited fields. The position of an inherited field should be the same in objects of the inheriting class as in objects of the parent class, such that field accesses can be performed by the same simple code independent of the dynamic type of a reference.

Since Java objects are typically small (Dieckmann finds average sizes between 12 and 23 bytes per object [DH99]), a simple linked list of blocks can be used to represent Java objects of arbitrary sizes, where one word per block is reserved for the link. The first block will contain the required type information and the first fields. If a second block is needed, the link field will point to a second block containing more fields. More blocks can be used if needed.

For a fixed block size of 16 bytes and a word size of 32 bits, **Figure 7.1** shows the structure of an object with seven fields of one word each. It is important that, using this object layout, fields can be added in a child class without changing the position of inherited fields, so that an access to a field does not require knowledge about the actual class of the object.

The time $O(p)$ required to access a field in an object is linear in the position p of the field in the object, instead of constant $O(1)$ for a classical representation of objects. The position p and hence the access time can be determined statically. We will see that an average field access requires little more than a single memory access.

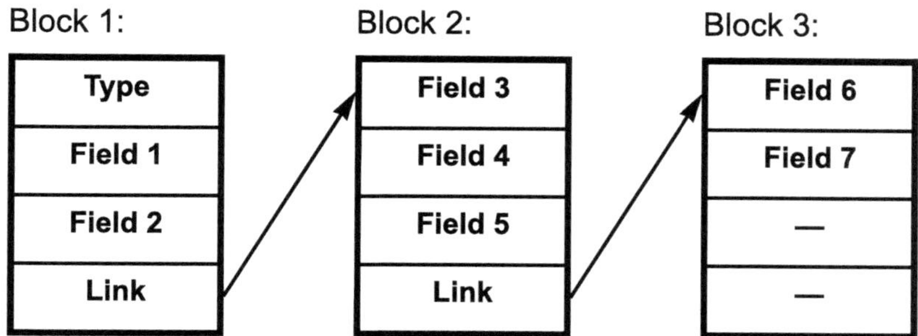

Figure 7.1: Object with 7 fields composed out of three blocks of 16 bytes each.

To avoid the linear access time *O*(*p*), a tree structure can be used. Such a tree requires at least two link entries in each block. Due to these links, fewer fields can be stored in the first block. For fields with larger positions *p* the access time becomes logarithmic *O*(ln(*p*)). Early experiments have shown that the average access time decreases when a tree is used for objects since accesses to fields with low offstes are much more frequent. The measurements that are presented at the end of this chapter show that most field accesses are in fact to fields in the first block.

7.3.2 Building Arrays out of Blocks

Arrays can be arbitrarily large, so representing arrays as a linked list would impose a high cost on array accesses: the time required to access an element of an array of *size* elements would be in *O*(*size*) compared to *O*(1) for the traditional representation of an array as a contiguous range of memory. The representation proposed here is a tree structure similar to the list structure proposed in [Rounce91]. The number of branches or array elements per node is the highest possible power of two permitted by the block size. The array data is stored in the leaf nodes only.

A Java array needs information on its type and length, which are stored in the array header. To ease the access to the elements, it is useful to also store the depth of the tree representation with each array. **Figure 7.2** illustrates an array of 11 elements of one word each, again for a block size of 16 bytes.

Using this tree structure gives a performance in *O*(ln(*size*)) for element accesses. This logarithmic access time may be shocking compared to the traditionally constant cost, but a usually low upper bound for the access time can be found for any given system; e.g., in a system with 32-byte blocks (i.e., 8 words of 32 bits each) and a heap of 16MBytes, the tree depth will never exceed 7.

The code required to access an element in such an array can use a small loop to traverse the depth of the tree until a leaf block is reached. A possible implementation in *C* is given in **Listing 7.1**.

The value *node_width* used in this code is a constant power of two specifying the number of words in a node of the tree. The code is for 16-byte blocks, as in the example from **Figure 7.2**, but it can be changed to work with different sizes by changing the *#define*'s. For a block size of 32 bytes the constants *node_width* and *log2_node_width* have to be

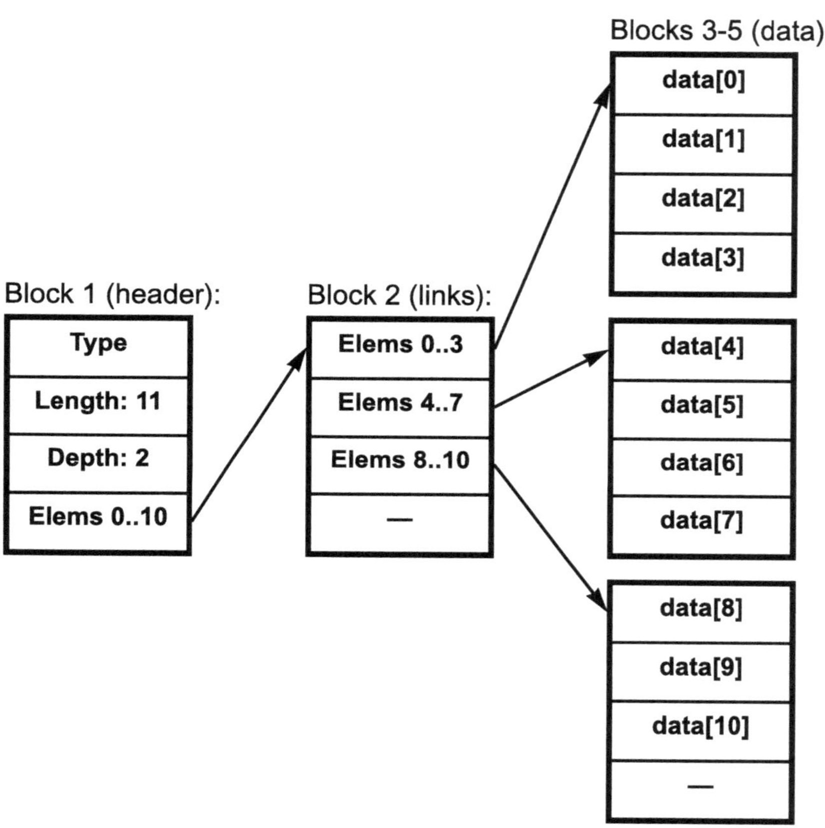

Figure 7.2: Tree representation of an array of 11 word elements composed out of five blocks of 16 bytes.

changed to 8 and 3, respectively. If the element size is different from the machine word size, the code needs to be adjusted accordingly.

The array access code can be implemented efficiently in machine code. As an example, **Listing 7.2** shows the assembly-code that could be produced for the ARM processor [ARM96]. The code is sufficiently short to be inlined, avoiding additional call overhead for array accesses.

```
#define node_width 4       /* 4 words in block   */
#define log2_node_width 2  /* log2(node_width)   */

word readArrayElement(block *array, int index) {
   block **ptr = &(array->elements);
   int d = array->depth * log2_node_width;
   while (d != 0) {
      int t = (index >> d);
      ptr = ptr[t];
      index = index - (t << d);
      d = d - log2_node_width;
   }
   return ((word *) ptr)[index];
}
```

Listing 7.1: C-Code to access array elements

```
-- rA      points to the array
-- rI      contains the index
-- rD, rT  temporary values
-- rE      result

  ld     rD, [rA, #depth]      -- rD = rA->depth
  add    rE, rA, #elements     -- rE = &(rA->elements)
  adds   rD, rD, rD            -- rD = rD*lg2_node_width
  beq    end                   -- if (rD==0) goto end
loop:
  mov    rT, rI, LSR rD        -- rT = rI >> rD
  ld     rE, [rE, rT LSL #2]   -- rE = rE[rT]
  sub    rI, rI, rT, LSL rD    -- rI = rI - (rT << rD)
  subs   rD, rD, #2            -- rD = rD-lg2_nd_width
  bne    loop                  -- if (rD!=0) goto loop
end:
  ld     rE, [rE, rI LSL #2]   -- rE = rE[rI]
```

Listing 7.2: ARM-Code to access array elements

Further optimizations are possible, e.g., the multiplication of the depth by *log2_node_width* can be avoided by storing the multiplied value instead of the depth with each array.

7.3.3 Supporting More Efficient Contiguous Arrays

Even though accesses to arrays that are represented as trees can be implemented in a surprisingly efficient way, the frequent use of arrays in typical Java applications causes the array access code to be one of the most important performance bottlenecks of this approach. Since frag-

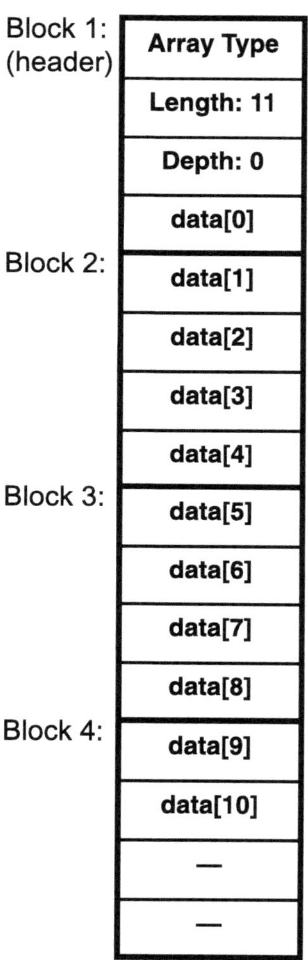

Figure 7.3: Contiguous representation of an array of 11 elements.

mentation is typically low [Johnstone97], it would be preferable to use a linear representation for arrays whenever possible. Such a linear representation is possible when setting the depth field in an array to zero as shown in **Figure 7.3** for the array from **Figure 7.2**. The array access code shown above does not need to be changed at all to support both array representations, trees and linear arrays. On an allocation of an array the linear structure can be used whenever a sufficiently large contiguous range of free blocks is available and can be found quickly enough. Otherwise, the tree representation can be used as a fall-back whenever the memory is too fragmented or searching for a suitable free range would be too expensive.

7.4 Implications for Hard Real-Time Garbage Collection, Optimizing Compilation and JVM Implementation

The use of fixed size blocks instead of a moving collector to avoid fragmentation has a number of important consequences for the implementation of a Java virtual machine and a compiler.

7.4.1 Updating References for Moved Objects

Moving garbage collectors are usually more complex to implement than non-moving ones. It is important to update all references to refer to the new location of a moved object. This updating requires all reference variables to be known to and modifiable by the collector, while for non-moving schemes it is sufficient that the garbage collectors finds one reference to each referenced objects, no matter how many other references to the same object may exist.

If this exact information is not available because, e.g., a compiler that is not garbage collection aware is used, conservative mechanisms have to be employed [Barlett88]. Objects must not be moved when a reference seems to exist to that object. In this case, defragmentation can only be partial, and fragmentation can still lead to unpredictable allocation failures.

A scheme using handles can be used to avoid the need to update all references. But this introduces a significant runtime overhead and conservatism may still be needed while direct accesses to objects are in use, e.g., by compiled code.

When fixed size blocks are used, objects are never moved and references do not need to be updated by the collector. It is sufficient if the garbage collector finds one reference of each object that is in use. There is no need for handles, and the compiler is free to use direct references to objects without informing the garbage collector or caring about changing object addresses as long as the compiler assures that at least one reference to each object that is accessed is known to the collector.

7.4.2 Dealing with Large Objects

An incremental moving collector typically has to move objects atomically. Since an object in a language such as Java may be an arbitrarily large array, moving an object atomically will introduce an arbitrarily long pause that will not be acceptable for hard real-time systems.

Incrementally moving an array as proposed in [DFS96] is likely to impose an unacceptable runtime overhead on array accesses, although a solution might be found here. Such a solution, however, will complicate both the garbage collector and the compiler or interpreter. To cope with this complication, hardware-assisted garbage collection algorithms that incrementally move arbitrarily large objects to their new locations have been proposed [Nilsen94].

Not moving larger objects and using the operating system's memory management unit for defragmentation has been proposed [HHMM98]. This solution may be satisfying for some systems, but it will complicate the implementation and introduce platform dependencies.

Another difficulty is scanning a large object for references during the garbage collector's mark phase. It may be desirable to scan one object atomically, i.e., not be interrupted by mutator activity. For large objects, this would also introduce long pauses that can be unacceptable.

In the presented approach that uses fixed size blocks, scanning can be done block-wise. This means that at some point during garbage collection, parts of the same object may have been scanned by the collector, while others have been found to be reachable and yet others have not yet been touched by the garbage collector at all. Since blocks all have the same small size, scanning a single block takes a small amount of time with a constant worst-case upper bound. The problems due to moving large objects never occur in this case since blocks are never moved.

7.4.3 Ease of Garbage Collector Implementation and Verification

An exact garbage collector requires detailed information on the layout of objects, their sizes and the location of references within each object. Often, it needs access to programming language specific data to obtain this information.

When fixed size blocks are used, the garbage collector does not need to know about the size or structure of objects (as shown in **Figures 7.1** through **7.3**). All it has to care about are blocks. To store the information on the location of references in a block, an additional bit array is sufficient. For 32 bytes per block on a 32-bit system, 8 bits per block are sufficient to store this information (one bit for each of the 8 words in a block).

Not dealing with objects directly takes a lot of complexity out of the implementation of the garbage collector, the implementation is clearer, simpler to verify and simpler to certify for critical applications.

Using blocks also gives an obvious measure for garbage collection progress and the state of the system: the number of blocks scanned, recycled, allocated, etc. Being able to measure progress easily permits the application of mechanisms that ensure sufficient garbage collection progress (see chapter 9).

7.4.4 Effects that are not directly Related to Memory Management

Moving garbage collectors also have implications on the implementation of a programming language that are not directly related to memory management. One example is a *hashCode* function, as defined in the Java standard API. In a system where objects do not move, *hashCode* can be implemented to be a simple function of the object's address in memory. It is guaranteed that the value remains constant during the lifetime of the object.

In an environment that moves objects, *hashCode* is more difficult to implement since an object's adress is not constant during the object's lifetime. To ensure that the *hashCode* value remains constant during the lifetime of an object, it has to be stored with the objects, requiring additional memory for every object.

Interfaces to non-garbage-collected languages such as JNI [SUN97] are another problem that is complicated by moving memory management systems. In a moving scheme, a direct reference to a movable object cannot be passed to code that is written in a language that does not support compacting GC. In a non-moving scheme, these references can be used directly and they remain valid as long as it is ensured that the garbage collector does not recycle the referenced memory.

7.5 The Jamaica Virtual Machine

The garbage collector in the Jamaica Virtual Machine (see section 4.8) is activated whenever an allocation is performed. The amount of garbage collection work is determined dynamically as a function of the amount of free memory in a way that sufficient garbage collection progress can be guaranteed while a worst-case execution time of an allocation can be determined for any application with limited memory requirements (see chapter 9). This approach requires means to measure allocation and garbage collection work. The use of fixed size blocks gives natural units here: the allocation of one block is a unit of allocation while the marking or sweeping of an allocated block are units of garbage collection work.

7.6 Choosing a Block Size

When using blocks of a fixed size, the most important decision to be made is to chose the block size. It is not at all clear which size is best for typical Java applications; it is indeed likely that different applications with different allocation behaviour perform best with different block sizes. The block size used by Jamaica is therefore configurable, it can be chosen between 16 and 128 bytes at build time.

The runtime performance and heap requirements of seven benchmarks from the SPECjvm98 benchmark suite have been analysed using 17 different fixed block sizes. Only one test from the benchmark suite, _200_check, is not included in the data since it is not intended for performance measurements but to check the correctness of the implementation.

For execution, the test programs were compiled and smart linked using the Jamaica builder. The programs were then executed on a single processor (333 MHz UltraSPARC-IIi) SUN Ultra 5/10 machine with 256MB of RAM running SunOS 5.7.

In addition to the performance of Jamaica, the performance using SUN's JDK 1.1.8, 1.2 and 1.2.2 [SUN_JDK] and their just-in-time compilers have been measured as well. However, these values are given for informative reasons only. A direct comparison of the garbage collector implementation is not possible due to a number of fundamental differences in the implementations (real-time vs. non-real-time garbage collection, static vs. just-in-time compilation, etc.).

7.6.1 Runtime Performance

First, the runtime performance of the example programs has been measured for 17 different block sizes. The results are shown in **Figure 7.4**. For the analysis, the heap size was set to 32MB for most tests. Only for compress, javac and mtrt it was set to 64MB, 72MB and 48MB, respectively, since these tests required more memory for some block sizes.

Block sizes that are powers of two cause a significantly better performance than other sizes. The main reason is the simplification of accesses to blocks and entries in the colour-vector and reference-bit-vector, where shift operations can be used instead of slow multiplications and divisions. Additionally, blocks with a size that is a power of two can be aligned with the system's cache lines, reducing cache misses.

Very small block sizes cause bad performance since a smaller block size causes more frequent splitting of an object into several blocks.

For larger block sizes, the performance of some tests either remains more or less constant (compress, mpegaudio, jack), while for the allocation intensive tests (jess, db, javac, mtrt) the performance decreases when the block sizes are increased. Larger blocks cause wasting of more memory, which causes more garbage collection work to recycle sufficient memory.

For all benchmarks, the best performance is achieved when using a power of two block size, but the optimal size differs between the tests: 32 bytes is optimal for jess, db, javac and mtrt, while 64 bytes is best for compress, mpegaudio and jack.

Compared to Sun's implementation, the performance of most tests for a 'good' block size is similar to that of JDK 1.1.8 or 1.2, while the performance of JDK 1.2.2 was improved significantly. One can expect that better optimization will improve the performance of Jamaica as well.

7.6.2 Memory Performance

Next, the heap requirements of the test applications were analysed. A special option '-analyse' of Jamaica instruments the garbage collector to run sufficiently aggressively to measure the required heap to a given accuracy. For all tests, this accuracy was set to 5%. During this analysis, all arrays are allocated in their tree representation, so that the result is the worst-case heap requirement for the case that no arrays could be

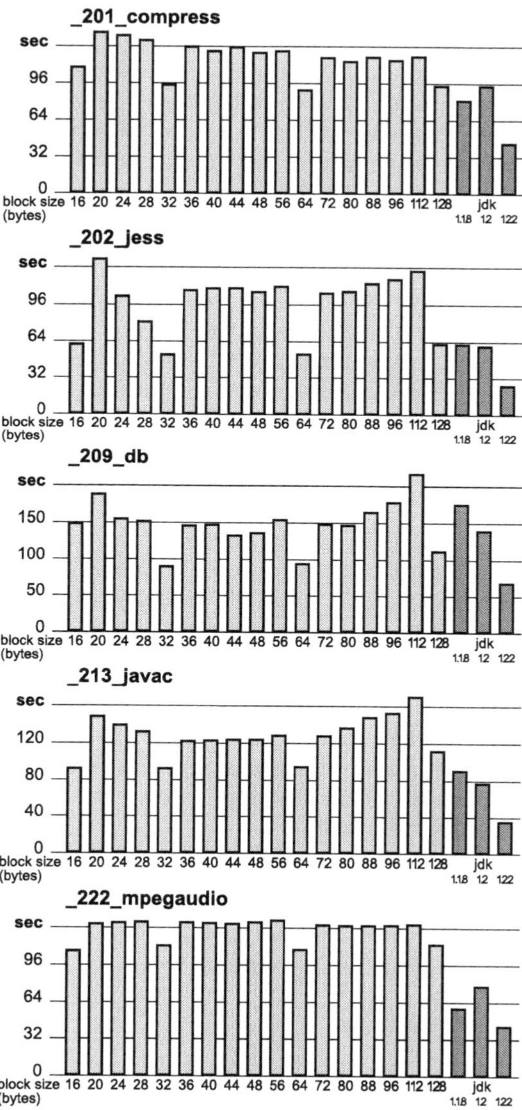

Figure 7.4a: Run-time performance of the SPECjvm98 benchmarks using Jamaica with different block sizes and Sun's JDK version 1.1.8, 1.2 and 1.2.2. Jamaica represents objects as lists and arrays as trees or contiguous ranges.

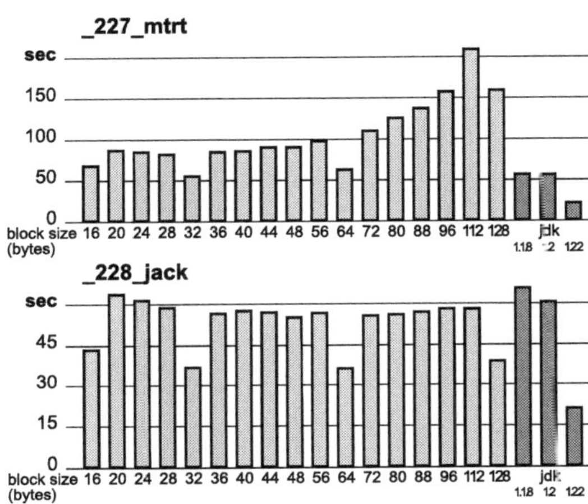

Figure 7.4b: Run-time performance of the SPECjvm98 benchmarks using Jamaica with different block sizes and Sun's JDK version 1.1.8, 1.2 and 1.2.2. Jamaica represents objects as lists and arrays as trees or contiguous ranges.

allocated in linear space due to fragmentation. The results of the memory analysis are shown in **Figure 7.5**.

For the JDK's, the minimum heap requirement was determined by gradually decreasing the heap size specified using the options *-ms* and *-mx* until the application failed with an out-of-memory error.

For all test programs, the space for the objects increases with the fixed size that was chosen. The reason for this is that a vast majority of the objects allocated are small, and bigger fixed sizes are of no use for these objects.

For most tests, the amount of memory required periodically drops at sizes that are powers of two. The reason is the tree representation of arrays that uses only the largest possible power of two number of words in each node or leaf of the tree. All the excess words are unused.

The smallest heap for most tests is possible with a block size of 32 bytes. The exceptions are the array-intensive tests compress and mpegaudio with the smallest heap for 128 or 64 byte blocks. In mtrt most objects that are allocated fit into a block of 20 bytes such that the smallest heap is attained using this block size.

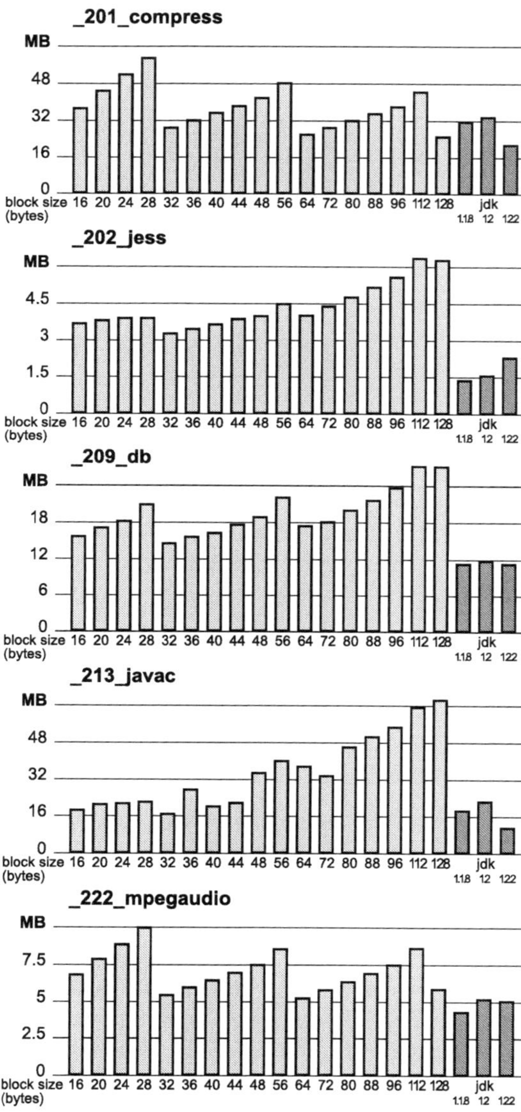

Figure 7.5a: Minimum heap required for different block sizes using Jamaica with different block sizes and Sun's JDK version 1.1.8, 1.2 and 1.2.2. For this measurement, Jamaica represents all arrays as trees.

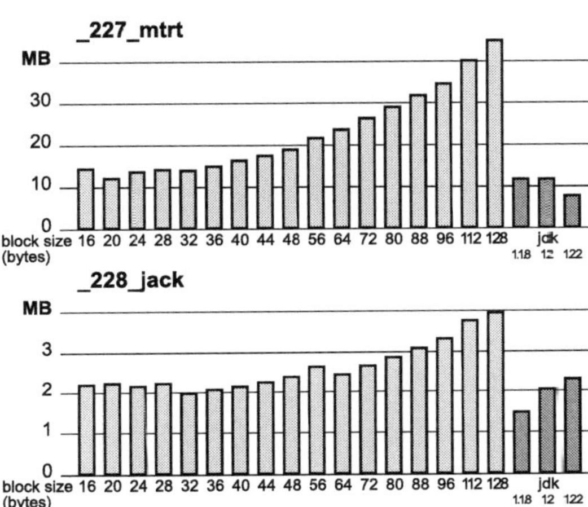

Figure 7.5b: Minimum heap required for different block sizes using Jamaica with different block sizes and Sun's JDK version 1.1.8, 1.2 and 1.2.2. For this measurement, Jamaica represents all arrays as trees.

7.6.3 Allocation and Memory Access Characteristics of the Benchmarks

To better understand the behaviour of the benchmark suite, the Jamaica compiler was instrumented to create additional code to collect information during the execution of the tests. First, the amount of memory allocated for objects and arrays was determined. For arrays, it was also recorded whether an array could be represented as a contiguous range of memory or whether the tree representation had to be used. The results are presented in **Figure 7.6**.

The tests compress and mpegaudio allocate most of their memory for arrays, while the other tests also allocate significant amounts for objects. The memory allocated for arrays in tree representation is insignificant for most tests, only compress and javac allocate a larger fraction of their arrays as trees. This result shows that fragmentation is not high during the execution of this set of benchmarks. Even the constant-time test to find a suitable range of free blocks for an array allocation is typically successful.

Next, the number of memory accesses required by the benchmarks to access objects and arrays on the heap was analysed. For an access to a field of an object, a single memory access is sufficient if the field resides in the first block used to represent the object. Two memory accesses are

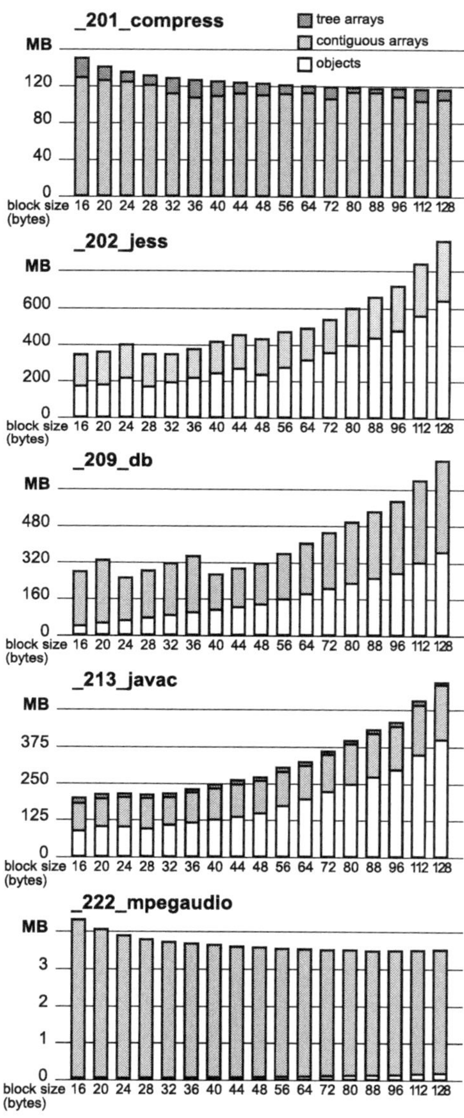

Figure 7.6a: Amount of memory allocated for contiguous arrays, tree arrays and objects for different block sizes

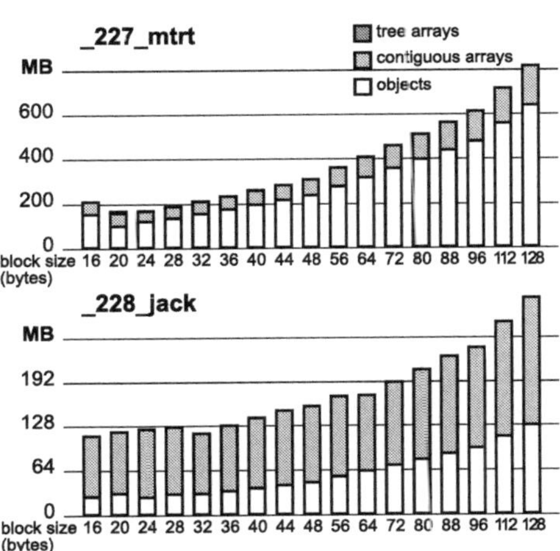

Figure 7.6b: Amount of memory allocated for contiguous arrays, tree arrays and objects for different block sizes

needed for fields in the second block (to read the link from the first block and to access the field itself), etc.

For accesses to arrays, the number of required memory accesses depends on the representation of the array: In contiguous representation, the array's depth needs to be read and checked, next the element itself can be accessed, so two memory accesses are needed. For an array in tree representation, the tree needs to be traversed. This traversal requires d memory reads for a tree of depth d. The depth and the element itself need to be accessed as well, so we get $2+d$ memory accesses in this case. **Figure 7.7** illustrates the total number of memory accesses required by the benchmarks. The number of memory accesses for objects changes significantly with the block size, while that for arrays is less affected by a change in the block size. Very small block sizes cause significantly more memory accesses for objects.

The average number of memory accesses required to access a field of an object or an array element was determined. The results are presented in **Figure 7.8**.

For object accesses, the average number of memory accesses is close to 1 for most block sizes. Only small blocks below 32 bytes cause the average number of accesses to rise significantly, up to around 2 memory accesses for a block size of 16 bytes. The low average number of memory accesses

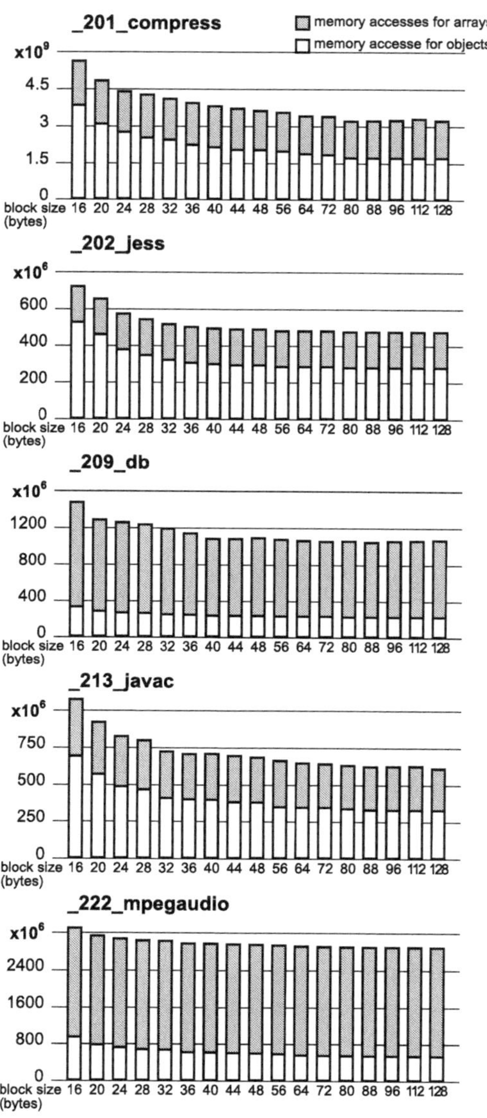

Figure 7.7a: Number of memory accesses performed for array elements and object fields using different block sizes

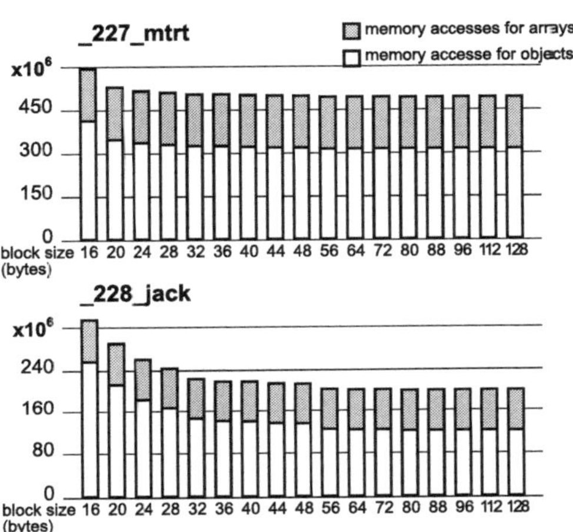

Figure 7.7b: Number of memory accesses performed for array elements and object fields using different block sizes

is due to the typically small size of objects in Java. Additionally, when fields of large objects are accessed, those fields with small offsets tend to be accessed more frequently than those with larger offsets.

For most tests, most array accesses are to arrays in contiguous representation, so the average number of memory accesses is 2 or just above 2. Only compress, db and javac have a significant number of accesses to arrays in tree representation. For very small block sizes, the average number of memory accesses reaches values close to 3, but for blocks of at least 32 bytes this value remains close to 2.

If these results are compared to a memory management system that moves objects and uses handles, one can see that object accesses need significantly fewer memory accesses in this approach: Close to a single memory access compared to 2 accesses to read the handle reference and the field itself. The average number of memory accesses required for array elements in our approach is slightly worse: Just above 2 accesses compared to exactly 2 when using handles.

7.6.4 Code Size for different Block Sizes

The additional code that is needed for field accesses when different block sizes are used has an impact on the size of the binary code of the application. The code sizes of the SPECjvm98 benchmarks when compi-

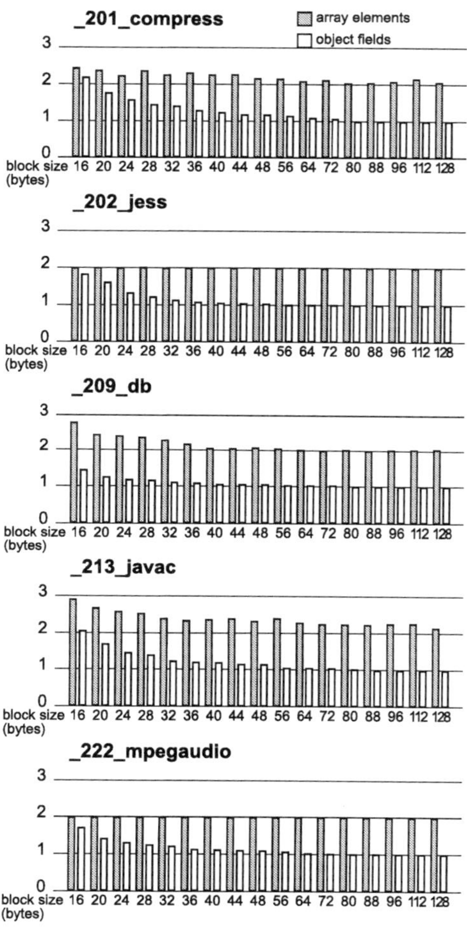

Figure 7.8a: Average number of memory accesses required to access object fields and array elements for different block sizes

led for different block sizes are presented in **Figure 7.9**. The values are the size of the *'strip'*ped binary files as compiled for SUN/SPARC. *'strip'* is a Unix command that removes unnecessary symbol information from binary files.

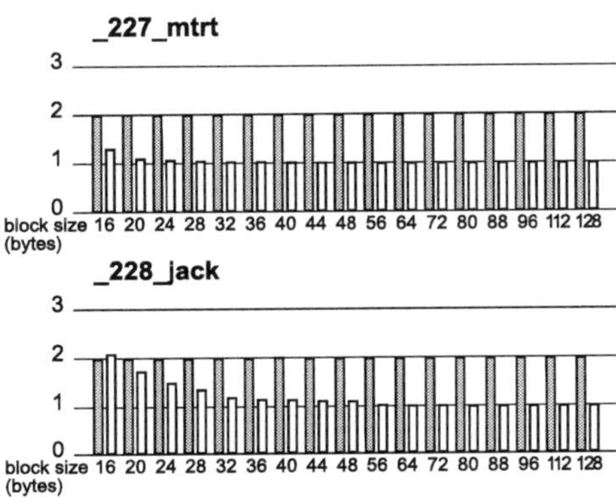

Figure 7.8b: Average number of memory accesses required to access object fields and array elements for different block sizes

The overall effect on the code size is small. When using a power of two for the block size, the binary file is typically a few percent smaller compared to sizes that are not powers of two. Else, the binary size typically does not change significantly, with the exception of very small block sizes that cause a slightly larger code size due to the more frequent splitting of objects into several blocks and hence the more complex code to access fields in these objects.

To be able to compare the code size overhead of using fixed size blocks to traditional object layouts, the compiler was instrumented to create code that assumes that all objects and arrays fit into a single block. The corresponding access code for fields or array elements always performs a single memory access in the first block; the array's depth is never loaded and checked in this version. The resulting code can not be executed since the allocator and garbage collector were not replaced, but it gives a reference for the code size when using a classical object model. The resulting code sizes are shown in **Figure 7.9** in the last column for block size ∞.

Compared to the traditional object model, using fixed size blocks causes the code size to be between 8.2% and 18.8% larger. The code size overhead is smallest for block sizes that are powers of two. In these benchmarks, the average code size is 11.3% larger for a block size of 32

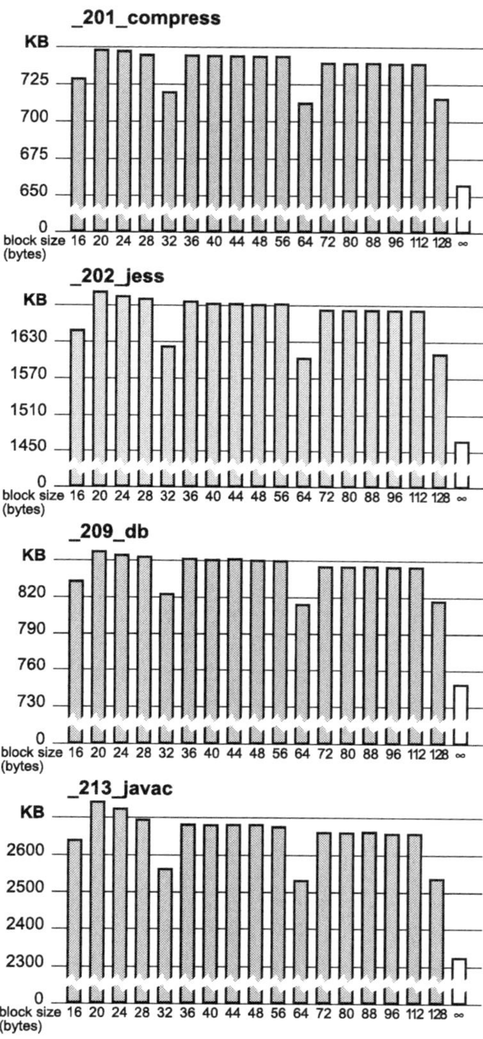

Figure 7.9a: Binary file size for compiled benchmarks using different block sizes and arbitrarily large blocks (∞).

bytes compared to the traditional object model. For 64 and 128 byte blocks, the average code size is 9.8% and 10.3%, respectively, larger.

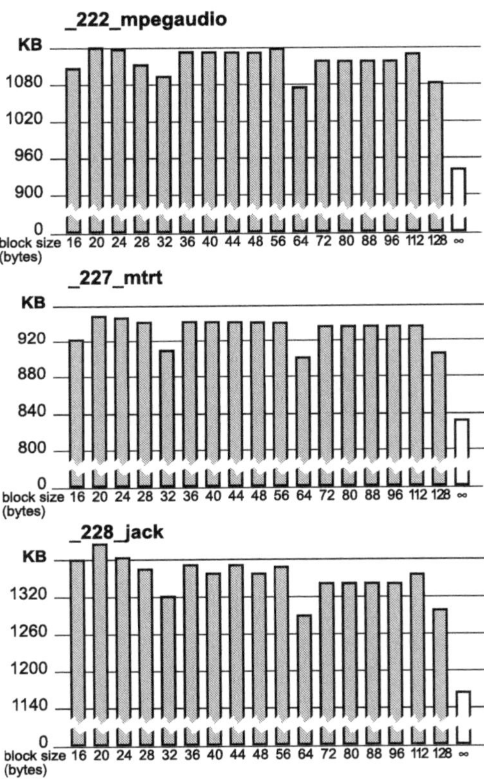

Figure 7.9b: Binary file size for compiled benchmarks using different block sizes and arbitrarily large blocks (∞).

In total, the additional code required for accesses to objects and arrays that are built out of blocks is relatively small compared to the total size of the application.

7.6.5 A Good Standard Block Size

A block size of 32 bytes has a good runtime performance and heap size requirement for most cases, so it seems to be a good size for most applications. However, since some applications achieve their optimal runtime or heap size performance with different sizes, an implementation should permit the selection of a different default size to best serve the application's needs.

Selecting a power of two as block size is strongly recommended due to the better runtime and heap-size performance in most cases.

7.7 Future Work

The performance of the proposed object model needs to be analysed with a much larger set of real Java applications. The main reason why this has not been possible is the small set of standard Java classes that have so far been implemented for Jamaica.

The applications that were analysed do not include any long running applications. It will be interesting to see how long running applications behave using this scheme, especially with respect to memory fragmentation and locality of reference: does the performance stay constant, or does gradual fragmentation of the memory occur and cause gradual decrease of the performance since more and more arrays have to be allocated using the tree representation and the blocks the objects are composed of are spread over the whole heap?

Of course, it would be interesting to apply the presented mechanism to other programming languages. A good candidate may be an implementation of Ada, since this language is widely used in hard real-time and safety-critical domains.

7.8 Conclusions

A new object model that uses fixed size blocks to avoid fragmentation has been presented. It has been applied to a new implementation of a Java virtual machine and a static Java compiler to analyse its behaviour. The results show that one can achieve performance that is comparable to that of current Java implementations using this scheme. Using this object model, one can give hard real-time guarantees that are difficult to achieve with any of the traditional mechanisms that fight fragmentation and that garbage collector implementation is simplified.

Even though the original main goal was to provide deterministic behaviour for a hard real-time implementation of Java, the elimination of fragmentation and the simplified garbage collector increase the total reliability of the implementation, so that applications that do not require hard real-time behaviour can be expected to benefit from it as well.

Vous faites partie d'une liste de quelques dizaines de milliers de personnes dans le monde qui les intéressent. Cette liste se divise en deux catégories: Ceux qu'ils éliment, et ceux qu'ils instrumentalisent. J'ai le plaisir de vous annoncer qu'ils vous placent apparemment dans la seconde catégorie. Votre Pamela bionique était chargée de la première phase de votre instrumentalisation. –mais encore...

–Enki Bilal: Le sommeil du monstre

8. GC Algorithm, Write Barrier and Heap Layout

So far, the presentation of the garbage collection mechanism that was developed during this thesis focused on the aspects for thread synchronization, root scanning and avoiding fragmentation. In this chapter, the overall algorithm that uses the presented techniques will be presented.

8.1 GC Algorithm

The basic garbage collection algorithm is a variant of the classical mark-and-sweep garbage collector as first described by John McCarthy [McCarthy60] and extended for incremental garbage collection by Dijkstra et al. [DLMSS78].

The algorithm associates a marking colour to every object. The colours *white*, *grey* and *black* are used for this purpose. The algorithm operates in two phases, mark and sweep. The mark phase starts with all objects marked *white* and terminates with all reachable objects marked *black*. During the succeeding *sweep* phase the remaining *white* objects are thus known to be unreachable garbage and their space can be freed and reused for new allocations.

At the beginning of the mark phase all objects are marked *white*. During the mark phase, objects are *shaded* to have darker colours (*grey* is darker than *white* and lighter than *black*).

The colours have the following meanings

white The object has not been found to be reachable yet

grey The object has been found to be reachable, but the objects referred to by this object may still be *white*.

black The object has been examined by the mark phase and all objects directly referred to by this object are either *grey* or *black*.

During the mark phase, the following invariant is respected by all modifications made by the garbage collector and the mutator:

INV No *black* object refers to a *white* object.

The mark phase starts with marking all objects that are reachable from a root reference *grey*. It then continues as long as there are *grey* objects. In each step of the mark phase, one *grey* object *o* is taken, all *white* objects that are referenced by *o* are shaded *grey* and *o* is shaded *black*. The mark phase finishes as soon as there are no *grey* objects left.

The invariant *INV* and the fact that all objects reachable from a root reference are shaded at the beginning of the mark phase ensures that objects that are *white* after the mark phase are garbage. The invariant ensures that they cannot be reached from a black object, while all objects reachable from roots have been shaded *black*.

Termination of the mark phase is trivially ensured by the fact that colours never become lighter, in every step of the mark phase one object is marked *black*, and all newly allocated objects are *black*.

One problem remains to be solved, though. This garbage collector must run incrementally while the application itself modifies the memory graph by assigning reference values to objects. The application is therefore also referred to as the *mutator*, it *mutates* the memory graph the garbage collector is scanning concurrently. A reference assignment may invalidate the invariant *INV* when a reference to a *white* object is stored into a *black* object. To ensure that the invariant holds even while the mutator modifies references, so called *write barrier* code is required to be executed whenever the mutator may invalidate the invariant. This code shades the *white* object *grey* whenever an assignment that may invalidate the invariant is performed.

During the sweep phase, the allocated objects are traversed and all *white* objects are added to the free list.

8.2 Root Scanning

An important modification to the original mark and sweep algorithm is the way root scanning is implemented. As has been shown in chapter 6, *Root Scanning*, there is only one single root reference. The root scanning task at the beginning of the mark phase hence becomes very simple. Only the single global root object needs to be marked *grey*.

This root scanning mechanism also avoids the difficulties the original algorithm had due to the fact that root references may be assigned new values by the application during the mark phase, which then may not be found by the collector. Any new root reference will be copied to the heap whenever the garbage collector may become active and it is ensured that this root reference is reachable from the single root reference.

8.3 Using Fixed Size Blocks

Instead of scanning objects, the algorithm works on single fixed size blocks only. The garbage collector is simplified significantly since it does not need to know the structure of large or complex objects. The use of fixed size blocks also gives a direct measure for garbage collection work: During one step of the mark phase, one *grey* block is shaded *black* and all *white* blocks reachable from this block will be shaded *grey*. During the sweep phase, one allocated block is regarded at a time. If it is *white*, the block will be added to the free list. Otherwise, its colour will be reset to *white*, such that all allocated objects are white at the beginning of the next garbage collection cycle.

8.4 Synchronization Points

The garbage collector operations on a single block is made atomic using synchronization points. After marking or sweeping each single block during the mark and sweep phases, respectively, a synchronization point allows preemption of the garbage collector and the activation of another thread.

The preempting thread may even itself cause garbage collection activity, which will again be executed as atomic marking or sweeping of single blocks.

8.5 Colour Encoding

For the efficient implementation of the garbage collector, it is required that shading of blocks and finding of *grey* blocks are efficient operations.

It is common to use a few mark bits for the encoding of the colours. The use of mark bits enables efficient shading, but the time required to find a *grey* object is linear in the number of allocated objects, causing the worst-case runtime of the mark phase to become quadratic in the number of allocated blocks. This is unacceptable for a garbage collector that has to give performance guarantees.

As an alternative, the use of double linked lists has been proposed by Baker [Baker91]. Using these lists permits constant-time implementation of shading and retrieval of *grey* objects. However, when a colour is associated with every fixed size block, and a small block size is used, the memory overhead is significant. For 32 byte blocks, the two link fields would require 8 bytes or 25% of additional memory on a 32 bit system.

An important observation one can make is that only *grey* blocks need to be found efficiently. The colour of *white* and *black* objects may as well be stored in a single field with every block.

The required operations for *grey* blocks are adding a block to the set of *grey* blocks and determination of an arbitrary *grey* block. For this, a single linked list is sufficient. What is required to create such a list is one additional machine word for each block to store the link in this list. For *white* and *black* objects, this word can be used to store the colour as a special value that is not a valid reference.

Using a single linked list for *grey* blocks, the write barrier code for the assignment $b.f = r$ of a reference r into field f of a block b becomes the code shown in **Listing 8.1**.

```
if (gc_mode != SWEEP) {
  if (colour(b) == black) {
    if ((r != null) && (colour(r) == white)) {
      colour(r) = grey_list;
      grey_list = r;
    }
  }
}
b.f = r;
```

Listing 8.1: Write barrier code for the store operation $b.f = r$ that tests the colour of b and r and adds r to the *grey* list.

The function *colour(r)* determines the word that is used to store the colour of block *r* or the successor of *r* in the *grey_list* in case *r* is a *grey* block. The variable *grey_list* refers to the head of the list of *grey* blocks.

As will be shown at the end of this chapter, the write barrier code needs to be executed only during the mark phase of the collector. No additional code is executed during sweep.

Shading *r* in the case that the colour of *b* is not *black* does not invalidate the invariant *INV*, so the test of *b*'s colour is not required. The write barrier code can be reduced to the code shown in **Listing 8.2**.

```
if (gc_mode != SWEEP) {
  if ((r != null) && (colour(r) == white)) {
    colour(r) = grey_list;
    grey_list = r;
  }
}
b.f = r;
```

Listing 8.2: Write barrier code for the store operation $b.f = r$ that tests only the colour of *r* and adds *r* to the *grey* list.

8.6 Heap Layout

The heap consists of a large array of blocks of all the same size, as has been explained in chapter 7. Nevertheless, additional space for the colour encoding is needed, and the garbage collector needs to know which fields of every block contain references that need to be traversed during the mark phase.

To store this additional information, two additional arrays exist parallel to the array of blocks. The first one is a bit-vector with one bit for every 4-byte word in the array of blocks (the size of a reference is 4 bytes). This bit indicates whether the corresponding word is a reference that needs to be traversed or data that can be ignored by the garbage collector. The second additional array contains one word for every block to hold the colour encoding for the corresponding block.

Figure 8.1 illustrates this heap layout with three arrays for blocks, the bits for reference identification and the colours.

For the determination of the colour of a block that is referred to by a reference *r*, this code can be used

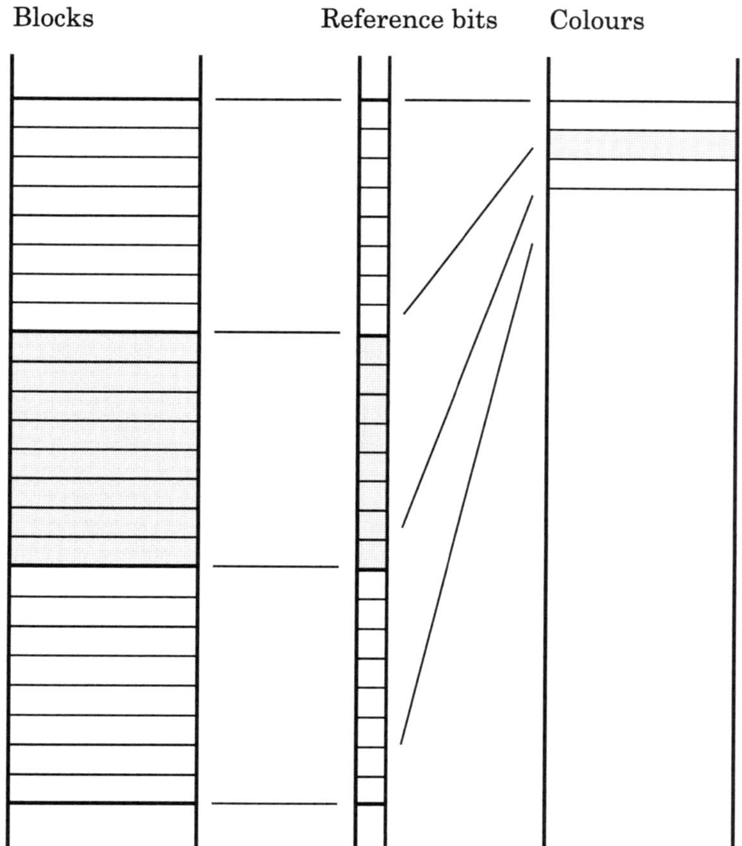

Figure 8.1: Heap layout using three arrays: Fixed size blocks, bit-vector to identify references and one word per block for the colour.

```
index = ((int32) r) - ((int32) blocks) / block_size;
colour = colours[index];
```

The code assumes that the type *int32* is of the same size as a reference. Using a runtime-constants *cb* and a compiletime-constant *cbShift* with

```
cbShift = log2(block_size / word_size);
cb = ((int32) colours) - (((int32) blocks) >> cbShift);
```

The code can be reduced to

```
colour = *(block**)(((int32) r) >> cbShift + cb);
```

The write barrier code for the assignment *b.f* = *r* that was shown in **Listing 8.2** becomes the code in **Listing 8.3**.

```
if (gc_mode != MARK) {
  if (r != null) {
    block**col = (block**)(((int32) r) >> cbShift+cb);
    if ((*col) == white)) {
      (*col) = grey_list;
      grey_list = r;
    }
  }
}
b.f = r;
```

Listing 8.3: Write barrier code for the store operation *b.f* = *r* using runtime-constant *cb* and compiletime-constant *cbShift* to determine the address of the colour entry.

This write barrier code can be translated into efficient machine code that uses simple arithmetic operations, three conditional branches and two memory accesses to read the colour value and write the link in the *grey* list in case the object referenced by *r* needs to be shaded. The code is short enough to be inlined such that additional call overhead is avoided.

8.7 Mark Phase Code

During the mark phase, a *grey* object is taken from the *grey* list and all *white* objects referred to by this object are shaded *grey*. The code required for this is a fairly simple loop over the block size shown in **Listing 8.4**.

```
block *b = grey_list;
block **col = (block**)((((word)b)>>cbShift)+cb);
grey_list = (*col);
(*col) = black;
for(i=0; i<block_size; i++) {
  if (isReference(b,i)) {
    block *n = b[i];
    if (n != null) {
      block **coln=(block**)((((word)n)>>cbShift)+cb);
      if ((*coln) == white) {
        (*coln) = grey_list; grey_list = n;
      }
    }
  }
}
```

Listing 8.4: Code used in mark phase to scan one *grey* object.

The code first takes the first block from the grey list. It determines the address of the colour entry corresponding to this block, removes it from the grey list and marks it *black*. Then all entries of the block are looked at. *isReference(b,i)* uses the reference-bit-vector to check if field *i* of block *b* is a reference. All entries that are references and that refer to a block whose colour is *white* are added to the grey list.

The code for scanning one *grey* object during the mark phase is short and efficient; a constant worst-case execution time for this code can be given.

8.8 Sweep Phase Code

The sweep phase traverses all the blocks. Blocks that are *white* will be added to the free list, blocks that are *black* will be reverted to *white*.

A special colour value *free* is used to indicate that a block is not allocated[1]. Contiguous ranges of free blocks are coalesced and the length of such a range is stored in the first block. These coalesced free blocks enable the garbage collector to jump over free ranges during the sweep phase. There are never two consecutive free ranges that have not been coalesced.

The code that is used to perform the sweep of one block at index *bx* is shown in **Listing 8.5.**

[1]Some publications use a new colour such as *blue* for free objects. Introducing a new term to describe free blocks does not seem to help understanding. Thus, no new term is introduced here, even though talking of *free* as if it was a colour is a misuse of the colour metaphor.

```
block *col = colours[bx];
if (col == free) {
  ...
  ... coalescing with previous free range if possible
  ...
  bx = bx + blocks[bx].freeRangeLength;
  col = colours[bx];
}

if (col == white) {
  colours[bx] = free;
  ...
  ... add block bx to free list
  ...
} else if (col == black) {
  colours[bx] = white;
}
bx = bx + 1;
```

Listing 8.5: Code used in sweep phase to sweep one block at index *bx*.

The code traverses all blocks using the index *bx* within the blocks array. This index is first used to determine the colour of the block. If it is *free*, the corresponding free range is skipped. Since consecutive free ranges are always coalesced, the first block following the free range is guaranteed to be allocated.

The colour of the allocated block is then checked. If it is *white*, the block is garbage and it is added to the free list. If it is *black*, the block's colour is reset to *white*, such that the next mark phase can start with all objects' colours reset to *white*.

No object can be grey during the sweep phase since there were no grey objects at the beginning of the sweep phase and the write barrrier does not shade objects during sweep.

The code that needs to be performed to sweep one block is also short. A constant worst-case execution time for this code can be given.

8.9 Garbage Collection Cycle Termination

Apart from the short worst-case execution times for marking or scanning of single blocks, it will be important in the next chapter to guarantee termination of a complete garbage collection cycle within bounded time.

During the mark phase, all reachable objects will eventually be marked *grey* and will have to be scanned by the mark code once during the current mark phase. The total execution time of the mark phase is in $O(R)$, where R is the number of reachable blocks found in this cycle. This number R includes all the blocks that were allocated during the mark phase and that were found to be reachable.

The sweep phase traverses all allocated blocks and free ranges. Not all free blocks are touched. Several consecutive free blocks in a free range are skipped in one step. The execution time of the sweep phase is in $O(A+H)$ with A blocks allocated and H free ranges.

Coalescing of free ranges ensures that there are no two consecutive free ranges. Since there are no two consecutive free ranges every free range is followed by an allocated block or the end of the heap. The number H of free ranges is consequently limited by the number of allocated blocks: $H \leq A+1$. Thus, the total execution time of the sweep phase is in $O(A)$, instead of $O(M)$ for a total heap size of M blocks if free ranges were not skipped. Blocks that are allocated during the sweep phase may need to be treated in the sweep phase as well, so A includes the memory that is allocated during the garbage collection cycle.

The total execution time of one garbage collection cycle consists of the sum of the execution times for the mark phase and the sweep phase. The required execution time t_{gc} is hence in $O(R+A)$. Since no reachable blocks are free, i.e., they are allocated and $R \leq A$, one can determine an upper bound for the execution time of the garbage collection cycle: $t_{gc} \in O(R+A) \subseteq O(2 \cdot A) = O(A)$.

A garbage collection cycle is finished in time linear in the number A of blocks allocated at the end of the cycle. The number of blocks that need to be scanned in the mark phase and the number of blocks touched in the sweep phase (including skipping of a free range) are both less or equal to A. This result is required to guarantee termination and sufficient progress of the algorithm as shown in the next chapter.

8.10 Correctness of the Garbage Collector

In this section, a sketch of a proof for the correctness of the garbage collector is given. A formal proof can be constructed with some effort. An example is the proof by Doligez and Gonthier [DG94] for their multiprocessor garbage collector.

For the garbage collector to be correct, the following conditions need to be guaranteed by the implementation:

C1 All blocks that are not reachable at the beginning of a cycle must be freed during the cycle.

C2 No reachable block is free.

The purpose of this section is to show that these conditions are satisfied by the presented algorithm. Any block has one of five colours. The colour of a block *A* is *colour(A)*. The colours are

free The block is not allocated.

white The block has not been found to be reachable yet.

white' Only during *sweep* phase: The block was found to be reachable, its colour has been reverted from *black*[2].

grey The block has been found to be reachable, but the blocks referenced by this block may still be *white*.

black The block has been found to be reachable and was examined by the mark phase. All blocks referenced by this block are shaded *grey* or *black*.

One block *G* is called the *global root block*. A block *B* is called *reachable* if and only if $B = G$ or, recursively, if a direct reference from *a reachable* block *C* refers to *B*.

In the proof, it will be shown that the invariant *I* that was partly introduced in section 8.1 will remain valid for all operations performed by the garbage collector or the application.

[2] *white'* is a colour that does not occur explicitly in the implementation. It is only needed for this proof. A block is considered to have colour *white'* if and only if the block's colour entry holds the value *white* and the garbage collector is in sweep phase and the block's memory address is less than the position of the next object that is touched by the sweep phase. A block is considered *white* if and only if the block's colour entry holds the value *white* and the garbage collector is not in sweep mode or the block's memory address is either greater or equal to the position of the next object that is touched by the sweep phase.

Using this definition of *white* and *white'* it becomes clear that the garbage collector can change the colour of all blocks that are *white'* to *white* in a single atomic operation *S3* at the end of the sweep phase: This colour change is done automatically since *white'* objects exist during sweep only.

I There is no reference from a block *A* to a block *B* with *colour(A)=black* and *colour(B)=white.*
No reachable block is *free.*

The atomic operations that the application can perform are:

A1 Store a reference to a reachable block *A* into a reachable block *B*. If the garbage collector is in *root_scanning* or *mark* phase and *colour*(*A*) is *white*, change the *colour* of *A* to *grey*.

This operation corresponds to the pointer write *B.f* = *A* for a field *f* of *B*.

A2 Remove a reference from a reachable block *A* to a reachable block *B*.

This operation corresponds to the pointer write *A.f* = *null* for a field *f* of *A*.

A3 Change the colour of a *free* block *A* to *white'* (in *sweep* phase if the block has already been touched) or *black* (otherwise) and store the reference to it into a reachable block *B*.

This operation performs the allocation of a block from free memory.

There are three phases of the garbage collector that perform different operations:

root_scanning phase:

R1 Mark the global root block *G grey*. Change phase to *mark.*

mark phase:

M1 If there is a *grey* block *A*, mark it *black* and mark all blocks B_i referenced by *A black* if *colour*(B_i)=*white.* If there is no *grey* block, change the phase to *sweep*.

sweep phase:

S1 Change the colour of a block *B* with *colour*(*B*)=*white* to *free*.

S2 Change the colour of a block *B* with *colour*(*B*)=*black* to *white'*.

S3 When the colour of all objects is either *white'* or *free*, change the colour of all objects that are *white'* to *white* and change phase to *root_scanning*.

A garbage collection cycle starts with the *root_scanning* phase. Let *U* be the set of blocks that are unreachable and not *free* at the beginning of this cycle. To show *C1*, it has to be ensured that all blocks in *U* are free after this cycle.

The following precondition holds at the beginning of the *root_scanning* phase:

R_{pre} All blocks are either *white* or *free*.
For all *B* in *U*: *colour(B)=white*.

This precondition and the invariant *I* hold at the beginning of the first cycle and, as will be shown below, will hold at the end of the *sweep* phase, i.e., at the beginning of the next cycle. During the *root_scanning* phase, any of operations *A1, A2, A3* and *R1* can occur. It can be shown easily that all of these operations keep *I* intact and all blocks in *U* stay unreachable. *A1* can change the colour of a reachable *white* block to *grey*. *A2* can introduce some new unreachable blocks. *A3* can change the colour of a *free* block to *black*. *R1* ensures that the global root block *G* is *grey* and terminates the *root_scanning* phase.

The resulting precondition of the *mark* phase is

M_{pre} All blocks are either *white*, *grey*, *black* or *free*.
colour(G)=grey.
For all *B* in *U*: *colour(B)=white*.

This precondition implies the following invariant for the *mark* phase.

M_{inv} All blocks are either *white*, *grey*, *black* or *free*.
colour(G)=grey or *colour(G)=black*
For all *B* in *U*: *colour(B)=white*.

During the mark phase, any of the operations *A1*, *A2*, *A3* and *M1* can be performed. All of these operations keep M_{inv} and *I* intact. The only changes to the colour of a any block are from *white* to *grey* (through *A1* or *M1*) and from *grey* to *black* (*M1*) and from *free* to *black* (*A3*).

The *mark* phase finishes as soon as there are no *grey* blocks left. Since there are no *grey* blocks and the only possible change in colour for a *grey* block during the *mark* phase is to *black*, the global root block *G* must be *black*. In conjunction with *I*, it is ensured that all reachable blocks are *black*. Consequently, no *white* block is reachable and all *white* blocks can be freed. This results in the following precondition for the *sweep* phase.

S_{pre} All blocks are either *white*, *black* or *free*.
colour(G)=black.
For all reachable blocks B: *colour(B)=black.*
For all B in U: *colour(B)=white.*

The invariant during the *sweep* phase is

S_{inv} All blocks are either *white*, *white'*, *black* or *free*.
For all reachable blocks B: *colour(B)=black* or *colour(B)=white'*.
For all B in U: *colour(B)=white* or B was freed.

S_{pre} implies S_{inv}. During *sweep*, operations *A1*, *A2*, *A3*, *S1* and *S2* can occur. Any of these operations keep S_{inv} and I intact. During this phase, the colour of blocks may change from *white* to *free*, from *black* to *white'*, from *free* to *black*, and from *free* to *white'*.

The *sweep* phase finishes with *S3*, which is executed when there are no *white* or *black* blocks left. This condition combined with the invariant S_{inv} gives the precondition of *S3*.

$S3_{pre}$ All blocks are either *white'* or *free*.
For all reachable blocks B: *colour(B)=white'*.
For all B in U: B was freed.

S3 changes the colour of all blocks that are *white'* to *white*. The postcondition of *S3* is consequently

$S3_{post}$ All blocks are either *white* or *free*.
For all reachable blocks B: *colour(B)=white.*
For all B in U: B was freed.

All blocks in U have been freed, condition *C1* holds for this cycle. Additionally, the invariant I includes that no reachable block is *free*, which implies *C2*. What is left to show is that this also holds for the next garbage collection cycle. This can be seen easily since $S3_{post}$ implies the precondition R_{pre}' of the next garbage collection cycle.

R_{pre}' All blocks are either *white* or *free*.
For all B in U': *colour(B)=white.*

U' is the set of blocks that are unreachable and not *free* at the beginning of the next cycle.

This completes the proof.

And someone will say
what is lost can never be saved.
–Smashing Pumpkins

9. When to Run the Garbage Collector

For garbage collection (GC) to be a generally accepted means of memory management it is required to prove its efficiency and effectiveness. This chapter presents a scheme that guarantees that an incremental garbage collector will complete its collection cycle before the system runs out of memory. The garbage collector is performing an incremental step whenever an allocation is performed. The work that has to be done by the collector in one incremental step is limited by a small constant depending on the percentage of total memory used by the application program. This result then permits one to find a suitable trade-off between memory demand and GC overhead.

This chapter is partly based on an earlier presentation at the International Symposium on Memory Management 1998 in Vancouver [Siebert98]. It corrects an important mistake in the original publication.

9.1 Introduction

The reason for applying an incremental garbage collector (as opposed to a disruptive one) is to reduce pauses imposed by the collector and instead spread the collection work over small increments. Each increment must make enough progress to satisfy allocation requests as long as there is garbage to be recycled, yet cause a delay of bounded duration.

Most garbage collection algorithms traverse all or part of the memory allocated by the application before any garbage is freed. This traversal and the freeing of the encountered garbage is called a GC cycle. An incremental collector splits the work into many tiny parts that are performed during the execution of the application program, either in parallel in a separate thread or by occasionally stopping the application.

This chapter describes a way to execute the incremental work of the garbage collector at allocation time such that all allocation can be satisfied and the allocation time is bounded.

Throughout this chapter, memory is measured in units. These may be bytes, the minimum object size, whole objects (in a system with only a single size-class), blocks as presented in chapter 7, or any other memory unit. It is assumed (for now) that the heap has a fixed size of M units. The part of the memory that is known to be free is F. The other memory that is not free is referred to as allocated memory: $A = M - F$. The memory actually used by the application program is the reachable memory R. So we have the following variables describing the memory usage:

	M	size of memory (known to the GC)
	F	size of free memory (known to the GC)
(1)	$A = M - F \leq M$	size of allocated memory (known to the GC)
(2)	$R \leq A$	reachable memory (unknown at runtime)

To simplify the analysis, we normalize these values:

(3)	$f = F/M$	free fraction of memory
	$a = A/M = 1 - f$	allocated fraction of memory
	$r = R/M \leq a$	reachable fraction of memory

During a GC cycle, the collector traverses the allocated memory A (or at least the reachable memory R) once or a small constant number of times. Possible algorithms have been presented by Dijkstra et. al. [DLMSS78] for a Mark and Sweep collector or by Baker [Baker78] for a copying collector. To generalize the different terms used, the term *to scan* is used here to refer to garbage collector activity. For a mark-and-sweep collector, scanning means marking and sweeping of the heap, while in a copying collector, scanning stands for copying allocated memory. In a garbage collector that requires several traversals of the heap, such as mark-and-sweep, scanning all allocated memory means performing both, the complete mark phase and the complete sweep phase.

The details of the collection algorithm and its incremental implementation are not dealt with in this chapter. There are only two requirements for the alogrithm: The collector finds all garbage that exists at the beginning of the collection cycle (which implies that it is exact); and during each increment of GC work progress is made so that at the latest after scanning all allocated memory, a GC cycle is finished. This progress is measured in the number of units of scanned memory. In more detail, the requirements on the GC algorithm are:

Let all garbage collection cycles be numbered starting with 1 for the first cycle. Let g_c be the fraction of garbage found (and therefore memory recycled) by the collector during GC cycle c:

G_c	amount of garbage found during GC cycle c
$g_c = G_c/M$	fraction of garbage found during GC cycle c

At the beginning of GC cycle c the amount of allocated memory is A_c units and the amount of reachable memory is R_c. The amount of garbage is A_c–R_c. The GC algorithm has to guarantee that, during cycle c, it will detect at least those garbage objects that were garbage at the beginning of the cycle, but it may as well find more garbage that was created during the cycle. So we have the requirements

	$G_c \geq A_c - R_c$	garbage memory at the beginning of cycle c is guaranteed to be found during cycle c
(4)	$g_c \geq a_c - r_c$	fraction of garbage found during cycle c

During GC cycle c, the application program will continue executing and it will allocate Q_c units of memory.

Q_c	amount of memory allocated during cycle c
$q_c = Q_c/M$	fraction of memory allocated during cycle c

At the end of each GC cycle c, the garbage found during the cycle will be added to the free memory, while the memory allocated during the cycle has become allocated memory. So we can use

(5)	$a_{c+1} = a_c + q_c - g_c$	allocated memory at the beginning of cycle $c+1$

to determine the fraction of memory allocated at the beginning of the next cycle.

A useful indicator for the progress made in an incremental step of the GC cycle is the amount of allocated memory scanned by the collector: Even if a scan traverses only the reachable memory R (as is typically the case for a copying collector), one can still use the allocated memory A to measure progress, since R is usually unknown, but R is known to be less than or equal to A. The progress function may indicate less progress than is actually made, so the cycle may finish earlier than anticipated.

P Function that returns the amount of allocated memory that is scanned in an increment.

The collector guarantees that a GC cycle is finished at the latest when the sum of the progress made in each increment reaches the amount of allocated memory (i.e., if a new GC cycle starts at GC increment $i=n$ and the progress made in each increment is P_i, then $\Sigma_{i=n..m} P_i \geq A$ implies that the cycle must have finished at increment m).

In this chapter, free memory is considered to be available for any allocation, i.e., not fragmented and therefore unusable. A non-fragmenting object layout as the one presented in chapter 7 can be used to deal with fragmentation. Alternatively, the garbage collector has to compact the memory, or the system can use only equally sized objects. In an environment that is not safety-critical, one may as well optimistically assume that fragmentation won't be a problem.

For the collector to be non-disruptive, the progress P must be small and bounded. But it must also be large enough that the GC can guarantee to find and recycle sufficient garbage memory such that all allocation requests by the application can be satisfied. A useful function for P, that gives the amount of scanning work at the time an object is allocated, will be presented here.

9.2 Simple Schemes for Time Distribution between Application and Collector

A simple scheme for distributing the available processing power between the application and the collector would be to allocate a fixed fraction of total CPU time to a collection process, e.g. *10%* or *25%*. On a multi-processor system, it is also tempting to allocate one processor for the collector, while leaving the remaining ones for the main application. This scheme ensures that only a limited amount of time will be spent for GC and it ensures non-disruptiveness during normal execution. But it is difficult to prove that sufficient GC work will be done for the system not to run out of free memory, so the danger of having to halt the application for a complete GC cycle persists. Its likelihood can be reduced by increasing the percentage of time spent on GC, but there is no guarantee that sufficient progress will be made as long it has not been proven.

Furthermore, this method will spend a fixed fraction of CPU time collecting garbage, even if this is not required because the application uses little memory or allocates no memory for a long period of time. Since no

GC work has to be performed as long as the application does not allocate memory, a better scheme may base the amount of work to be performed by the collector on the amount of memory allocated by the application. Here, a fixed ratio can be selected as well: after each allocation of n units of memory, we can have the collector scan $P \cdot n$ units of allocated memory, where P is a constant, e.g., between 3 and 10. This policy avoids wasting time for GC work while the application is not allocating memory, and the incremental work to be performed by the collector on an allocation is small and bounded. But there is no guarantee that the system won't run out of free memory.

As has been shown in a survey by Wilson [Wilson92], for an application with a maximum fraction of reachable memory k (i.e., the amount of reachable memory is always less than or equal to this constant: $r \leq k$), completion of the GC cycle can be guaranteed by selecting $P \geq 2 \cdot k/(1-k)$. Note that Wilson assumes that objects that are allocated during the GC cycle are scanned (are allocated *black*) and that only reachable objects need to be scanned. Some collectors, e.g., the one presented in this thesis, however, scan all allocated memory.

Since k depends on the application program, this solution cannot be applied directly in a generic garbage collector that has no special knowledge about the application program, as is usually the case in a Java virtual machine. Selecting $P = 2/(1-k)$ can be used instead:

Theorem 1: Using the constant progress function

(6) $$P = 2/(1-k)$$

for the amount of garbage collection work after the allocation of one unit of memory in an incremental garbage collector that requires linear time in the amount of allocated memory to complete one GC cycle and the fraction of reachable memory is bounded by k, all allocation requests can be satisfied.

Proof:

In the proof, an upper bound for the fraction of memory allocated at the beginning of all garbage collection cycles is determined first. This upper bound can then be used to show that the fraction of allocated memory does not exceed the available memory.

It will first be shown by induction on c that the amount of memory a_c allocated at the beginning of a cycle c is bounded by

(7) $$a_c \leq k \cdot ((P-1)/(P-2))$$

There is no allocated memory at the beginning of the first cycle. $a_o = 0$ establishes the base case. The garbage found during cycle c is

(8) $\quad g_c \geq \max(0, a_c - k)$
$\qquad\quad \geq a_c - k.$

Cycle c terminates after a fraction q_c of memory has been allocated. It can be shown easily that q_c is bounded by

(9) $\quad q_c \leq a_c/(P-1) \qquad$ upper bound for q_c

The fraction of memory scanned in cycle c is $q_c \cdot P$. The garbage collector guarantees that the cycle has terminated when the scanned memory $q_c \cdot P$ exceeds the amount of memory $a_c + q_c$ that is allocated meanwhile

$$q_c \cdot P \geq a_c + q_c$$

For $q_c = a_c/(P-1)$, the cycle c has terminated since

$$\begin{aligned} & q_c \cdot P \geq a_c + q_c \\ \Leftrightarrow \quad & (a_c/(P-1)) \cdot P \geq a_c + a_c/(P-1) \\ \Leftrightarrow \quad & \text{true} \end{aligned}$$

Consequently, (9) gives an upper bound for q_c. This upper bound can be used to estimate the allocated memory a_{c+1} at the beginning of the next cycle

$$\begin{aligned} a_{c+1} & = a_c + q_c - g_c \\ & \leq a_c + a_c/(P-1) - (a_c - k) && \text{replacing } q_c \text{ (9) and } g_c \text{ (8)} \\ & \leq k/(P-2) + k && \text{using (7)} \\ & = k \cdot ((P-1)/(P-2)) \end{aligned}$$

Which shows that (7) holds for $c+1$ *and* completes the induction.

The total fraction of allocated memory a is bounded by the fraction a_c of memory allocated at the beginning of a cycle plus the maximum fraction q_c of memory allocated during this cycle:

$$\begin{aligned} a & \leq a_c + q_c \\ & \leq a_c + a_c/(P-1) && \text{using (9)} \\ & = a_c \cdot P / (P-1) \\ & \leq k \cdot (P/(P-2)) && \text{using (7)} \end{aligned}$$

With $P = 2/(1-k)$ from (6) we get

$$
\begin{aligned}
a \quad & \leq k\cdot((2/(1-k))/((2/(1-k))-2)) \\
& = k\cdot(2/(2-2\cdot(1-k))) \\
& = k/k \\
& = 1
\end{aligned}
$$

The fraction of allocated memory never exceeds the total amount of memory. Thus, the memory recycled by the garbage collector is sufficient to satisfy all allocations made by the application.

This completes the proof.

In a system that uses the constant progress function from (6), not all memory M has to be allocated from the operating system at the beginning. Instead, these allocations can be delayed until an allocation cannot be satisfied using memory freed by the collector. The guarantee for sufficient GC progress then ensures that the maximum fraction of reachable memory will reach the fraction k that was preselected for calculation of P. So, when $k = 1/3$ was selected, which results in $P = 3$, the total memory requested from the operating system will never exceed three times the amount of reachable memory. Accordingly, the amount of reachable memory can be guaranteed to be at least 90% of the total memory by selecting $P = 2/(1-0.9) = 20$. The delayed allocation of system memory permits a trade-off between GC overhead and memory usage even for applications with unknown memory requirement. Using a constant factor P to determine GC work, however, will cause a constant and high GC overhead that is actually needed only during the time of highest memory demand by the application.

9.3 Flexible Time Distribution between Application and Collector

A better progress function results when exploiting the information available on the current state of the memory. Since the collector is required to make progress only when the application allocates memory, the required collection work after an allocation should be found. A function P shall be derived that gives the required progress rate measured in units of allocated memory scanned by the garbage collector per unit of memory allocated.

An easily determinable indicator for the state of the memory is the current amount of free memory F. The allocation of one unit of memory reduces the free memory by just this unit: $F' = F - 1$. Running out of free memory must be avoided, so a GC cycle should be finished (and have freed some memory) before F becomes zero. That means the cycle has to finish during the next F allocations. We do not want to make an assumption on what state the GC is in; in the worst case it has just begun a new cycle. A complete cycle may scan all allocated memory A. If we wanted to spread the work during this cycle evenly over the next F allocations, we would have to scan at least A/F units of memory for every allocation of a unit of memory. We use $(A/F)+1$ as progress function. Scanning one extra unit on every step is necessary for the proof of sufficient progress below.

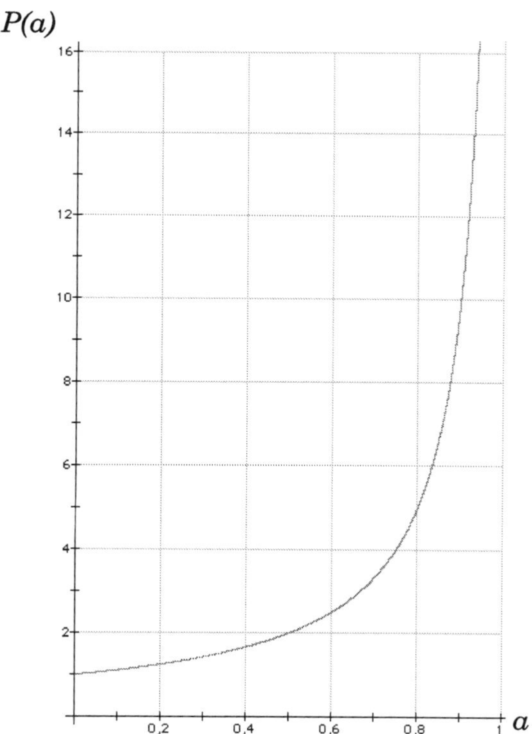

Figure 9.1: Progress to be made by collector on allocation as a function of allocated memory: $P(a) = 1/(1-a)$.

$P = (A/F) + 1$ Progress rate of the GC for the allocation of one unit of memory

With a few conversions using (1) and (3) we get P as a function of the fractions of free memory f or allocated memory a:

(10) $P(a) = 1/(1-a) = 1/f$

With this simple scheme, the work to be done by the GC is small as long as there is sufficient free memory, but it increases hyperbolically as we run out of memory. **Figure 9.1** shows the graph for $P(a)$.

In the next section, it will be shown that using this scheme for any application whose reachable memory is always less than the total memory, sufficient memory will be freed before the free memory is exhausted. Next, an upper bound for P will be given that shows that the actual overhead to be done on every allocation is bounded and small.

9.4 Guaranteeing Sufficient Progress

For a collector to be non-disruptive or real-time, the overhead of each incremental step must be bounded. Yet enough progress must be made to free some allocated memory before the free memory is exhausted. First, I will show that sufficient progress is guaranteed if the application program always uses less than the total heap memory for reachable objects.

It has to be guaranteed that the system never runs out of free memory, i.e.,

(11) $f > 0$

always holds. Thus, there must be an upper bound k for the fraction of reachable memory r with

(12) $r \leq k$ with $0 \leq k < 1$.

This upper bound k depends on the application, it is not known to the collector.

For the following analysis, an additional constraint on k is needed:

(13) $k \geq \frac{1}{4}$

Requiring this lower bound for k imposes no additional requirement on the application program.

Assuming the fraction of allocated memory is a_c when a new collection cycle c starts. We want to determine how much memory q_c has to be allocated for this cycle to finish. The cycle has finished if the sum of the progresses from (10) made on all allocations is sufficient to scan all allocated memory a_c and all memory q_c allocated meanwhile. This is the case when this equation holds:

$$(14) \qquad a_c + q_c \le \sum_{i=1}^{q_c \cdot M} P(a_c + i/M)/M$$

To estimate q_c, a function U of a_c will be determined that gives an upper bound for q_c such that equation (14) holds.

To find U, the transition to infinitesimal memory units is made. The sum from equation (14) can be approximated using an integral. $P(a)$ is monotonously increasing, such that the integral is larger or equal to the sum. This is illustrated in **Figure 9.2.**

$$\int_{a_c}^{a_c+q_c} P(a)\,\mathrm{d}a \le \sum_{i=1}^{q_c \cdot M} P(a_c + i/M)/M$$

To find a q_c for which equation (14) holds, it is hence sufficient to find a solution for this strengthened inequality for q_c:

$$(15) \qquad a_c + q_c \le \int_{a_c}^{a_c+q_c} P(a)\,\mathrm{d}a$$

The integral can be removed using the logarithm:

$$a_c + q_c \le \int_{a_c}^{a_c+q_c} 1/(1-a)\,\mathrm{d}a$$

$$= \ln(1-a_c) - \ln(1-a_c-q_c)$$

so we get for q_c:

$$a_c + q_c \le \ln((1-a_c)/(1-a_c-q_c)))$$

which is equivalent to

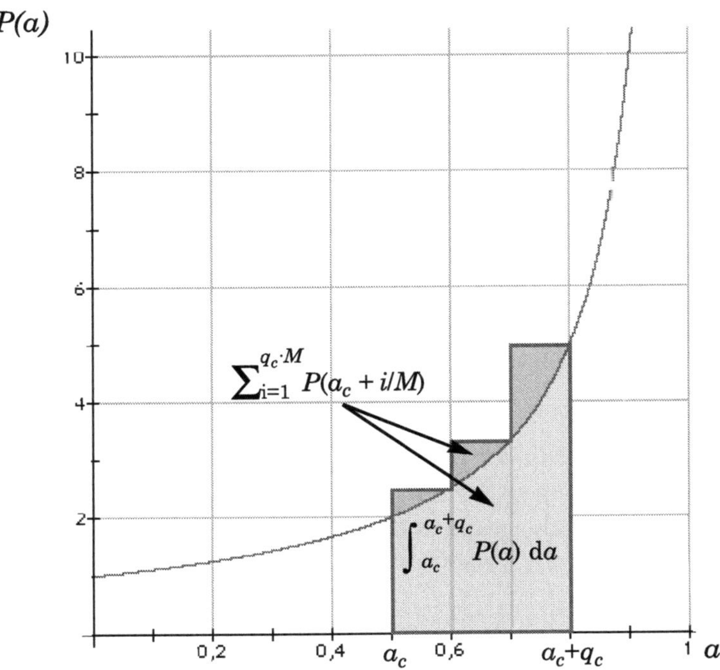

Figure 9.2: Transition to infinitesimal cumulative progress.

$$(q_c - 1 + a_c)\cdot e^{(q_c-1+a_c)} \geq (a_c-1)/e$$

This equation has a solution in terms of Lambert's W function [CG-HJK96], which is a solution $y = W(x)$ of $y \cdot e^y = x$. A plot of $W(x)$ is shown in **Figure 9.3**.

To apply Lambert's W function, y is substituted by $(q_c - 1 + a_c)$ and x is substituted by $(a_c-1)/e$:

$$(q_c - 1 + a_c) \leq W((a_c-1)/e)$$

We get an upper bound $U(a_c)$ for q_c for which inequality (15) holds

$$q_c \leq U(a_c)$$

with

$$U(a_c) = 1 - a_c + W((a_c-1)/e)$$

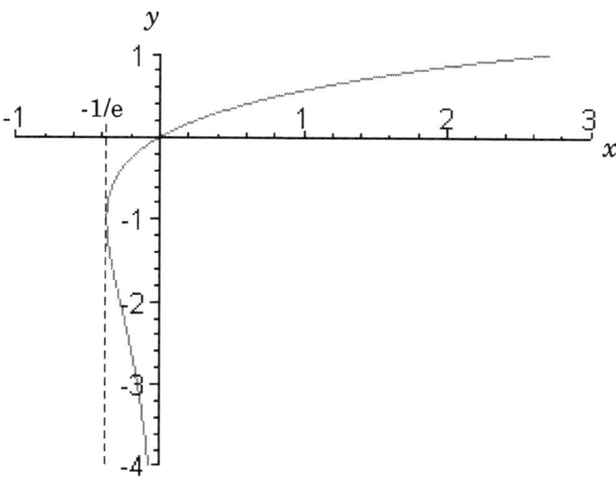

Figure 9.3: Plot of $y \cdot e^y = x$. For $x > -1/e$ and y > –1 this curve is the graph of Lambert's *W* function .
(source: [Corless00])

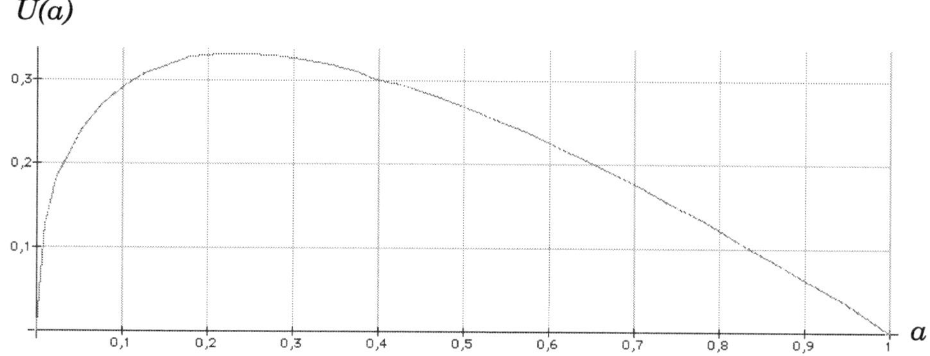

Figure 9.4: Amount of allocation required to complete GC cycle: $U(a) = 1 - a + W((a-1)/e)$

Since (15) implies (14), $U(a_c)$ is an upper bound for the fraction q_c of allocation that is done during GC cycle c. Whenever a collection cycle starts while the amount of allocated memory is a_c, this cycle will be finished before $U(a_c)$ memory has been allocated. **Figure 9.4** illustrates this function.

Theorem 2: Using the progress function

$$P(a) = 1/(1-a) = 1/f$$

to determine the garbage collection work after the allocation of one unit of memory in an incremental garbage collector that requires linear time in the amount of allocated memory to complete one GC cycle, the amount of allocated memory a_c at the beginning of the cycle will be less or equal to $k+U(k)$.

(16) $$a_c \leq k + U(k)$$

Where k is an upper bound for the fraction of reachable memory.

Proof:

The graph shown in **Figure 9.4** gives a motivation for constraint (13): For $k \geq \frac{1}{4}$ the function $U(k)$ is decreasing[1], the derivative $U'(x)$ is negative for $k \leq x \leq 1$. This fact is required in the proof.

The proof shows that the theorem holds after every cycle c. It trivially holds for the first cycle c=0 with a_c=0 since $k + U(k)$ is positive.

Depenping on the fraction of reachable memory at the beginning of cycle c, two cases are distinguished:

First case:

(17) $$a_c \leq k$$

The amount of memory to be allocated before the next cycle finishes is bounded by $U(a_c)$:

$$q_c \leq U(a_c)$$

Applying (5) enables us to determine the fraction of allocated memory after this cycle:

[1]The exact maximum of $U(k)$ is slightly less than 0.25, the exact value cannot be expressed as a closed term.

$$\begin{aligned} a_{c+1} &= a_c + q_c - g_c \\ &\leq a_c + q_c \\ &\leq a_c + U(a_c) \\ &= a_c + 1 - a_c + W((a_c - 1)/e) \\ &= 1 + W((a_c - 1)/e) \end{aligned}$$

Since $W(x)$ increases monotonically for $x \geq -1/e$, we get:

$$\begin{aligned} a_{c+1} &\leq 1 + W((k - 1)/e) \\ &= k + 1 - k + W((k - 1)/e) \\ &= k + U(k) \end{aligned}$$

Second case:

(18) $$a_c > k$$

Since $r_c \leq k < a_c$ implies $r_c < a_c$, some garbage will be found in this cycle using estimate (4):

$$g_c \geq a_c - r_c \geq a_c - k > 0$$

The amount of memory q_c allocated before the next cycle finishes is bounded by $U(a_c)$:

$$q_c \leq U(a_c)$$

Applying (5) enables us to determine the fraction of allocated memory after this cycle:

(19) $$\begin{aligned} a_{c+1} &= a_c + q_c - g_c \\ &\leq a_c + U(a_c) - (a_c - k) \\ &= k + U(a_c) \end{aligned}$$

The monotonicity of $U(x)$ for $k \leq x \leq 1$ and (18) enable us to continue the estimation of a_{c+1} from (19)

$$\begin{aligned} a_{c+1} &\leq k + U(a_c) \qquad \text{with } k \geq \tfrac{1}{4} \text{ and } a_c > k \\ &\leq k + U(k) \end{aligned}$$

These two cases and the starting condition $a_0 = 0$ yield that a_c is bounded by $k + U(k)$.

This completes the proof.

An upper bound of allocated memory for the application that is independent of the state of the collector follows from theorem 2:

Corollary 1: The amount of allocated memory a is bounded by

(20) $$a \leq a_{max}$$

with

(21) $$a_{max} = 1 + W(W((k-1)/e)/e)$$

independent of the current state of the garbage collector.

Proof:

Since every cycle takes at most $U(a_c)$ allocations to finish, the upper bound on a_c from (16) implies an upper bound of allocated memory at the end of every cycle, and therefore a total upper bound for the allocated memory:

(22) $$\begin{aligned} a &\leq a_c + q_c \\ &\leq a_c + U(a_c) \\ &= a_c + 1 - a_c + W((a_c - 1)/e) \\ &= 1 + W((a_c - 1)/e) \\ &\leq 1 + W((k + U(k) - 1)/e) && \text{transformations}^2 \\ &= 1 + W(W((k-1)/e)/e) \\ &= a_{max} \end{aligned}$$

Figure 9.5 illustrates a_{max} as a function of the upper bound of reachable memory k. **Table 9.1** presents the maximum fractions of allocated memory for some selected maximum fractions of reachable memory.

***k*:**	0.0	0.3	0.4	0.5	0.6	0.7	
a_{max}:	0.0	0.838	0.876	0.906	0.931	0.952	
***k*:**	0.75	0.8	0.85	0.9	0.95	0.975	1.0
a_{max}:	0.961	0.970	0.978	0.985	0.993	0.997	1.0

Table 9.1: Upper bound for the maximum amount of allocated memory

[2]The following simple transformations show:

$$\begin{aligned} & 1 + W((a_c - 1)/e) \\ = \; & k + U(k) + (1 - (k + U(k)) + W((k + U(k) - 1)/e)) \\ = \; & k + U(k) + U(k + U(k)) \\ = \; & k + U(k) + 1 - k - U(k) + W((k + U(k) - 1)/e) \\ = \; & 1 + W((k + U(k) - 1)/e) \\ = \; & 1 + W((k + 1 - k + W((k-1)/e) - 1)/e) \\ = \; & 1 + W(W((k-1)/e)/e) \end{aligned}$$

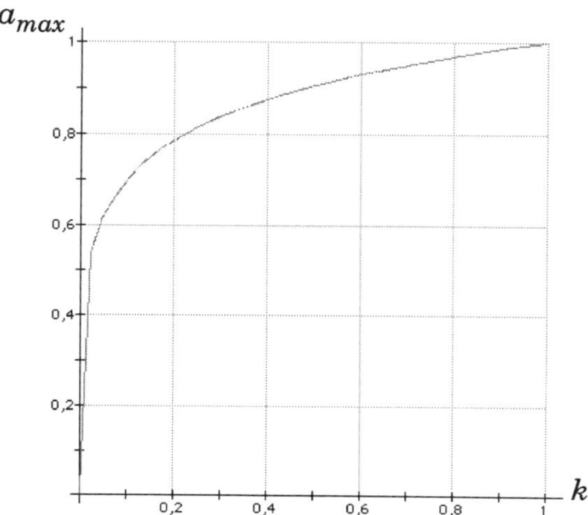

Figure 9.5: Upper bound for the maximum amount of allocated memory $a_{max} = k + U(k) + U(k + U(k))$

9.5 Upper Bound for Work to be Done by GC on Allocation

With the upper bound for the allocated memory a as given in (20), one can use (10) to determine an upper bound for the progress the current GC cycle has to make on the allocation of one unit of memory:

(23) $$P_{max} = 1/(1-a_{max})$$
$$= -1 / \mathrm{W}(W((k-1)/e)/e)$$

Figure 9.6 shows this progress function. Some values for P_{max} are given in **Table 9.2**.

For an application that uses at most 80% of the total memory as reachable objects, at most 33.1 units of allocated memory must be scanned by the collector on every unit allocation. The average amount of memory to be scanned is significantly lower. The maximum is only reached at the end of the collection cycle that causes the highest amount of allocated memory. At the beginning of the next cycle, garbage is recycled and a lower progress is sufficient. Of course, whenever the amount of reachable

k:	0.0	0.3	0.4	0.5	0.6	0.7	
P_{max}:	1.0	6.173	8.085	10.67	14.47	20.71	
k:	0.75	0.8	0.85	0.9	0.95	0.975	1.0
P_{max}:	25.67	33.10	45.45	70.11	144.0	291.8	∞

Table 9.2: Upper bound for required GC progress per unit of memory allocated

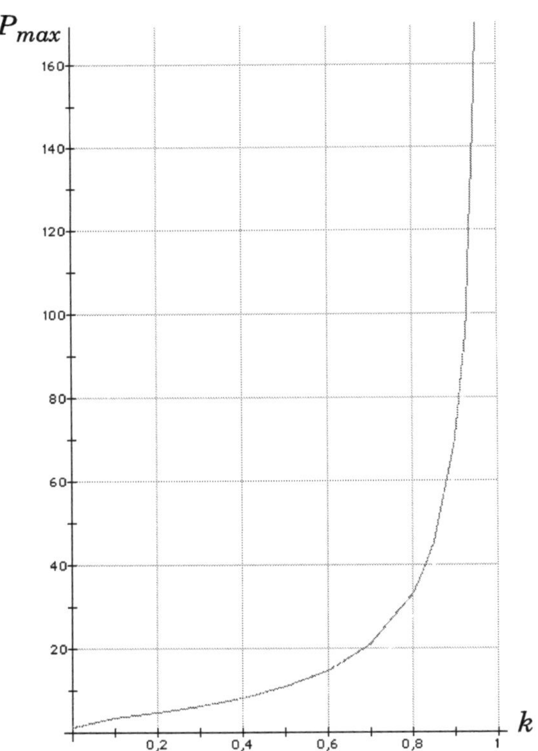

Figure 9.6: Upper bound for required GC progres per unit of memory allocated
$P_{max}(k) = 1/W(W((k-1)/e)/e)$

memory is less than 80% of the total memory, less collection work will be required.

9.6 Exploiting these Results

A straightforward implementation of the scheme results in little garbage collection overhead for applications that use a fraction of less than about 80% of the availabe memory. The overhead increases dramatically when the memory requirements of the application come close to 100% of the available memory. Applications that use all or nearly all of the available memory will encounter a noticeable slowdown by the collector. The scheme has the pleasant feature that adding memory to such a system will prevent this slowdown and will also reduce the required GC work on all applications.

A system that provides means to dynamically enlarge the heap size provides another application of this scheme. Here, a reasonable trade-off between garbage collection time and memory demand can be found as follows. Whenever the required progress of the collector reaches a certain upper bound, the memory manager may decide that it would be better to allocate some additional memory from the operating system instead of performing too much collection work. The relation between the maximum fraction of allocated memory a_{max} and k as shown in (21), **Table 9.1** and **Figure 9.5** can serve as an upper bound for the amount of unused memory:

Assuming that the work to be done by the garbage collector on an allocation of one unit of memory should never be more than scanning 20.71 units of memory. This will be the case when the allocated memory reaches $a = 0.952$. From **Figure 9.5** we see that this amount of allocated memory can only be attained by an application whose reachable memory is at least 70% of the total memory. In this situation, at least 70% of the total memory must have been reachable by the application; the amount of unused memory is at most 30%.

If the memory manager decides to allocate more memory from the operating system whenever a reaches 0.952, it can guarantee the upper bound of $P \leq 20.71$ for the collection work, while also guaranteeing not to waste more than 30% of the total memory (assuming that the amount allocated from the operating system is small compared to the total memory).

Table 9.3 shows this trade-off between memory usage and GC overhead for several selected values of P_{max}, a_{max}, k_{min} and wasted memory

P_{max}:	1.0	6.173	8.085	10.67	14.47	20.71	
a_{max}:	0.0	0.838	0.876	0.906	0.931	0.952	
k_{min}:	0.0	0.3	0.4	0.5	0.6	0.7	
w_{max}:	100%	70%	60%	50%	40%	30%	
P_{max}:	25.67	33.10	45.45	70.11	144.0	291.8	∞
a_{max}:	0.961	0.970	0.978	0.985	0.993	0.997	1.0
k_{min}:	0.75	0.8	0.85	0.9	0.95	0.975	1.0
w_{max}:	25%	20%	15%	10%	5%	2.5%	0%

Table 9.3: Trade-off between maximum GC overhead P_{max} and wasted memory w_{max}. Also shown is maximum amount of allocated memory a_{max} in this case and lower bound k_{min} for the reachable memory of the application program.

w_{max}. If we allow a significant GC overhead of scanning up to 291.8 units of memory per unit allocated, we can reduce the amount of wasted memory to 2.5%. When limiting the collection work to 6.173 times the allocated memory, up to 70% of the total memory may be unused by the application program.

9.7 Experimental Results

Experiments were performed to verify the assumption that the dynamic adjustment of garbage collection activity as presented in section 9.3 performs better in the average case than selecting a constant value P for the garbage collection progress as described for the simple scheme in section 9.2. For the measurements, the tests from the SPECjvm98 [SPEC98] benchmark suite were used and compiled with the static compiler of the Jamaica virtual machine that will be presented in more detail in the next chapter.

Two tests were excluded: *_200_check* is not intended for performance measurements, and *_227_mtrt* uses multi-threading in a way that makes it impossible to predict the maximum amount of reachable memory during a program run accurately.

For the test, the maximum amount R_{max} of reachable memory during the execution of the test applications was first determined. The mechanism that will be described in section 11.3 was used. The amount was measured with an accuracy of 5%, i.e., the result gives an upper bound for the amount of reachable memory that is at most 5% higher than the actual maximum amount of reachable memory used by the application.

Based on this maximum amount of reachable memory, the test applications were run with different heap sizes with the garbage collector performing collection work at allocation time that is either determined dynamically or fixed statically. In dynamic mode, the progress function $P(a) = 1/(1-a)$ from (10) was used, while in static mode a constant garbage collection progress $P = 2/(1-k)$ from (6) as described section 9.2 was chosen.

The tests where run with 23 different heap sizes M such that $k = R_{max}/M$ varied from 0.289 to 0.980. The resulting execution times are shown in **Figure 9.7**.

The measurements show that there is a significantly longer execution time when using static mode and a large fraction of the memory is actually used for reachable objects (for $k > 0.9$).

For larger heap sizes, i.e., smaller k, the execution time of static mode is larger in most cases in allocation intensive tests such as *_213_javac*. The difference becomes smaller with growing heap size. For larger heaps, there is little difference in average execution time when comparing static and dynamic garbage collection progress.

The runtime of tests that perform few allocations are hardly affected by the progress mode of the garbage collector or the heap size. *_222_mpegaudio* is an example for this.

In summary, dynamic garbage collection progress provides better average case performance compared to static progress on allocation intensive tests. The difference in performance becomes larger as the heap size gets closer to the minimum required heap size. In cases with little allocation and large heap, there is little difference in runtime performance between dynamic and static garbage collection progress.

In a hard real-time system, worst-case execution time is typically more important than average-case execution time. **Figure 9.8** illustrates the worst-case garbage collection progress for the heap sizes examined with the benchmarks. In static mode, the worst-case and average case are the same since the amount of garbage collection work is constant. In a hard real-time system, the static mode may be preferred even though its average case performance is worse, since the worst-case execution times

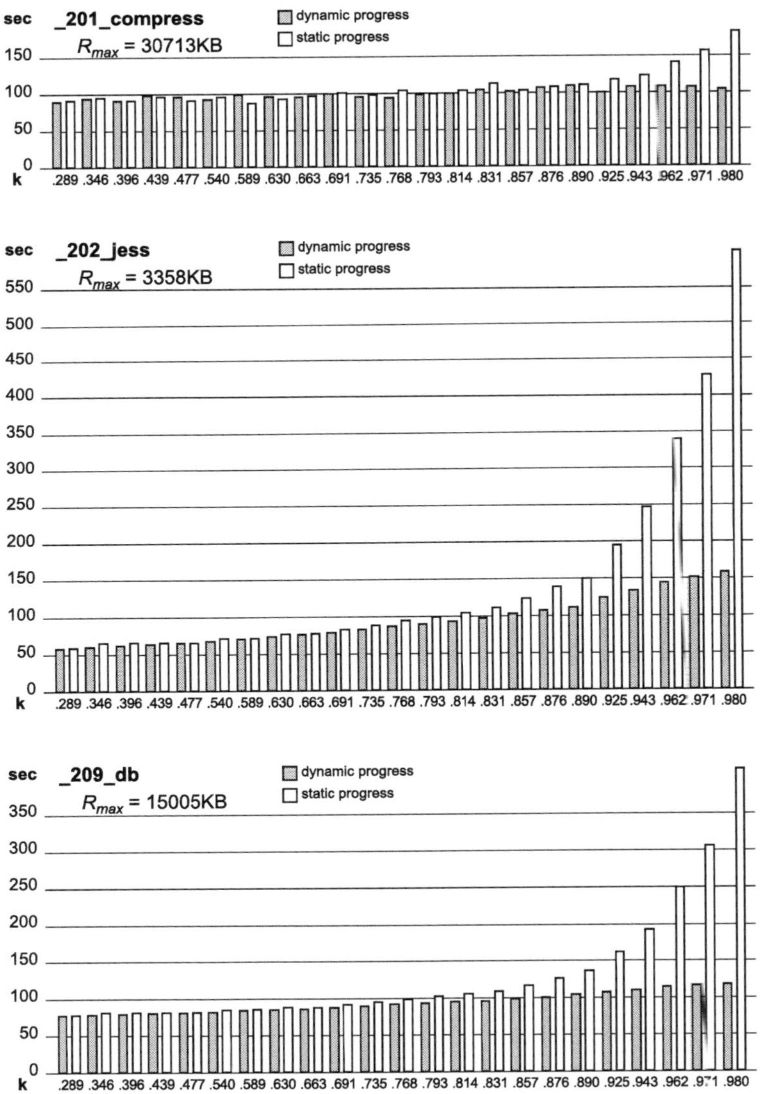

Figure 9.7a: Runtime performance of SPECjvm98 benchmarks using different heap sizes and running GC in dynamic and static mode.

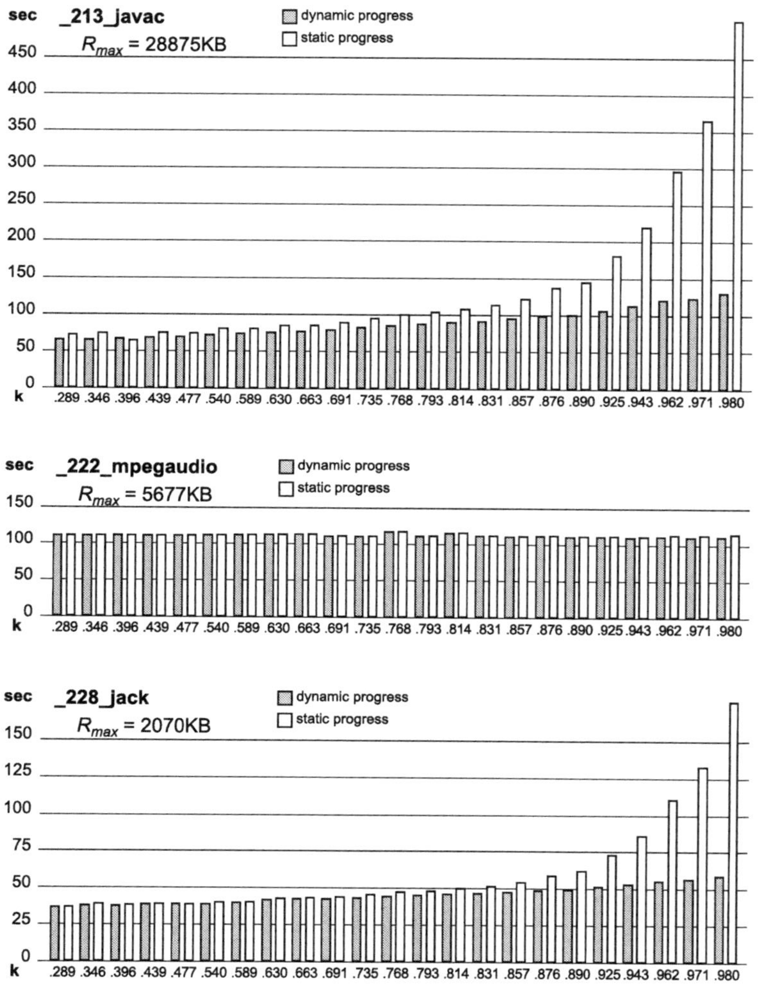

Figure 9.7b: Runtime performance of SPECjvm98 benchmarks using different heap sizes and running GC in dynamic and static mode.

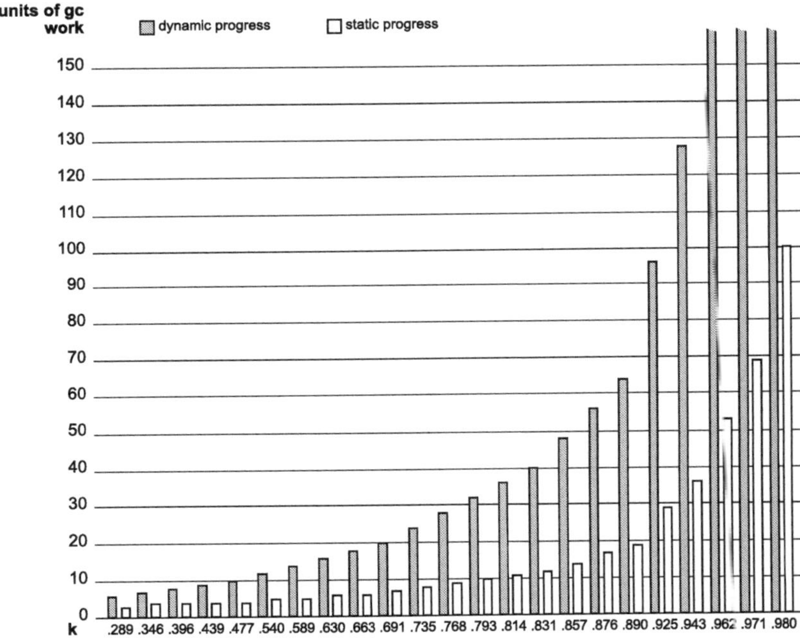

Figure 9.8: Worst-case garbage collection overhead on an allocation for different heap sizes and running GC in dynamic and static mode.

of the garbage collection work for an allocation is lower. The difference in these worst-case execution times is largest when the heap size is smallest. For a heap usage of only 28.9% ($k = 0.289$), the worst-case execution time of an allocation in dynamic mode is two time the one in static mode. For a heap usage of 98% ($k = 0.980$), an allocation in dynamic mode may even take 3.84 longer in the worst case compared to static mode.

9.8 Acknowledgements

Thanks go to Sumeer Bhola for pointing me to an important error in the original publication of this chapter in the ISMM'98 proceedings.

Don't like Jamaica, I love 'er,
–10CC

10. Deterministic Execution of Java's Primitive Operations

For the application of Java in real-time and safety-critical application domains, an analysis of the worst-case execution times of primitive Java operations is necessary. All primitive operations must either execute in constant time or have a reasonable upper bound for their execution time. The difficulties that arise for a Java virtual machine and a Java compiler in this context will be presented here. These difficulties include the implementation of the of Java's class and interface model, class initialization, monitors and automatic memory management. A new Java virtual machine and compiler that solves these difficulties have been implemented and the performance has been analysed.

This chapter is based on an earlier presentation at the Java Virtual Machine Research and Technology Symposium 2001 (JVM '01) in Monterey [SW01].

10.1 Introduction

Java is becoming increasingly popular for software development, even in application domains well beyond the original target domain of the language. The driving force is the high productivity, code quality, security and platform-independence that typically goes along with the use of Java. Java is promoted even as a development tool for real-time critical systems that require deterministic execution [JCons00, RT-JEG00], even though there are several obstacles to be overcome to achieve deterministic execution of Java code. Deterministic execution in real-time systems means being able to predict the execution time of the code, or, to at least be able to give a good upper bound for the execution time.

An important source for indeterministic execution time are processor caches. Providing good and reliable estimates of the execution time with the presence of caches will be left for future research.

The most obvious source for indeterministic execution is garbage collection. Realtime embedded systems such as in industrial automation, avionics or automotive applications often require short response times. Blocking garbage collectors cause long pauses that are hard to predict and unacceptable for these applications.

Although incremental garbage collection techniques can help reduce the likelihood for a garbage collection pause, they can not guarantee it. It can still occur that the collector does not make sufficient progress. Consequently, the system can fail or require long pauses to recycle memory or defragment the heap. Techniques to provide deterministic garbage collection were presented in the preceeding chapters of this thesis.

A deterministic implementation of Java must provide means to determine worst-case execution times for Java's primitive operations. The dynamic structure of Java, with inheritance, virtual method calls and multiple-inheritance for interfaces, poses several difficulties for the implementation. The time required for calls or type checks must be limited and statically determinable.

Further difficulties are caused by the dynamic nature of Java's class loading and initialization mechanism. Finally, Java's monitor and exception mechanism pose further difficulties for a deterministic implementation.

10.2 Related Work

Research on object oriented language implementation so far focused on high average-case runtime performance. A predictable runtime cost that is required in realtime systems is of little importance for classical Java applications.

For the application of Java in realtime systems, Nilsen identifies mechanisms to determine conservative worst-case execution times for code sequences that exclude recursion and unbounded loops as a key enabling technology [Nilsen96, NR95]. The determination of worst-case execution times is not straightforward for all of Java's primitive operations; this chapter will describe how a Java implementation can permit this analysis. The other enabling technologies listed by Nilsen are execution time measurement, rate-monotonic analysis [LL73], static cyclic schedules and real-time garbage collection.

Different approaches for the implementation of dynamic dispatching in the context of single- and multiple-inheritance have been proposed. Zendra et. al. suggest specific dispatch functions instead of virtual function tables [ZCC97]. Typical implementations of C++ use several virtual function tables per object and direct references to sub-objects to implement multiple inheritance. To improve the average performance of virtual calls, inline caching has been suggested [DS84].

Yang et. al. [Yang99] and Bacon et. al. [BKMS98] present techniques to inline monitors in objects and reduce the average runtime cost for monitor operations. Their approaches, however, cannot avoid high worst-case overhead in the case of contention.

10.3 The Jamaica Virtual Machine

Jamaica is a new virtual machine implementation for Java, an overview of this Java implementation was given in section 4.8. The following sections describe the deterministic implementation of the Java bytecodes, monitors and exceptions in Jamaica.

10.3.1 Executing Bytecodes

Most Java bytecode instructions can be implemented directly as a short sequence of machine instructions that executes in constant time when cache effects are ignored. Even in the presence of processor caches, a worst-case execution time can be determined easily. These operations include accesses to local variables and the Java stack, arithmetic instructions, comparisons and branches.

The bytecode instructions for which a deterministic implementation is not straightforward will be described in detail in this section.

10.3.1.1 Loading String Constants

One needs to be careful when loading string constants with the *ldc* bytecode instruction. The string object must have been created in advance to avoid high allocation overhead on the first access. The implementation achieves predictable execution time by creating all constant string objects at class load time. During execution, loading the string's address is all that needs to be done.

10.3.1.2 Class Initialization

The semantics of Java require that on the first access to a static field, a static method or the first creation of an instance of a class the corresponding class be resolved and its static initializer be executed. In a standard Java implementation, the first resolution of a class also causes the class to be loaded, a complex operation that may take a lot of time. All primitive operations that cause class resolution consequently have long worst-case execution times. Once the referred class is initialized, the actual execution time of these operations is typically short.

This problem is not easy to solve without changing Java's semantics. The Java virtual machine specification [LY99] explicitly allows early loading and resolution of classes, as long as the semantics of Java are respected. It does not, however, allow early execution of static initializers, since this would change the control flow.

To avoid the overhead of loading and linking a class during class resolution, the Jamaica virtual machine recursively loads and links all classes that are referenced by the root class (the class containing the method *main)* at system initialization. If later during execution of the system additional classes are loaded using *java.lang.Class.forName()* or the reflection API, this process is repeated and all referenced classes are loaded as well.

What is left at the first reference to a class is the execution of its static initializer. The user is free to perform arbitrarily complex calculations within the static initializer, so a worst-case execution time for this operation can not be guaranteed by the Java implementation unless the static initializer is relatively simple, e.g., code that contains no method calls or loops.

Even for simple static initializers, the call overhead causes fairly bad worst-case execution times for simple operations such as an access to a static field. The user can avoid this overhead by explicitly causing early initialization of the referred class during system startup. This early resolution can be achieved by explicitly referencing all accessed classes within a class's static initizalizer.

The resulting overhead for operations that cause class resolution is then reduced to the overhead of checking the initialization state of the class.

This can be done by reading a single field in the class's descriptor and a conditional branch.

It is planned to improve the Jamaica compiler such that explicit early initialization can be detected statically such that the test can be avoided in most cases.

10.3.1.3 Method Invocation

The invocation of methods in the context of class extension and interface implementation is another difficulty for a deterministic implementation of Java. There are four different bytecode instructions for the invocation of methods.

Static Calls

Two call instruction avoid dynamic binding altogether: *invoke_static* and *invoke_special*. The first one is used to call static methods, while *invoke_special* is used for instance methods, but uses static binding instead of dynamic binding (this is used for object initialization or when explicit calls to a certain class' method is needed as in *super.method()*). The lack of dynamic binding semantics in these two bytecode instructions makes the implementation straightforward. Control flow can directly switch to the called method since the target method is known.

Virtual Calls

A call using *invoke_virtual* is slightly more difficult to implement since the dynamic type of the target object needs to be taken into account. If the called method was redefined by the dynamic type of the target, that redefined method needs to be called.

The standard method of implementation provides deterministic execution time. A virtual call is implemented with a method table that is part of the type descriptor of each object (**Figure 10.1**). Each method is assigned a unique index in the method table. Inherited methods keep their unique indices in the new class. Methods defined within a class are assigned the next available index, while methods that redefine inherited methods inherit the index of the original method. Every method is recorded in the method table at its index, while inherited methods that were redefined are replaced by their redefined versions. Using this technique, a virtual call can be performed in constant time.

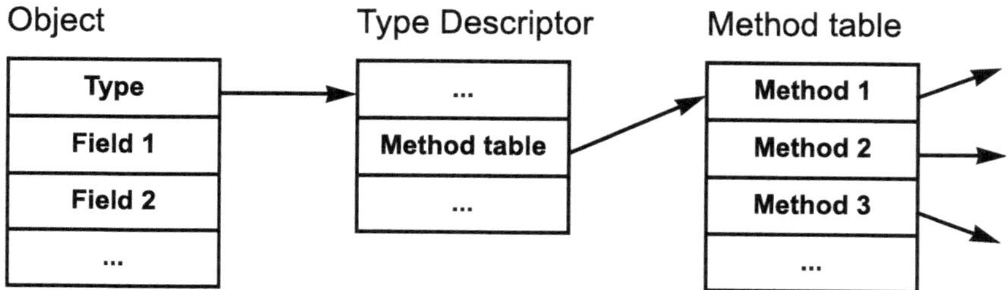

Figure 10.1: Method table used for dynamic binding of virtual calls

Interface Calls

The most difficult to implement calls are calls to interface methods via the bytecode operation *invoke_interface*. The reason is that multiple inheritance makes it impossible to assign constant indices to the methods as in the case of virtual calls. A dynamic search for the called method is typically made in this case. This causes a call overhead that depends on the number of methods in a class or the number of interfaces implemented by a class. Therefore calls to interface methods are significantly less efficient in many Java implementations.

The representation of classes and interfaces that was chosen for the Jamaica implementation permits constant-time calls to interface methods. Every interface is assigned a unique identifier *interface_id,* starting at 0 for the first interface loaded. Each method within an interface is assigned an *interface_method_index* similar to the index assigned to methods of normal classes. The class descriptor of every class that implements one or several interfaces contains a reference to an array of references. This array is referred to as *implements* array. For each interface that is implemented, the *implements* array contains a valid reference at the interface' *interface_id.* This reference points to an array of the methods defined in the interface and implemented in the class, with each method at its *interface_method_index* (**Figure 10.2**). All entries in the *implements* array that correspond to interfaces that are not implemented by the class are set to *null.* For the call of an interface method, all that is needed is to read the *implements* array from the target object's type descriptor, index this array at the interface's *interface_id* and finally read the method at the *interface_method_index.* Compared to virtual methods, there is only one additional indirection needed. Calls to interface methods are performed in constant time.

Nevertheless, there is an important disadvantage of this approach: the size of the implements array is linear in the total number i of interfaces, and the total memory required for a system with c classes is therefore in $O(c{\cdot}i)$. The memory usage is quadratic in the size of the code. With the applications executed using Jamaica, this has not caused any difficulties, but it may be a problem for large applications.

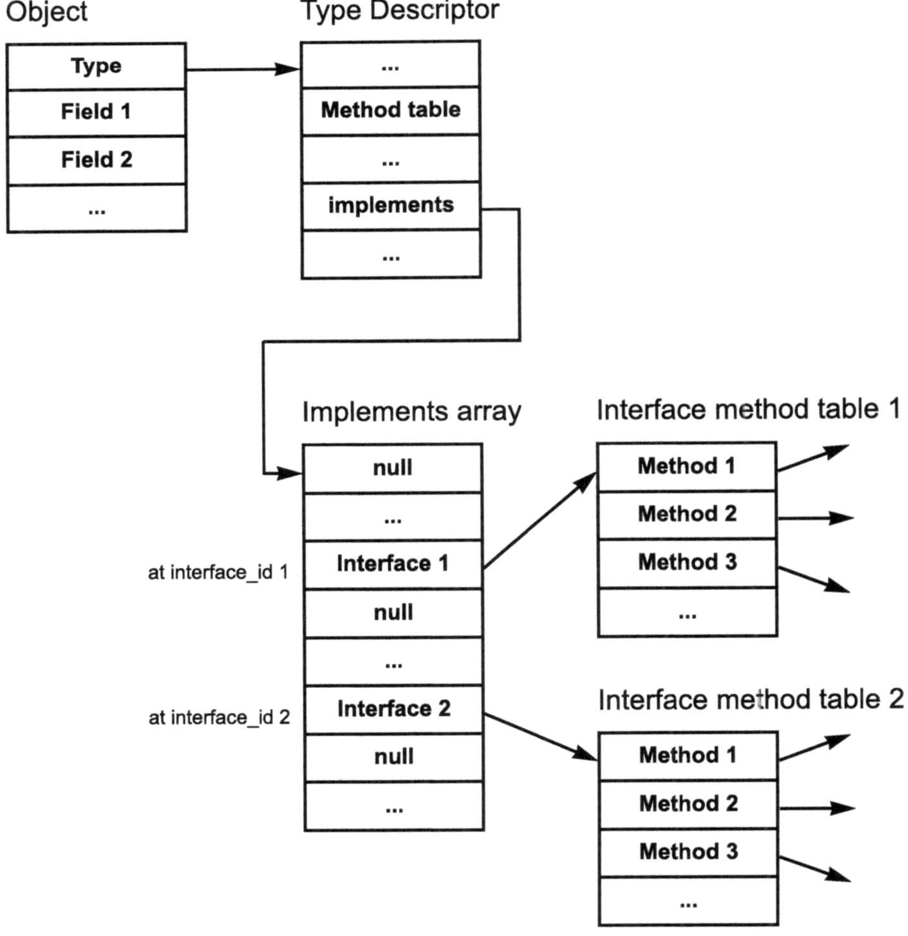

Figure 10.2: Interface call using implements array

The memory overhead can be reduced using some simple optimizations. It is sufficient if the size of the *implements* array is reduced to *interface_id*+1 for the largest *interface_id* of all the interfaces implemented. In addition, all classes that do not implement any interfaces can share one single empty *implements* array. Jamaica uses these optimizations.

Dynamic loading of interface classes can also be handled using this mechanism. New interface classes will be assigned new *interface_ids* and classes implementing these interfaces will get sufficiently large *implements* arrays. In the context of class garbage collection, care must be taken to ensure that unused *interface_ids* will be reused, so that the size of the *implements* arrays does not grow without bound.

One can imagine that the typically high additional overhead for calls due to multiple inheritance may be the only reason for the existence of interfaces. Using the scheme presented here, the overhead is minimal compared to a virtual call using single inheritance. If Java allowed multiple inheritance for normal classes, there would be no need for interfaces at all. A single concept, the class, could be used to model interfaces and classes. This would remove the often difficult decision whether to model a concept using an abstract class or an interface. The former is more powerful by allowing the implementation of some methods, while the latter is more flexible and allows multiple inheritance. Eiffel has shown that a single concept using multiple inheritance is sufficient and that efficient implementation of multiple inheritance is possible [Meyer92].

Additional Call and Return Overhead

Apart from the overhead needed to determine which method is called, a call requires setting up a new stack frame. Later, this stack frame has to be removed when the method returns. Unlike in languages such as *C* or *C++*, the creation and removal of the stack frame is not a constant time operation. The reason is that reference values on the stack frame must be known to the garbage collector. Each entry in the stack frame that is reserved for a memory reference must be at least initialized at the start of a method call and also perhaps cleaned up at the end of the call. Consequently, the overhead for creation or removal of a stack frame is linear in its size.

10.3.1.4 Type Checking

Another problem area for a deterministic implementation that is closely related to dynamic calls is dynamic type checking. There are two situations in Java code that require dynamic determination of the type of a reference: explicit type tests using the *instanceof* operator and type casts. Consequently, there are two bytecode operations, *instanceof* and *checkcast,* for these two purposes. The first of these, *instanceof*, tests if a referenced object is of a certain type and produces a *boolean* result, while *checkcast* causes an exception if the type test fails and does nothing otherwise. Furthermore, there are three categories of types in Java that have to be treated differently in the type check: classes, interfaces, and arrays.

Type Checking for Classes

The most common case for a type check is checking whether or not a referenced object is an instance of a certain class. As an example, assume the following *if*-statement.

```
if (r instanceof A) {
  System.out.print("r is of class A");
}
```

The straightforward implementation of this type check would traverse the inheritance-chain of the object referenced by *r* until either class *A* is found or the root object *java.lang.Object* has been reached. This implementation requires time linear in the depth of the inheritance tree, a worst-case execution time for the type check is difficult to determine.

A simple modification of the representation of inherited classes permits constant-time type checking for classes. Every class has a fixed position in the inheritance tree and a fixed distance to class *java.lang.Object.* All classes in the inheritance tree that are on the path from a class *C* to *java.lang.Object* are referred to as *C*'s ancestors. *C*'s ancestors include the classes *C* and *java.lang.Object.* The number of ancestors of class *C* is the depth of *C* in the inheritance tree. Any class descriptor can now be equipped with a reference to an array of all ancestors, as shown in **Figure 10.3**. Each ancestor that resides at position *depth* in the inheritance tree is stored at position *depth*–1 in this *ancestors* array. Now, the type check can be done in constant time. All that is needed is a check of the *ancestors* array's entry at the position corresponding to the class' depth.

C-code that performs the *instanceof*-check shown above would look like this.

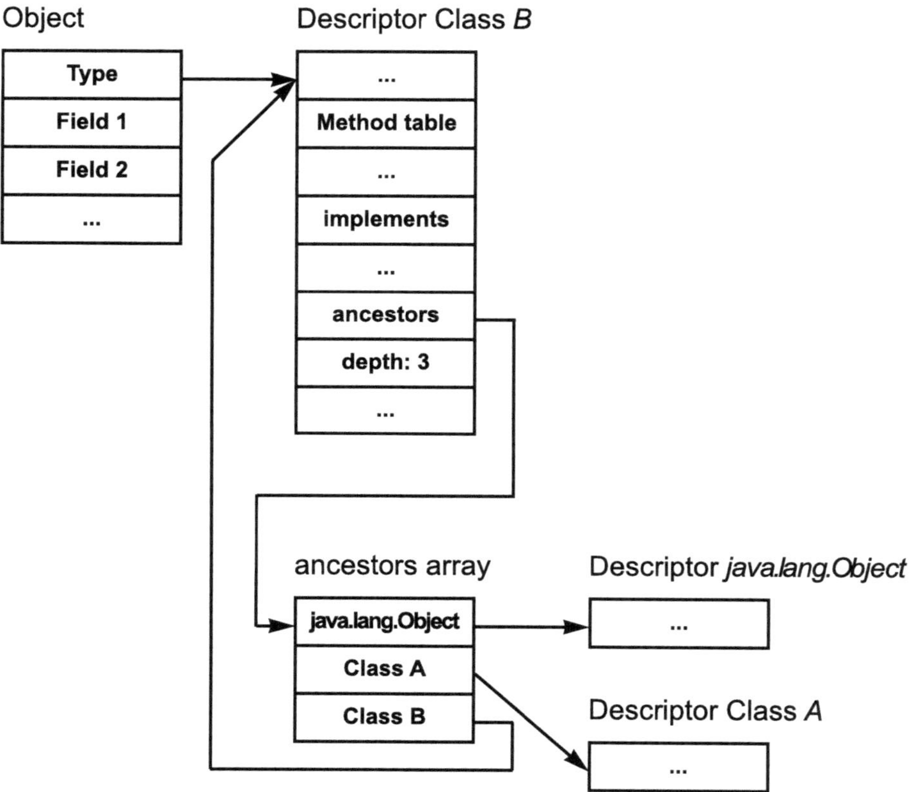

Figure 10.3: Type checking for classes using ancestors array. Class *B* extends class *A* which inherits directly from class *java.lang.Object.*

```
if ((r != null)
 && (r->type->ancestors.length       >= A->depth)
 && (r->type->ancestors[A->depth-1] == A   ))
{
  System.out.print("r is of class A");
}
```

The code requires reading the referenced object's class descriptor, the *ancestors* array, the array length and one element in the array. The depth of class *A* and the class descriptor of class *A* are also required in this test, but these values are runtime constants and can be inlined by a compiler.

Type Checking for Interfaces

The *ancestors* array approach used for class types cannot be used directly for interfaces since a class may implement several interfaces that reside at the same *depth* in the inheritance tree. What is needed is an array with a unique entry for every interface that is implemented by a class. Fortunately, such an array was already introduced for the efficient implementation of interface calls: the *implements* array.

Thus, for a type check of the form

```
if (r instanceof I) {
  System.out.print("r is of interface I");
}
```

all that is needed is to check whether the *implements* array of *r* has an entry for interface *I*. In C-like code, this may look as follows.

```
if ((r != null)
 && (r->type->implements.length >  I->id)
 && (r->type->implements[I->id] != null ))
{
  System.out.print("r is of interface I");
}
```

The code requires reading the class descriptor reference, the implements array, its length and the entry corresponding to the interface *I*. The *interface_id* that is required is a runtime constant.

Type Checking for Arrays

The type checking semantics for arrays are defined recursively. The examined type must be an array. If this is the case, the type checking continues for the element type of the array. A straightforward implementation of this definition requires execution time linear in the number of dimensions of the array. Nevertheless, a constant-time implementation of type checking for multidimensional arrays is possible. One need only store the dimension count and a reference to the final non-array element type with the array type.

This can be illustrated using the following code sequence.

```
if (r instanceof A[][][]) {
  System.out.print("r is A[][][]");
}
```

All that is required for this test is to check whether the object referred to by *r* is an array of dimension three and the base element type *A*. The C-code may look like as follows.

```
if ((r != null)
 && (r->type->dimensions == 3)
 && (r->type->elemnt->ancestors.length       >= A->depth)
 && (r->type->elemnt->ancestors[A->depth-1] == A         ))
{
  System.out.print("r is A[][][]");
}
```

The code checks the correct number of dimensions of the array and then type checks the element class as described above.

Care needs to be taken when checking arrays of class *java.lang.Object* or interfaces *java.lang.Cloneable* and *java.io.Serializable*. The class *java.lang.Object* is an ancestor of all arrays and the two interfaces are implemented by all arrays. To implement the type check for these arrays correctly, the check must additionally succeed whenever the dimension of the examined type is higher than that with which the array type is compared.

10.3.1.5 Switch Statement

The Java bytecode provides two different operations for switch-statements: *tableswitch* and *lookupswitch*. For a switch-statement with case-entries that are similar values, *tableswitch* is used. It permits a constant-time table lookup for the statement sequence that needs to be executed.

For switch-statements, that extend over a large range of values with unused intervals, *tableswitch* would require a large table. In this case, *lookupswitch* is used in the bytecode. This instruction uses a sorted table of case-value and target address pairs. The lookup binary searches this table, hence the runtime is logarithmic in the number of case-labels in the switch statement.

The Java implementation of the interpreter has little choice here but to implement the binary search. Converting a *lookupswitch* into a constant-time *tableswitch* may require too much memory for the table. The user of the system must therefore be careful when using switch-statements with case-entries that stretch over a large range of values. It is up to the Java compiler (e.g., *javac*) to create either of these instructions.

A Java compiler that generates native code can use perfect hashing here. During compilation time, a conflict-free hash function is computed that maps the case-values to target addresses. The jump is then executed in $O(1)$. As shown by Mehlhorn, such a hash table of size $3n$, where

n is the number of case-labels, can be computed in cubic time [Mehlh84]. Future versions of Jamaica that generate native code will use perfect hashing here. The currently generated *C* code uses *C*'s switch statement and relies on the *C* compiler's implementation.

10.3.1.6 Memory Allocation

The most difficult problem to be solved by a deterministic implementation of Java is to provide deterministic behaviour of dynamic memory allocation. The implementation must guarantee a hard upper bound for the execution time of an allocation. The implementatio of Jamaica's memory management system has been explained in detail in the earlier chapters. The garbage collector implementation will be evaluated in more detail in the next chapter.

10.3.1.7 Memory Accesses

The use of fixed size blocks to represent Java objects and arrays has an important impact on the code that is required to access object fields and array elements.

Field Accesses

Since a linear list of blocks is used to represent objects, the number of memory references required is linear in the offset of the field within the object. Fields that reside in the first block can be accessed using a single memory access, while fields in the second block require two memory accesses, etc.

Fortunately, most Java objects are small and even for larger objects the fields that are accessed most frequently are typically the first fields with the lowest offsets (see chapter 7). For any field, the position can be determined statically and hence the number of memory accesses required can as well be determined statically.

Array Accesses

With array accesses, the situation is a bit more complex since arrays are represented as trees. The trees use the highest branching factor allowed by the block size. For a block size of 32 bytes on a 32-bit system, this means that the branching factor is 8. Even large arrays can be represented in a fairly shallow tree. For a given system with a bounded heap size h, the maximum depth d_{max} for these trees can be determined statically using the following term (for a block size of 32 bytes).

$$d_{max} = \lceil ln_8(h \ / \ 32) \rceil$$

For a heap of 32MB the resulting maximal depth is 7. For an array access, one additional memory access is required to read the array's depth and one reference is needed to read the actual element. So the total number of memory accesses is d_{max}+2, or 9 for a heap size of 32MB.

This bound on the number of memory accesses enables the determination of a worst-case execution time for array accesses. Even though this time is much higher than that of a classical linear array representation, it will be shown below that the overall performance of the system is comparable to that of traditional Java implementations.

10.3.2 Monitors

Several publications have presented efficient implementations of Java monitors that reduce the memory overhead of inlined monitors and the runtime overhead in the most common cases. Yang et. al. [Yang99] proposed inlining the monitor and reserving one word per object for the monitor. This word consists of three sub-word sized integers that represent the nest count (the number of time the monitor was entered by the same thread), the owner thread and a list of waiting threads. The nodes of this list are stored in a hashtable and they are only used if threads are actually waiting for a monitor.

Bacon et. al. [BKMS98] reserve 24 bits per object for the monitor. They distinguish two different representations for monitors: inlined and inflated. Inlined monitors use the monitor value to store an identifier for the owner thread and a nest count. Inflated monitors use the 24 bits as a monitor id that functions as a reference to a monitor object on the heap. Monitors that are never subject to contention remain in inlined representation, while monitors that are subject to contention will be converted to their inflated representation and will remain in this representation until the object dies.

The disadvantage of these monitor representations is their unpredictable runtime behaviour due to the use of heap allocation or a hashtable for monitors that are subject to contention.

The Jamaica monitor implementation avoids the need to dynamically allocate monitor storage on the heap or stack altogether. Monitors are always inlined, using 16 or 32 bits per object (16 bits are sufficient in systems with few threads and a limited nest count). As long as no threads are waiting for a monitor, it is sufficient to record the owning thread's identifier and the nest count in the inlined monitor (**Figure 10.4**). As soon as a thread tries to acquire a monitor that is owned by a different thread, a queue of waiting threads needs to be created.

An important observation one can make is that no thread can ever be waiting for more than a single monitor. Hence, instead of creating independent node objects for the waiting queue, one may as well reserve some additional fields in the thread object itself and create a queue of thread objects for all waiting threads. Since a thread may own several

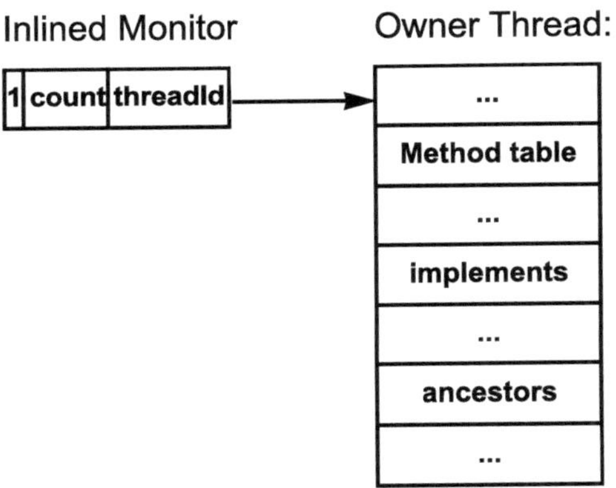

Figure 10.4: Inlined monitor owned by one thread.

monitors simultaneously, the owning thread itself must not be part of this queue, only the waiting threads can be linked to the monitor. One bit in the inlined monitor indicates that a waiting queue exists. In this case, the nest count and owning thread's identifier are copied into reserved fields of the threads in the waiting queue. The identifier of the first thread in the queue is stored in the inlined monitor (**Figure 10.5**).

The result is a monitor implementation that is efficient for the most frequent cases of monitor operations. Code for entering a monitor that is not owned by any thread or that has already been acquired by the current thread and code for exiting a monitor that has no other threads waiting is inlined. The operations that involve waiting threads do not require dynamic creation of a monitor object. All that needs to be done is queuing and unqueuing the waiting threads and performing the actual wait or resume. However, wait times depend on the application and are not predictable by the virtual machine implementation.

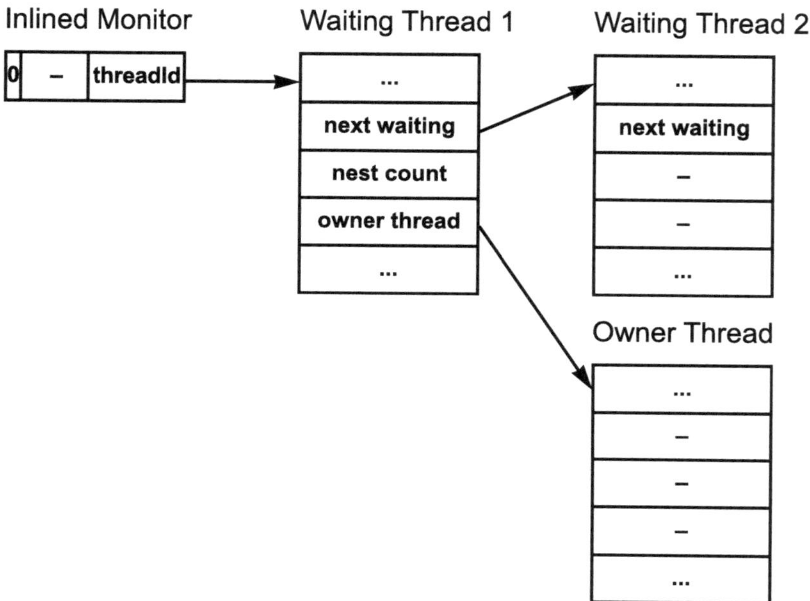

Figure 10.5: Monitor owned by one thread with two waiting threads.

10.3.3 Exceptions

Java's exception mechanism enables control flow from an active method back to a method with an exception handler that lies an arbitrary number of stack frames above the current position in the call chain. Throwing an exception that is handled by another method therefore requires removal of all active stack frames that lie in between the method causing the exception and the method handling it. This removal of stack frames includes removing all local references in these stack frames from the garbage collector's root set, which is an operation linear in the number of active stack frames and in the number of root references.

The execution time for throwing an exception is therefore not constant and it is at least difficult to find a constant-time implementation for exception handling. Using a mechanism like C's *setjmp* and *longjmp* enables constant-time change of the control flow that is required for exceptions, but it does not provide means to remove the information required for accurate garbage collection.

In the Jamaica implementation, the execution time of throwing an exception is therefore linear in the size of the stack frames between the exception throwing point and the corresponding exception handler. Since exceptions are not supposed to be used for normal control flow, but for exceptional control flow only, this behaviour should be acceptable even when deterministic execution in the non-exceptional case is required.

10.4 Performance Comparison

To evaluate the overall performance of the deterministic Java implementation Jamaica and to compare it to traditional Java implementations, the SPECjvm98 benchmark suite [SPEC98] has been run using Jamaica and several versions of SUN's JDK [SUN99, SUN00] with JIT compiler enabled (JDK 1.1.8; Classic VM build JDK-1.2-V, green threads, sunwjit; and Solaris VM build Solaris_JDK_1.2.2_05, native threads, sunwjit). Only one test from the benchmark suite, *_200_check*, was excluded from the analysis since it is not intended for performance measurements but to check the correctness of the implementation (and Jamaica passes this test).

For execution, the test programs were compiled and smart linked using the Jamaica builder. The programs were then executed on a single processor (333 MHz UltraSPARC-IIi) SUN Ultra 5/10 machine equipped with 256MB of RAM running SunOS 5.7.

The results of the performance measurements are shown in **Figure 10.6**. For the measurements, the heap size was set to 32MB for all tests but *_201_compress*. This test required more memory to execute and was run with a heap size of 64MB.

Compared to Sun's implementation, the performance of the deterministic implementation is similar to that of JDK 1.1.8 or 1.2, while the performance of JDK 1.2.2 was improved significantly. Since Jamaica is still a young implementation and not much effort has been spent on improving and tuning the compiler's optimization techniques, one can expect that better optimization in the compiler will improve the performance of Jamaica further. Another source for future performance enhancements will be direct generation of machine code instead of using *C* as an intermediate language as is done currently. Using *C* does not permit optimal code selection for primitives such as write barrier code or garbage collector root reference information. Direct generation of machine code permits selection of better code for these primitives, e.g., by assigning certain registers for specific purposes.

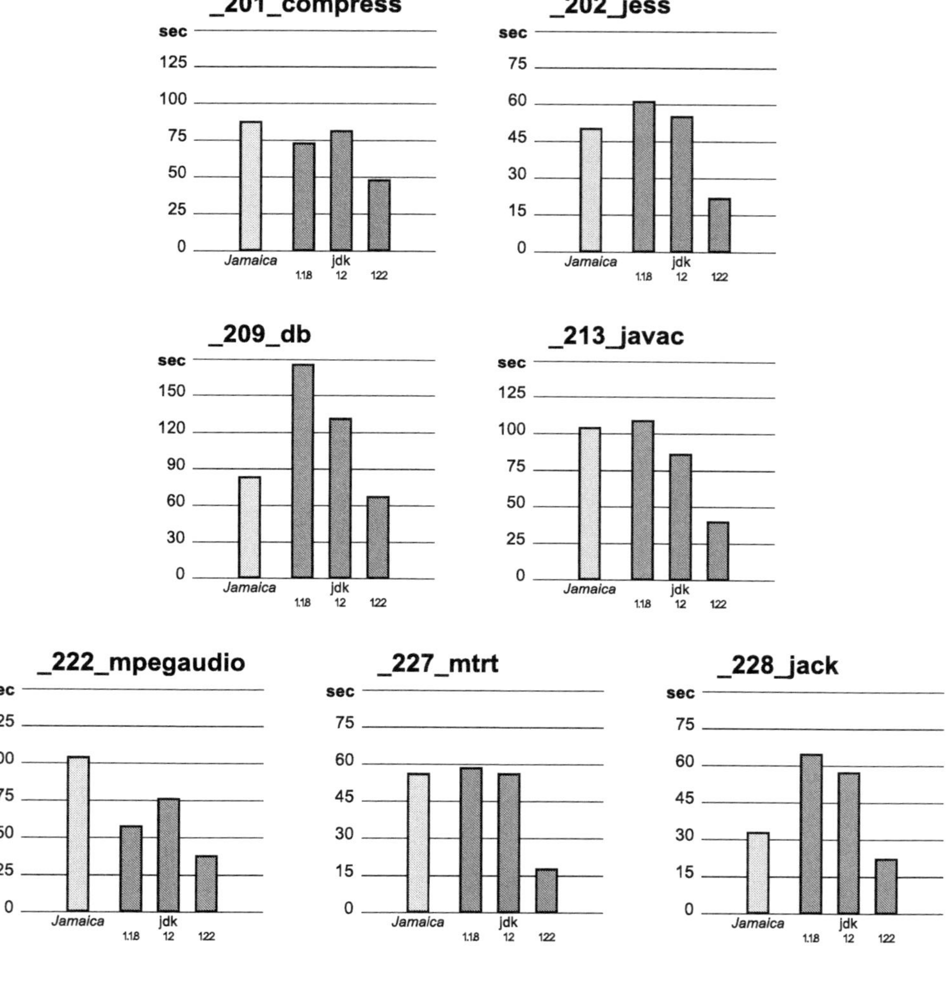

Figure 10.6: Runtime performance of the SPECjvm98 benchmarks using Jamaica and JDK 1.1.8, 1.2 and 1.2.2

10.5 Conclusions

In this chapter the Jamaica implementation of Java has been presented. The deterministic implementation of Java's primitive operations in this implementation has been explained. The implementation permits static analysis of the execution time of its primitive operations that is not possible with current Java implementations. This enables the use of Java in application domains that require deterministic behaviour of the implementation.

The performance of the implementation has then been measured and compared to different versions of Sun's JDK implementation using the SPECjvm98 benchmark suite. The results show that performance that is comparable to Sun's implementations can be reached. These results are encouraging to further improve the implementation and to further reduce the performance gap compared to non-deterministic Java implementations.

10.6 Future Work

The deterministic implementation of a programming language's primitive operations provides only the basis for further analysis of the code. Tools for automatic determination of worst-case execution times can be build on top of this. For an accurate analysis that is not too conservative, mechanisms to model the system's cache memories and the effects of modern superscalar processors on the execution time need to be developed.

11. Evaluation of the Garbage Collector

The implementation of the garbage collector described throughout this text will be analysed in this chapter. The worst-case execution time of a unit of allocation work will be determined for the PowerPC processor. The result will then be used to determine worst-case execution times for allocations with different configurations, i.e., with different fractions of the total heap size used as reachable memory by an application.

Then, a technique to automatically determine an upper bound for the amount of reachable memory used by an application will be presented. Its use will be illustrated using a small benchmark as an example.

At the end of this chapter, the worst-case execution times of memory accesses and root saving will be determined.

11.1 Assumptions and Simplifications

For an accurate worst-case execution time analysis of the garbage collection code, a sophisticated technique that takes cache effects and instruction pipelining into account would be ideal. An automatic tool to perform this analysis using a technique such as that presented by Lim et. al. [LBJR+94] would be a good choice. A tool for the determination of the worst-case execution time that is based on abstract interpretation, such as PAG [FMW96, FW97], would be an even better alternative.

Unfortunately, such a tool was not available for this analysis. Instead, a less accurate manual analysis using a simplified machine model had to be used here.

For the analysis of the implementation, the generated machine code for a PowerPC board [Motorola96] was analysed. A processor speed of 200MHz is assumed. All instructions are assumed to be performed in a single clock cycle, with the exception of memory accesses that cause cache misses. There is only a single 4-way associative cache with 32 bytes per cache line. The cache miss penalty is 14 clock cycles (Hennessy and Patterson [HP96] describe typical values for the miss penalty in 1995 workstations as 8-66 clock cycles).

Similar to the simplification made by Hopp [Hopp01] for cache behaviour analysis, the instruction cache effects are ignored, i.e., cache misses in the instruction cache and conflicts between data and instructions in a unified cache are not taken into account. Writes are treated as reads (write-allocate-strategy). The last-recently-used (LRU) strategy is assumed for cache line replacement.

It is assumed that no interrupts occur and no thread switches are caused. This is a reasonable assumption for the highest priority thread in many real-time systems. For other threads, the additional cost for interrupt handling or preemption by a higher priority thread must be considered as well.

11.2 Worst-Case Execution Time of an Allocation

In chapter 9, *Garbage Collector Activation*, it has been shown how the garbage collector has to be run such that sufficient garbage collection progress is guaranteed and a worst-case execution time for an allocation can be given.

To determine this worst-case execution time, one first needs to know the worst-case execution time of basic garbage collector operations. To find these times, the machine code that was generated for the main garbage collector loop is analysed to find the overhead of one increment of garbage collection work. The analysis was done for a block size of 32 bytes or 8 machine words. First, the worst-case execution time of marking and sweeping of a single block is determined. Then, a function for the worst-case execution time for several units of garbage collection work is determined.

The analysis is done for the PowerPC processor with the garbage collector code compiled for Linux using *gcc*.

11.2.1 Marking one Block

Listing 11.1 gives the assembly code produced for the marking of one block of memory. A flowchart for this code is shown in **Figure 11.1**. This flowchart lists the number of machine instructions in each basic block. Since a block consists of eight words, the backward branch is executed no more than seven times.

```
.L205:
   mr 7,6                  # b (r7) = g
   lwz 9,68(31)
   srwi 11,7,5
   lbzx 8,9,11             # r (r8) = refs(b)
   srwi 10,7,3
   cmpwi 0,8,0
   lwzx 6,10,30            # g (r6) = (*col);
   stwx 28,10,30           # (*col) = black;
   bc 12,2,.L207           # while (r) {
.L208:
   andi. 24,8,1
   bc 12,2,.L209           #    if (r & 1) {
   lwz 11,0(7)             #      n (r11) = b[0];
   cmpwi 0,11,0
   bc 12,2,.L209           #      if (n != null) {
   srwi 9,11,3             #        coln (r9/r30) = COLOUR(n)
   lwzx 0,9,30             #        r0 = (*coln)
   cmpwi 0,0,0
   bc 4,2,.L209            #        if ((*coln) == white)
   stwx 6,9,30             #          (*coln) = g;
   mr 6,11                 #          g = n;
                           #        }
                           #      }
.L209:                     #    }
   srwi. 8,8,1             #    r (r8) = r >> 1
   addi 7,7,4              #    b = &(b[1])
   bc 4,2,.L208            # }
.L207:
```

Listing 11.1: Assembly code for marking one block.

The code has a small loop that is executed for all 8 words of a block. The longest execution path occurs when all words in the examined block are references, all of these references are non-*null* and they all refer to *white* blocks. For this case, the code for marking one block needs to execute 121 machine instructions of the following kinds:

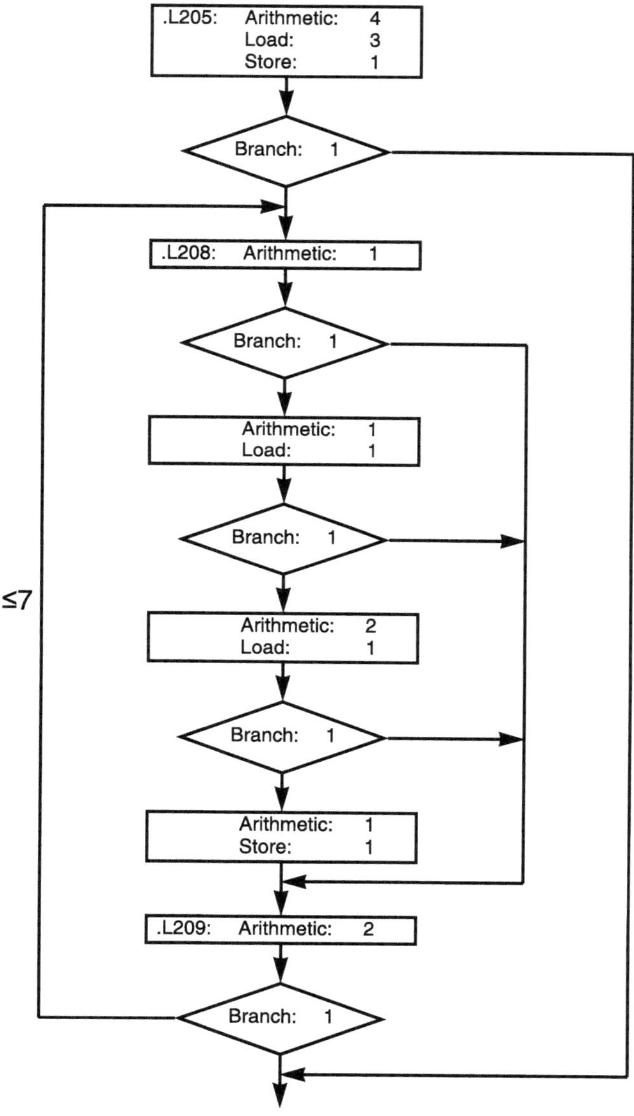

Figure 11.1: Flowchart for machine code for marking one block of 8 words.

Arithmetic (move, add, shift, compare, etc.):	4+7·8	= 60
Load:	3+2·8	= 19
Store:	1+1·8	= 9
Branch:	1+4·8	= 33

The 8 loads of all the words in the block are all in the same cache line since blocks are aligned with cache lines, only the first one can cause a cache-miss. All stores are to cache lines that have previously been loaded (the colour values), so these do not cause cache-misses. Thus, there is potential for at most 12 cache-misses.

Assuming that all instructions take a single clock cycle (pipeline effects are ignored), and the cache miss penalty is 14 clock cycles, the total worst-case execution time becomes m_{mark} = 121 instructions or c_{mark} = 121+12·14 = 289 cycles.

In addition to the code for marking every single block, there is loop overhead when several blocks are marked. This loop overhead includes testing the end condition of the mark loop and allowing for thread switches. The overhead is

Arithmetic (move, add, shift, compare, etc.):	8
Load:	2
Store:	0
Branch:	2

Assuming the memory accesses are cache-misses, the additional loop overhead is m_{mark_loop} = 12 instructions or c_{mark_loop} = 12+14·2 = 40 cycles.

11.2.2 Sweeping one Block

Correspondingly, one can analyse the overhead required during the sweep phase for one block. **Listing 11.2** gives the assembly code for sweeping, while **Figure 11.2** shows the corresponding flowchart with number of arithmetic (A), load (L), store (S) and branch (B) instructions in each basic block. The basic blocks that are part of the longest execution path through the code are shaded.

```
.L229:
  slwi 9,8,2
  lwzx 11,9,27     # col (r11) = colours[bx];
  cmpwi 0,11,2
  bc 4,2,.L230     # if (col == free) {
  cmpwi 0,6,0
```

```
    slwi 0,8,5
    lwzx 5,30,0      #   rL (r5) = bs[bx].freeRangeLen;
    add 9,0,30
    bc 12,0,.L231    #   if ((lf >= 0) &&
    add 0,6,7
    cmpw 0,8,0
    bc 4,2,.L231     #      (bx (r8) == (lf (r6)+lfl (r7)))) {
                     #        /* coalesc with prev. range */
    lwz 10,4(9)      #      nf (r10) = bs[bx].nextFreeRng;
    slwi 9,6,5
    add 7,7,5        #      lfl (r7) = lfl (r7) + rL (r5)
    cmpwi 0,10,0     #      (nf (r10) == 0) ?
    add 11,9,30
    stwx 7,9,30      #      bs[lf].freeRangeLen = lfl;
    stw 10,4(11)     #      bs[lf].nextFreeRng = nf;
    bc 12,2,.L233    #      if (nf != 0) {
    stw 11,8(10)     #        nf->prevFreeRng = &(bs[lf]);
    b .L233          #      }
  .L231:             #   } else {
    mr 6,8           #      lf (r6) = bx (r8);
    mr 7,5           #      lfl (r7) = rangeLength (r5);
  .L233:             #   }
    cmplw 0,7,4      #
    bc 4,1,.L234     #   if (lfl (r7) > large (r4)) {
    slwi 9,6,5
    add 0,30,9
    stw 0,48(31)     #      gcenv->largeFree = &(bs[lf]);
    mr 4,7           #      large (r4) = lfl;
  .L234:             #   }
    add 8,8,5        #   bx = bx + rangeLength;
    slwi 9,8,2
    cmpw 1,8,28
    lwzx 11,9,27     #   col (r11) = colours(r27)[bx (r8)];
  .L230:             # }
    bc 4,4,.L235     # if (bx < nb) {
    cmpwi 0,11,3
    bc 4,2,.L236     #   if (col (r11) == reserved) {
    slwi 0,8,5
    lwzx 9,30,0
    add 8,8,9        #          bx = bx + bs[bx].freeRangeLen;
    b .L235
  .L236:             #   } else {
    cmpwi 0,11,0
    bc 4,2,.L238     #      if (col (r11) == white) {
    cmpwi 0,6,0
    slwi 5,8,5
    li 0,2
    add 10,30,5
    stwx 0,9,27      #         colours[bx] = free;
    bc 4,0,.L239     #         if (lf (r6) < 0) {
                     # /* b becomes the first free block */
    lwz 9,44(31)     #           fL = gcenv->freeList;
    stw 11,8(10)     #           b  ->prevFreeRng = null;
    cmpwi 0,9,0
    stw 9,4(10)      #           b  ->nextFreeRng = fL;
    stwx 25,30,5     #           b  ->freeRangeLen = 1 (r25);
```

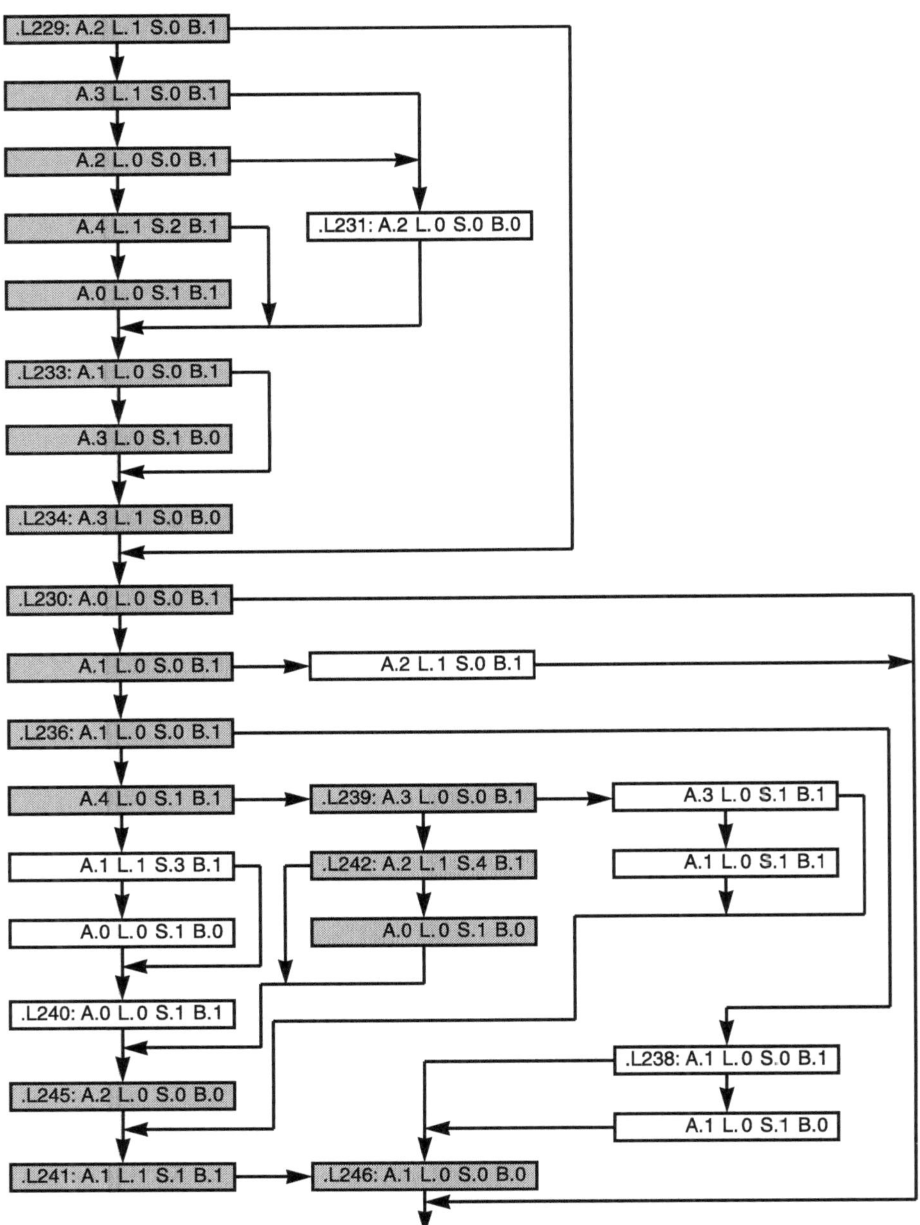

Figure 11.2: Flowchart for machine code for sweeping one block.

```
  bc 12,2,.L240   #           if (fL != null) {
  stw 10,8(9)     #             fL->prevFreeRng = b;
.L240:            #           }
  stw 10,44(31)   #           gcenv->freeList = b;
  b .L245         #           lf = bx; lfl = 1;
.L239:            #         } else {
  add 0,6,7
  cmpw 0,8,0
  slwi 9,6,5
  bc 4,2,.L242    #          if (bx == (lf+lfl)) {
                  #  /* coalesc with previous free range */
  addi 7,7,1      #            lfl++;
  cmplw 0,7,4
  stwx 7,9,30     #            bs[lf].freeRangeLen = lfl;
  add 9,9,30
  bc 4,1,.L241    #            if (lfl > large) {
  stw 9,48(31)    #              gcenv->largeFree=&(bs[lf]);
  mr 4,7          #              large = lfl;
  b .L241         #            }
.L242:            #          } else {
  add 9,9,30
  lwz 11,4(9)     #            nf = bs[lf].nextFreeRng;
  stw 9,8(10)     #            b ->prevFreeRng=&(bs[lf]);
  stw 11,4(10)    #            b ->nextFreeRng = nf;
  cmpwi 0,11,0
  stwx 25,30,5    #            b ->freeRangeLen = 1;
  stw 10,4(9)     #            bs[lf].nextFreeRng = b;
  bc 12,2,.L245   #            if (nf != null) {
  stw 10,8(11)    #              nf->prevFreeRng = b;
.L245:            #            }
  mr 6,8          #            lf = bx;
  li 7,1          #            lfl = 1;
.L241:            #          }
  lwz 9,4(31)
  addi 9,9,1
  stw 9,4(31)     #          gcenv->numFree++;
  b .L246         #        }
.L238:
  cmpwi 0,11,-1
  bc 4,2,.L246    #      } else if (col == black) {
  li 0,0
  stwx 0,9,27     #        colours[bx] = white;
.L246:            #      }
  addi 8,8,1      #      bx (r8) = bx (r8) + 1;
.L235:            #    }
```

Listing 11.2: Assembly code for sweeping one block (including skipping of free ranges and coalescing free ranges).

The code uses several conditional branches to distinguish all possible cases (coalescing free ranges, new head of free list, new largest free range, etc.). The longest possible execution path through this code uses 62 machine instructions:

Arithmetic (move, add, shift, compare, etc.):	33
Load:	6
Store:	11
Branch:	13

Six of the eleven stores are known to be cache-hits since the same cache line was accessed just before the write. The remaining five stores and all six loads have to be assumed to be cache-misses, so in total there may be up to 11 cache-misses.

Assuming that all instructions take a single clock cycle, and the cache miss penalty is 14 clock cycles, the total worst-case execution time becomes m_{sweep} = 63 instructions or c_{sweep} = 63+11·14 = 217 cycles.

In addition to the code for sweeping every single block, there is loop overhead when several blocks are swept. This includes testing the end condition of the sweep loop and allowing for thread switches. The overhead is

Arithmetic (move, add, shift, compare, etc.):	10
Load:	2
Store:	0
Branch:	2

Assuming the memory accesses are cache-misses, the additional loop overhead is m_{sweep_loop} = 14 instructions or c_{sweep_loop} = 14+14·2 = 42 cycles.

11.2.3 Overhead for Phase Changes

An additional overhead is incurred whenever the garbage collection phase changes between mark phase and sweep phase. The most expensive change is the start of the mark phase which includes code for constant-time root scanning. This code is shown in **Listing 11.3**.

```
.L199:              # case JAMAICA_GCSTATE_START:
  lwz 10,72(31)     #   r (r10) = gcenv->roots;
  lwz 11,64(31)
  srwi 9,10,3       #   c (r9/r11) = &COLOUR(gcenv,r);
  lwzx 0,9,11
  cmpwi 0,0,0
  bc 4,2,.L200      #   if ((*c) == white) {
  lwz 0,40(31)
  stwx 0,9,11       #     (*c) = gcenv->greyList;
  stw 10,40(31)     #     gcenv->greyList = r;
.L200:              #   }
  li 0,3
  stw 0,52(31)      #   gcenv->gcState=JAMAICA_GCSTATE_MARK;
                    #   /* case fall through to mark */
```

Listing 11.3: Code for constant-time root scanning

The overhead for this additional code is

Arithmetic (move, add, shift, compare, etc.):	3
Load:	4
Store:	3
Branch:	1

All stores are to memory locations that have just before been loaded, so they can be assumed to be cache-hits. The second load of *64(r31)* is a cache-hit since it directly follows the load of *72(r31)* in the same cache line. The remaining 3 loads are potential cache misses and the total additional overhead becomes m_{rs} = 11 machine instructions or c_{rs} = 11 + 3·14 = 53 cycles.

11.2.4 Total Overhead for an Allocation

Now, one can calculate the total runtime overhead for an allocation, when this allocation requires the garbage collector to make progress that corresponds to scanning of P blocks of memory. Since the garbage collector has two phases, mark and sweep, scanning of one block corresponds to marking or sweeping of two blocks (such that scanning of all allocated blocks corresponds to marking and sweeping of all allocated blocks). The more expensive of these two activities is marking with 121 machine instructions or 289 cycles per block. Additionally, a phase change may occur and one has to consider the additional overhead of 11 machine instructions or 53 cycles.

The total number of machine instructions $m(P)$ and cycles $c(P)$ can hence be calculated as

$$m(P) = m_{rs} + 2 \cdot (m_{mark} + m_{mark\_loop}) \cdot P = 11 + 266 \cdot P$$

$$c(P) = c_{rs} + 2 \cdot (c_{mark} + c_{mark\_loop}) \cdot P = 53 + 658 \cdot P$$

As shown in chapter 9, an upper bound P_{max} can be given for P if the total memory used by the application is limited and is less than the heap size. For an application that requires 512KB of memory (i.e., the application uses no more than 512KB as reachable memory), **Table 11.1** illustrates possible heap sizes and the resulting worst-case execution times for the garbage collection work on an allocation of one block of memory. The clock frequency used to determine the execution time is 200MHz.

These values do not include the call overhead for the allocation and the calculation of *P(a)*, which can be done using simple arithmetic and one division.

heap size M	**mem. used** k	**GC units** P_{max}	**instructs.** m_{max}	**cycles** c_{max}	**µsec**
569KB	90%	71	18897	46771	233.86
640KB	80%	34	9055	22425	112.13
732KB	70%	21	5597	13871	69.34
854KB	60%	15	4001	9923	49.62
1024KB	50%	11	2937	7291	36.46
1280KB	40%	9	2405	5975	29.88
1707KB	30%	7	1873	4659	23.30

Table 11.1: Possible heap sizes and the corresponding worst-case execution times for the garbage collection work required for the allocation of one block.

11.3 Analysis of an Application's Required Heap Size

An important input for the determination of the worst-case overhead of garbage collection as shown in the previous section is the amount of memory required by the application, i.e., the maximum amount of reachable memory during its execution. The determination of an upper bound on the amount of reachable memory is difficult in practice since all allocations by the application and the underlying runtime system have to be taken into account. It is desirable to have automatic tools that simplify this task.

11.3.1 Exact Determination of Maximum Reachable Memory

One means to determine the exact amount of memory required by an application is to run a complete garbage collection cycle before every allocation and record the maximum amount of allocated memory during the execution of a test run of the applications. This approach produces an exact result, but it causes a significant slowdown of the application during the test run. In the worst case that no garbage is found, this analysis requires time quadratic in the number of allocations.

11.3.2 Determination of an Upper Bound for Reachable Memory

In practice, the exact estimation is not required. A sufficiently accurate upper bound for the amount of reachable memory can instead be used to configure the system. The automatic determination of an upper bound that is within a certain percentage d of the actual maximum amount of reachable memory causes significantly less runtime overhead during the test run of the application.

For this analysis, the garbage collector is run such that the amount of allocated memory a never exceeds the maximum amount of reachable memory r_{max} plus the allowed margin $d \cdot r_{max}$:

(1) $a \leq (1 + d) \cdot r_{max}$

Since the amount of allocated memory is never less than the amount of reachable memory, the maximum amount of allocated memory a_{max} during the test run will then give an estimate for r_{max} of accuracy d:

(2) $r_{max} \leq a_{max} \leq (1 + d) \cdot r_{max}$

Theorem 1: To ensure (1), it is sufficient to perform P_d units of garbage collection work for every unit of memory allocation with

(3) $P_d = 2/d + 2$

Proof:

Using the progress function P_d given in (3), a garbage collection cycle that started when the amount of allocated memory was a_c will finish as soon as the cumulative garbage collection scanning work exceeds the amount of allocated memory a_c and the amount of memory allocated meanwile q_c. On every allocation of one unit of memory, P_d units of collection work are performed, so that the collection cycle ends at the latest when the collection work exceeds the sum of the originally allocated memory plus the memory allocated during the current cycle.

$$a_c + q_c \geq q_c \cdot P_d$$

This gives the following upper bound for the amount of allocation during this cycle.

$$(4) \qquad q_c \leq a_c \,/\, (P_d - 1) = (d \,/\, (2 + d)) \cdot a_c$$

The amount a_{c+1} of memory allocated after this cycle is the sum of a_c and q_c minus the amount g_c of garbage found during this cycle:

$$a_{c+1} = a_c + q_c - g_c$$

First, it will proven by induction over the garbage collection cycle c that the amount a_c of memory allocated at the beginning of a cycle is bounded by

$$(5) \qquad a_c \leq (1 + d/2) \cdot r_{max}$$

This limitation for a_c will then be used to find an upper bound for the allocated memory a.

For the first collection cycle, no memory is allocated so far such that a_0 is equal to 0 and (5) trivially holds. For the following cycles with $c > 0$ two cases have to be distinguished:

First case:

$$(6) \qquad a_c \leq r_{max}$$

All allocated memory may be reachable, so the collector might not find any garbage during this cycle.

$$g_c \geq \max(0, a_c - r_{max}) = 0$$

Nevertheless, an upper bound for a_{c+1} can be determined:

$$\begin{aligned} a_{c+1} &= a_c + q_c - g_c && \text{using (4)+(6)} \\ &\leq r_{max} + (d \,/\, (2 + d)) \cdot r_{max} - 0 \\ &= (1 + (d \,/\, (2 + d))) \cdot r_{max} \\ &\leq (1 + d/2) \cdot r_{max} \end{aligned}$$

which shows (5) for a_{c+1}.

Second case:

$$(7) \qquad r_{max} < a_c \leq (1 + d/2) \cdot r_{max}$$

The allocated memory is more than the amount of reachable memory, so garbage will be found during this cycle:

(8) $\quad g_c \geq a_c - r_{max} \geq 0$

This recycled memory allows the determination of an upper bound for a_{c+1} as follows.

$$\begin{aligned}
a_{c+1} &= a_c + q_c - g_c && \text{using (4)+(8)}\\
&\leq a_c + (d / (2 + d)) \cdot a_c - a_c + r_{max} \\
&= (d / (2 + d)) \cdot a_c + r_{max} && \text{using (7)}\\
&\leq (d / (2 + d)) \cdot (1 + d/2) \cdot r_{max} + r_{max} \\
&= [\, 1 + (d / (2 + d)) \cdot ((2 + d) / 2)\,] \cdot r_{max} \\
&\leq (1 + d/2) \cdot r_{max}
\end{aligned}$$

This shows (5) for a_{c+1}.

The fraction of allocated memory at the beginning of a garbage collection cycle hence never exceeds $(1 + d / 2) \cdot r_{max}$. The fraction of allocated memory at the end of one cycle, before the garbage found during this cycle is freed, gives an upper bound for the amount of allocated memory. This amount is the amount a_c of memory allocated at the beginning of the cycle

$$a_c \leq (1 + d/2) \cdot r_{max} \qquad \text{from (5)}$$

plus the amount q_c of memory allocated during this cycle

$$q_c \leq (d / (2 + d)) \cdot (1 + d/2) \cdot r_{max} \qquad \text{from (4)}$$

The resulting upper bound for the allocated memory is consequently

$$\begin{aligned}
a &\leq a_c + q_c \\
&\leq (1 + d/2) \cdot r_{max} + (d / (2 + d)) \cdot (1 + d/2) \cdot r_{max} \\
&= [1 + d/2 + (d / (2 + d)) \cdot (1 + d/2)] \cdot r_{max} \\
&= [1 + d/2 + (d / (2 + d)) \cdot ((2 + d)/2)] \cdot r_{max} \\
&= [1 + d/2 + (d / 2)] \cdot r_{max} \\
a &\leq (1 + d) \cdot r_{max}
\end{aligned}$$

This completes the proof.

With this, it is possible to run the garbage collector using the the progress function P_d from (3) such that the maximum amount of allocated memory a_{max} gives an estimation for the maximum amount of reachable memory r_{max} that lies within r_{max} and $(1 + d) \cdot r_{max}$.

```
> ./CaffeineMarkEmbeddedApp
Sieve score = 2118 (98)
Loop score = 3157 (2017)
Logic score = 23340 (0)
String score = 319 (708)
Float score = 1705 (185)
Method score = 3509 (166650)
Overall score = 2584

### Application used at most 232582 bytes for the Java
### heap (accuracy 5%).
### Non-Java heap memory used: 13214 bytes.
###
###                          Worst case allocation overhead:
###      heapSize            dynamic GC          static GC
###      799k                6                   3
###      670k                7                   4
###      587k                8                   4
###      531k                9                   4
###      490k                10                  4
###      434k                12                  5
###      399k                14                  5
###      374k                16                  6
###      356k                18                  6
###      342k                20                  7
###      322k                24                  8
###      309k                28                  9
###      300k                32                  10
###      292k                36                  11
###      287k                40                  12
###      278k                48                  14
###      273k                56                  17
###      269k                64                  19
###      259k                96                  27
###      254k                128                 36
###      250k                192                 53
###      247k                256                 69
###      245k                384                 100
>
```

Figure 11.3: Result of measured required heap size for the embedded Caffeine benchmark.

11.3.3 Configuring the Heap Size and Garbage Collector

When using Jamaica, a special option *-analyze* instructs the builder tool to run the garbage collector such that the reachable memory is measured with a given accuracy. The technique that was described in the previous section is used for this.

If instrumented like this, the result of the measurement is printed to standard output after the execution of the application. Apart from the actual amount of memory used, a list of possible heap sizes and the corresponding worst-case execution times of an allocation measured in units of garbage collection work is given. **Figure 11.3** shows the output of the embedded Caffeine benchmark [Pendr97] when run after it was built using the option *'-analyze 5'*, i.e., the required heap size is measured with an accuracy of 5%. The table with suggested heap sizes shows the worst-case number of units of garbage collection work for dynamic and static determination of garbage collection work.

Of course, this measurement cannot be used to predict the heap size required by a run of an application with arbitrary input data or indeterministic behaviour as it may be introduced through the use of threads or other timing dependent mechanisms.

For applications whose memory demand depends on the input data, the automatic analysis can nevertheless be useful. It can be employed to determine the memory requirements for all the internal data structures that are created during the startup of the application, such that for the determination of the complete memory needs only the memory dependent on the input data needs to be calculated manually. If the algorithms used require memory that is monotonous with the size of the input data, the automatic measurement can be used to measure the memory required to treat the largest input that the application is supposed to handle.

In multi-threaded applications, it may be required to measure the memory needs of each thread individually, and then calculate the total memory demand for the whole application using these measurements.

11.4 Worst-Case Execution Time of Memory Accesses

Apart from allocation of objects, the execution time of accesses to memory is also affected by the garbage collector. All accesses have to take the object model that is based on fixed size blocks into account. Writes of reference values in addition need to perform write barrier code. The worst-case execution times of these operations will be determined here.

11.4.1 Field Accesses

Depending on the position of a field within the linked list of blocks that form the object, a number of link references need to be traversed before the field itself can be accessed. For a field at position p, where p gives the byte offset of the field in a classical (linear) representation of the object, the number of links $l(p)$ that need to be traversed is

$$l(p) = \lfloor p \,/\, (block\_size - word\_size) \rfloor.$$

For a block size of 32 bytes on a system with 32 bits per word, this becomes

$$l(p) = \lfloor p \,/\, (32 - 28) \rfloor = \lfloor p \,/\, 28 \rfloor$$

Listing 11.4 illustrates the PowerPC code required to read a field that occupies one word at position 68 of an object for a block size of 32 bytes. This code can be used for reference and non-reference values

```
lwz    rLink ,28(rObj)
lwz    rLink ,28(rLink)
lwz    rValue,12(rLink)
```

Listing 11.4: Code to access a field at position 68 in object *rObject* for a block size of 32 bytes. The field is stored in register *rValue*. Register *rLink* is used to traverse the link values.

The number of machine instructions m_{read_field} required for the access to a word-size field is

$$m_{read\_field}(p) = l(p) + 1 = \lfloor p \,/\, 28 \rfloor + 1$$

The number of cycles c_{read_field} required for this access assuming all memory accesses are cache misses is

$$c_{read\_field}(p) = (14+1)\cdot(l(p) + 1) = 15\cdot(\lfloor p \,/\, 28 \rfloor + 1)$$

The code to store a non-reference value is similar to the code for reading a value. The links have to be traversed before the field can be stored. The code is illustrated in **Listing 11.5.**

```
lwz    rLink ,28(rObj)
lwz    rLink ,28(rLink)
stw    rValue,12(rLink)
```

Listing 11.5: Code to write a non-reference field to position 68 in object *rObject* for a block size of 32 bytes. The value from register *rValue* is stored in the field. Register *rLink* is used to traverse the link values.

The numbers of machine instructions $m_{write\_non\text{-}reference\_field}$ and cycles $c_{write\_non\text{-}reference\_field}$ required for the write to a word-size non-reference field is equal to the numbers for reading the field:

$$m_{write\_non\text{-}reference\_field}(p) = l(p) + 1 = \lfloor p / 28 \rfloor + 1$$

$$c_{write\_non\text{-}reference\_field}(p) = (14+1)\cdot(l(p) + 1) = 15\cdot(\lfloor p / 28 \rfloor + 1)$$

When a reference field needs to be written, the write barrier code needs to be executed. This results in the more complex code illustrated in **Listing 11.6** for writing a reference field at position 68.

```
  lwz    rLink ,28(rObj)   # link = obj->link;
  lwz    rLink ,28(rLink)  # link = link->link;
  cmpwi  0,rValue,#0       #
  bc     12,2,label        # if (value != null) {
  lwz    rCB,cb(rEnv)      #   cb = rEnv->colourBase;
  srwi   rColR,rValue,#3   #   colR = value >> 3;
  lwzx   rCol,rColR,rCB    #   col = (*(cb+colR));
  cmpwi  0,rCol,#0         #
  bc     4,2,label         #   if (col == white) {
  lwz    rGrey,grey(rEnv)  #     grey = rEnv->greyList;
  stwx   rGrey,rColR,rCB   #     (*(cb+colR)) = grey;
  stw    rValue,grey(rEnv) #     rEnv->greyList = value;
                           #   }
label:                     # }
  stw    rValue,12(rLink)  # link->field = value;
```

Listing 11.6: Code to write a reference field to position 68 in object *rObj* for a block size of 32 bytes. The value from register *rValue* is stored in the field. Register *rLink* is used to traverse the link values. The write barrier code is to be executed to maintain the garbage collector invariant.

The worst-case execution time to write a reference field has to consider the write barrier code overhead as well. Assuming that all memory accesses are cache misses, the numbers of machine instructions $m_{write\_reference\_field}$ and cycles $c_{write\_reference\_field}$ become

$$m_{write\_reference\_field}(p) = l(p) + 1 = \lfloor p / 28 \rfloor + 11$$

$$c_{write\_reference\_field}(p) = (14+1)\cdot(l(p) + 6) + 5 = 15\lfloor p / 28 \rfloor + 95$$

11.4.2 Array Accesses

Accessing an array element requires traversal of the tree of blocks that is used to represent the array. The code for such an access is illustrated in **Listing 11.7** for an array of words.

```
   lwz    rD,8(rArray)        # d = array->depth;
   andi   rD,rD,#15           # d = d & 15;
   muli   rD,rD,#3            # d = d * 3;
   addi   rE,rArray,#16       # e = &(array->elements);
   slwi   rI,rI,#2            # i = i << 2;
   cmpwi  0,rD,#0             #
   bc     12,2,end            # if (d != 0) {
loop:                         #   do {
   slw    rT,rI,rD            #     t = i >> d;
   andi   rT,rI,#31           #     t = t & 31;
   lwzx   rE,rE,rT            #     e = (*(e+t));
   srw    rT,rT,rD            #     t = t << d;
   subf   rI,rT,RI            #     i = i - t;
   addi   rD,rD,#-3           #     d = d - 3;
   cmpwi  0,rD,#0             #
   bc     4,2,loop            #   } while (d != 0);
end:                          # }
   lwzx   rValue,rE,rI        # value = (*(e+i))
```

Listing 11.7: Read an element from index *rI* of an array of words *rA*. First, the depth is determined, and then the elements of the array are traversed. This code is also applicable to arrays in contiguous representation.

The worst-case execution time of an array access depends on the depth of the array. Assuming that all memory accesses are cache misses, the numbers of machine instructions and cycles are

$$m_{read\_array}(d) = d \cdot 8 + 8$$

$$c_{read\_array}(d) = d \cdot (8+14) + 8+2 \cdot 14 = d \cdot 22 + 36 .$$

The depth d of an array of *size* bytes can be determined using

$$d_{size}(size) = \lceil \ln_8(size \, / \, 32) \rceil$$

The size can never be larger than the available heap h, so the depth may never exceed $d_{max}(h)$:

$$d_{max}(h) = \lceil \ln_8(h \, / \, 32) \rceil$$

For a heap size of 32MB, the resulting maximal depth is 7. The worst-case execution times for this case are thus

$$m_{read\_array\_32MB\_heap} = 64$$

$$c_{read\_array\_32MB\_heap} = 190\ .$$

The code to write an element to an array of non-reference words is similar to the code to read such an array. The only difference is that the element is written and not read. **Listing 11.8** shows the required code.

```
  lwz    rD,8(rArray)       # d = array->depth;
  andi   rD,rD,#15          # d = d & 15;
  muli   rD,rD,#3           # d = d * 3;
  addi   rE,rArray,#16      # e = &(array->elements);
  slwi   rI,rI,#2           # i = i << 2;
  cmpwi  0,rD,#0            #
  bc     12,2,end           # if (d != 0) {
loop:                       #   do {
  slw    rT,rI,rD           #     t = i >> d;
  andi   rT,rI,#31          #     t = t & 31;
  lwzx   rE,rE,rT           #     e = (*(e+t));
  srw    rT,rT,rD           #     t = t << d;
  subf   rI,rT,RI           #     i = i - t;
  addi   rD,rD,#-3          #     d = d - 3;
  cmpwi  0,rD,#0            #
  bc     4,2,loop           #   } while (d != 0);
end:                        # }
  stwx   rValue,rE,rI       # (*(e+i)) = value
```

Listing 11.8: Write element at index *rI* of an array of words *rA*. First, the depth is determined, and then the elements of the array are traversed. This code is also applicable to arrays in contiguous representation.

The worst case execution time for writing a non-reference element to an array of words is equal to that for read accesses:

$$m_{write\_non\text{-}reference\_array}(d) = d \cdot 8 + 8$$

$$c_{write\_non\text{-}reference\_array}(d) = d \cdot 22 + 36$$

$$m_{write\_non\text{-}reference\_array\_32MB\_heap} = 64$$

$$c_{write\_non\text{-}reference\_array\_32MB\_heap} = 190\ .$$

The code to write an element to an array of references needs to perform write barrier code not to invalidate the garbage collector invariant. **Listing 11.9** shows the required code.

```
  lwz    rD,8(rArray)        # d = array->depth;
  andi   rD,rD,#15           # d = d & 15;
  muli   rD,rD,#3            # d = d * 3;
  addi   rE,rArray,#16       # e = &(array->elements);
  slwi   rI,rI,#2            # i = i << 2;
  cmpwi  0,rD,#0             #
  bc     12,2,end            # if (d != 0) {
loop:                        #   do {
  slw    rT,rI,rD            #     t = i >> d;
  andi   rT,rI,#31           #     t = t & 31;
  lwzx   rE,rE,rT            #     e = (*(e+t));
  srw    rT,rT,rD            #     t = t << d;
  subf   rI,rT,RI            #     i = i - t;
  addi   rD,rD,#-3           #     d = d - 3;
  cmpwi  0,rD,#0             #
  bc     4,2,loop            #   } while (d != 0);
end:                         # }
  cmpwi  0,rValue,#0         #
  bc     12,2,label          # if (value != null) {
  lwz    rCB,cb(rEnv)        #   cb = rEnv->colourBase;
  srwi   rColR,rValue,#3     #   colR = value >> 3;
  lwzx   rCol,rColR,rCB      #   col = (*(cb+colR));
  cmpwi  0,rCol,#0           #
  bc     4,2,label           #   if (col == white) {
  lwz    rGrey,grey(rEnv)    #     grey = rEnv->greyList;
  stwx   rGrey,rColR,rCB     #     (*(cb+colR)) = grey;
  stw    rValue,grey(rEnv)#        rEnv->greyList = value;
                             #   }
label:                       # }
  stwx   rValue,rE,rI        # (*(e+i)) = value
```

Listing 11.9: Write element at index *rI* of an array of references *rA*. The write barrier code needs to be executed when the value is written.

Compared to non-reference arrays, the worst case execution time is augmented by the write barrier code overhead:

$$m_{write\_reference\_array}(d) = d \cdot 8 + 18$$

$$c_{write\_non\text{-}reference\_array}(d) = d \cdot 22 + 116$$

$$m_{write\_reference\_array\_32MB\_heap} = 74$$

$$c_{write\_reference\_array\_32MB\_heap} = 270\ .$$

11.5 Worst-Case Execution Time of Root Saving

For the constant-time root scanning phase that was described in chapter 6, it is required that local references that survive a GC-point be saved to the heap. The code required to save such a reference needs to execute write barrier code. GC points are either synchronization points or call points.

To enable the garbage collector to recycle an object refered to by a local reference, the copy that was saved to the heap must be removed at the end of the lifespan of the variable. This requires additional code.

Listing 11.10 shows the code required to save a reference from register *rRef* at the beginning of its lifespan; **Listing 11.11** shows the corresponding code to remove this reference at the end of the lifespan.

```
  cmpwi  0,rRef,#0           #
  bc     12,2,label          # if (ref != null) {
  lwz    rCB,cb(rEnv)        #   cb = rEnv->colourBase;
  srwi   rColR,rRef,#3       #   colR = ref >> 3;
  lwzx   rCol,rColR,rCB      #   col = (*(cb+colR));
  cmpwi  0,rCol,#0           #
  bc     4,2,label           #   if (col == white) {
  lwz    rGrey,grey(rEnv)    #     grey = rEnv->greyList;
  stwx   rGrey,rColR,rCB     #     (*(cb+colR)) = grey;
  stw    rRef,grey(rEnv)     #     rEnv->greyList = ref;
                             #   }
label:                       # }
  stw    rRef,28(rRoots)     # rRoots[7] = ref;
```

Listing 11.10: Code to save the local reference *rRef* at position 7 of the current frame in the roots array. This code needs to be executed at the definition of *rRef* if the lifespan of this value contains a GC-point.

```
  subf   r0,r0,r0            #
  stw    r0,28(rRoots)       # rRoots[7] = null;
```

Listing 11.11: Code to remove the local reference *rRef* from position 7 of the current frame of the roots array.

The worst-case execution time of saving a references comprises the time required for the write barrier code and the time to store the reference itself. The worst-case number of machine instructions $m_{save\_reference}$ is 11. Assuming all memory accesses are cache misses, the number of cycles $c_{save\_reference}$ in the worst case is 95:

$$m_{save\_reference} = 11$$

$$c_{save\_reference} = 6 \cdot 14 + 11 = 95\ .$$

The code to clear a saved reference at the end of its lifespan is simple, it requires 2 instructions and 16 cycles assuming it causes a cache miss:

$$m_{clear\_reference} = 2$$

$$c_{clear\_reference} = 1 \cdot 14 + 2 = 16\ .$$

Every method that saves local references to root arrays allocates a range of root arrays for use by the current method at the entry of the method. All references that are saved are assigned a fixed index in this array. The code to allocate and deallocate this range is simple. It is shown in **Listing 11.12**. The total code of the method is extended by 4 instructions. Three of these instructions are accesses to the heap, so in case of cache misses, they will require 46 machine cycles:

$$m_{alloc\_and\_dealloc\_roots} = 4$$

$$c_{alloc\_and\_dealloc\_roots} = 3 \cdot 14 + 4 = 46\ .$$

The memory accesses in this code are required only because *C* is used as an intermediate language and *C* does not permit to chose a register globally that always refers to the current position in the roots array.

Determining worst-case execution times of a code sequence that uses the presented code to save references is possible with the presented execution times. Doing this manually, however, is not an easy task since the code is added automatically by the compiler and it is not obvious where the compiler choses to insert the code.

Nevertheless, the presented worst-case execution times can serve as a basis for the implementation of automatic tools for the determination of the worst-case execution times of more complex code sequences that contain calls and synchronization points.

```
#
# Allocate range of roots array
#
lwz     rRoots,roots(rEnv) # rRoots = rEnv->roots;
addi    rTemp,rRoots,#36    # rTemp = rRoots+36
stw     rTemp,roots(rEnv)   # rEnv->roots = rTemp;

#
# ..method body..
#

#
# Deallocate range
#
stw     rRoots,roots(rEnv)   # rEnv->roots = rRoots;
```

Listing 11.12: Code to allocate and deallocate a range of references in the roots array. This code is executed at entry and exit of every method that needs to save references.

11.6 Worst-Case Execution Time of Other Operations

The worst-case execution time of the remaining basic operations that are implemented deterministically as described in chapter 10 can be determined accordingly.

The detailed determination of these worst-case execution times is not presented here. The times can be determined in a straightforward way.

For real-time system development using Java, a detailed list of the worst-case execution times of all operations is nevertheless useful. Such detailed information is unfortunately not even available for most development systems that are currently employed for the construction of real-time systems using traditional languages such as C or C++. Instead, measurements and safety margins are used to compensate for this lack of information on execution time.

塵も積もれば山となる。

Even a little bit of dust can form a mountain.
–Japanese saying

12. Conclusions and Future Work

12.1 Conclusions

This dissertation dealt with the issues related to the application of modern object oriented programming languages with automatic memory for the development of real-time systems. Even though a significant number of publications on previous research on automatic memory management for real-time systems exists, a number of difficulties for an implementation remained unsolved. Techniques to solve theses difficulties on a single processor in an implementation of Java have been presented in this thesis.

In contrast to previous approaches for the application of Java in the real-time domain, the presented solution does not restrict the use of the Java language for providing real-time guarantees. Instead, even real-time code can make full use of dynamic memory allocation. Timing guarantees can be given for heap-related operations like creation of new objects.

12.1.1 Techniques

The following techniques have been presented and analysed in this thesis.

Constant-Time Root Scanning

The difficult task of finding references in execution stacks of all running threads has been solved by ensuring that all live references that are used locally are automatically copied to a dedicated data structure on the heap whenever the garbage collector may become active. The compiler and virtual machine automatically ensure that live references are copied to the heap. The data structures used for storing the copied references are all reachable from a single global root pointer. The root scanning phase is reduced to scanning this single root pointer.

Non-Fragmenting Object Model

A non-fragmenting object model based on fixed size blocks has been applied and analysed. This object model enables the use of fragmented memory and hence avoids the need to move objects for heap compaction. This solves all the difficulties that arise during compaction for updating references to the new addresses of moved objects and for moving objects of arbitrary sizes. The surprising result is that the non-fragmenting object model permits efficient runtime performance.

Garbage Collector Activation

A mechanism for activation of garbage collection work at the time of an allocation has been presented. The amount of garbage collection work performed is determined dynamically as a function of the size of the free memory. A proof is given that this work is sufficient to recycle enough memory and that an upper bound for this work can be given.

12.1.2 Implementation

An important goal of this work was to show the applicability of garbage collection for real-time system development using a full-featured implementation of a programming language including an optimizing compiler and standard libraries. It is not sufficient to theoretically show that garbage collection is applicable to real-time system development or to analyse a prototype of an implementation that has restrictions that prevent its application in a real programming language implementation.

Consequently, a full-featured Java virtual machine using the presented techniques was implemented. For competitive runtime performance, an optimizing static compiler for Java bytecode was implemented. The compiler generates *C* source code that is used as a portable assembly language. A number of Java's standard classes were implemented such that a large number of Java applications can be executed on the new system. Since many real-time systems are deeply embedded devices with tight ressource constraints, special tools to optimize the system's memory and processing power requirements have been implemented.

The performance of the implementation was analysed using the SPECjvm98 benchmark suite. The measured performance was compared to traditional Java implementations that do not provide real-time guarentees.

The resulting implementation is now used in a number of commercial software development projects for embedded systems.

12.1.3 Consequences

The results of this work show that modern object oriented programming languages with dynamic memory management can be used for the development of hard real-time systems. Thus, developers of real-time software can use modern software development tools that so far have not been applicable in this domain.

One can expect that the use of powerful dynamic languages in this domain will increase the productivity of the software development process and the quality of the software, just as the application of these languages improved the software development on desktop systems. These languages help the development of more complex systems that would be difficult to design with languages that are traditionally used in this domain.

12.2 Future Work

For the application of modern programming languages to hard real-time and safety-critical system development, guaratees on the effectiveness and performance of memory management and other primitive operations as presented in this thesis is an important prerequisite. Nevertheless, for the mainstream application, the determination of worst-case execution times for primitives is hardly sufficient. Automatic tools to find the execution times of more complex sequences of operations are needed.

An important problem to be solved here is the accurate determination of worst-case execution times while cache memories and pipelined superscalar architectures with complex pipelines are taken into account. As long as performance improvements through caches and modern processors are not taken into account in the analysis, the results are too conservative. Since accurate analysis of execution times is not currently possible, measurements are typically used to configure real-time systems. It is hard to guarantee that the resulting configuration is feasible if it is based on such measurements.

In the context of the garbage collection techniques presented here, the worst-case and average-case performance of the collector may be improved significantly if cache effects would be taken into account [KS00, Boehm00].

Another source for improvement may lie in different object layouts than those that were presented in chapter 7.

Compilers may perform a number of optimization that can improve the performance of the presented scheme. One idea is to specialize loops or even whole methods for certain representations of objects. As has been shown in chapter 7, most arrays can be represented in a contiguous range of memory. A compiler may create specialized versions of methods, such as those in class *Vector*, that are optimized for contiguous arrays and that are only used for accesses to these arrays. Regular traversal of arrays in tree representation could also be optimized by a specialized compiler.

Another promising direction is specialized hardware and hardware-software co-design in the context of the presented garbage collector. What parts of the garbage collection code, such as the write barrier or the collector loop, could be implemented in specialized hardware? May the overhead for synchronization points or root reference saving be reduced by such hardware? Can the hardware provide any features that facilitate the block structure of objects?

The presented memory management technique is currently restricted to single processor systems. This prevents the application in computation intensive domains that require scalability. An generalization of the techniques to parallel systems should be analysed.

Different memory management algorithms may bring surprising benefits when the presented techniques are applied. As an example, the application of the object model based on fixed size blocks to a reference counting scheme that performs deferred reference counting has been suggested by Tobias Ritzau [Ritzau01]. It allows constant allocation time that is independent of the fraction of reachable memory and that is applicable to real-time systems as long as no cyclic structures are used.

13. References

[ADEM98] Ole Agesen, David Detlefs, J. Eliot and B. Moss: *Garbage Collection and Local Variable Type-Precision and Liveness in Java™ Virtual Machines*, ACM SIGPLAN Conference on Programming Language Design and Implementation (PLDI), 1998

[AEL88] Andrew W. Appel, John R. Ellis and Kai Li: *Real-time Concurrent Collection on Stock Multiprocessors*, ACM SIGPLAN Conference on Programming Language Design and Implementation (PLDI), 1988

[AFGHS00] Matthew Arnold, Stephen Fink, David Grove, Michael Hind and Peter F. Sweeney: *Adaptive Optimization in the Jalapeño JVM*, OOPSLA, 2000

[AG98] Ken Arnold and James Gosling: *The Java Programming Language*, 2nd edition, Addison Wesley, 1998

[Agesen98] Ole Agesen: *GC Points in a Threaded Environment*, Sun Labs Tech report 70, 1998

[Anders94] L. Andersen: *Program Analysis and Specialization for the C Programming language*, PhD thesis, DIKU, University of Copenhagen, 1994

[Appel89] A.W. Appel: *Runtime Tags Aren't Necessary*, Lisp and Symbolic Computation, 2, pp. 153-162, 1989

[ARM96] *ARM Architecture Manual*, Advanced Risc Machines Ltd, Prentice Hall, 1996

[Baker78] Henry G. Baker: *List processing in Real Time on a Serial Computer*, Communications of the ACM 21,4 (April 1978), pp. 280-294.

[Baker91] Henry G. Baker: *The Treadmill: Real-time garbage collection without motion sickness*, Position paper for the OOPSLA'91 Workshop on Garbage Collection in Object-Oriented Systems, also in SIGPLAN Notices 27(3), pp. 66-70, March 1992.

[Barlett88] Joel F. Barlett: *Compacting Garbage Collection with Ambiguous Roots*, Digital Equipment Corporation, 1988

[BC99] Guy E. Blelloch and Perry Cheng: *On Bounding Time and Space for Multiprocessor Garbage Collection*, ACM SIGPLAN Conference on Programming Language Design and Implementation (PLDI), 1999

[BDS91] Hans-J. Boehm, Alan J. Demers and Scott Shenker: *Mostly Parallel Garbage Collection*, ACM SIGPLAN Conference on Programming Language Design and Implementation (PLDI), 1991

[BKMS98] David F. Bacon, Ravi Konuru, Chet Murthy, Mauricio Serrano: *Thin Locks: Featherweight Synchronization for Java.* ACM SIGPLAN Conference on Programming Language Design and Implementation (PLDI), 1998

[BLT98] Philippe Bernadat, Dan Lambright, Franco Travostino: *Towards a Resource-safe Java for Service Guarantees in Uncooperative Environments*, IEEE Workshop on Programming Languages for Real-Time Industrial Applications, Madrid, 1998

[BM90] Mats Bengtsson and Boris Magnusson: *Real-Time Compacting Garbage Collection*, OOPSLA, 1990

[Bobrow68] D.G. Bobrow: *Storage Management in Lisp*, Symbol Manipulation Languages, Techniques, North-Holland, 1968.

[Boehm88] Hans-Juergen Boehm: *Garbage Collection in an Uncooperative Environment*, Software Practice and Experience, Vol 18 (9), pp 807-820, September 1988

[Boehm93] Hans-Juergen Boehm: *Space Efficient Conservative Garbage Collection*, ACM SIGPLAN Conference on Programming Language Design and Implementation (PLDI), 1993

[Boehm00] Hans-J. Boehm: *Reducing Garbage Collector Cache Misses*, International Symposion on Memory Management (ISMM'00), Minneapolis, 2000

[Brooks84] Rodney A. Brooks: *Trading Data Space for Reduced Time and Code Space in Real-Time Garbage Collection on Stock Hardware*, Lisp and Functional Programming, pp. 256-262, ACM Press, 1984

[CGHJK96] R. M. Corless, G.H. Gonnet, D.E.G. Hare, D.J. Jeffrey, D. E. Knuth: *On the Lambert W Function*, Advances in Computational Mathematics, Volume 5, 1996, pp. 329-359

[Cheney70] C. J. Cheney: *A Nonrecursive List Compacting Algorithm*, Communications of the ACM 13, 11, pp. 677-678, November 1970

[Christop84] Thomas W. Christopher: *Reference Count Garbage Collection*, Software Practice & Experience, Vol 14(6), June 1984, pp. 503-507

[Corless00] R. M. Corless: http://kong.apmaths.uwo.ca/~rcorless/frames/PAPERS/LambertW/wplot1.html

[DFS96] Danny Dubé, Marc Feeley and Manuel Serrano: *Un GC temps réel semi-compactant*, Journées Francophones des Langages Applicatifs, JFLA, Janvier 1996

[DG94] Damien Doligez, Georges Gonthier: *Portable, Unobstrusive Garbage Collection for Multiprocesssor Systems*, ACM Symposium on Principles of Programming Languages (POPL), 1994

[DH99] Sylvia Dieckmann and Urs Hölzle: *A Study of the Allocation Behavior of the SPECjvm98 Java Bench-*

marks, 13th European Conference on Object-Oriented Programming (ECOOP'99), Lisbon, 1999

[Dijkstra65] Edsgar W. Dijkstra: *Cooperating Sequential Processes*, Technical Report EWD-123, Technical University Eindhoven, 1965

[DKLS+00] Tamar Domani, Elliot K. Kolodner, Ethan Lewis, Eliot E. Salant, Katherine Barabash, Itai Lahan, Yossi Levanoni, Erez Petrank and Igor Yanover: *Implementing an On-the-fly Garbage Collector for Java*, International Symposion on Memory Management (ISMM'00), Minneapolis, 2000

[DKP00] Tamar Domani, Elliot K. Kolodner and Erez Petrank: *A Generational On-the-fly Garbage Collector for Java*, ACM SIGPLAN Conference on Programming Language Design and Implementation (PLDI), 2000

[DL93] Damien Doligez and Xavier Leroy: *A concurrent, generational garbage collector for a multithreaded implementation of ML*, POPL, 1993

[DLMSS78] Edsgar W. Dijkstra, L. Lamport, A. Martin, C. Scholten and E.Steffens: *On-the-fly Garbage Collection: An Exercise in Cooperation*, Communications of the ACM, 21,11 (November 19778), pp. 966-975

[DMH92] Amer Diwan, Eliot Moss and Richard Hudson: *Compiler Support for Garbage Collection in a Statically Typed Language*, ACM SIGPLAN Conference on Programming Language Design and Implementation (PLDI), 1992

[DS84] L. Peter Deutsch and Allan M. Schiffman: *Efficient Implementation of the Smalltalk-80 System*, Conference Record of the Eleventh Annual ACM Symposium on Principles of Programming Languages, pp. 297-302, Salt Lake City, UT, January, 1984

[Edwards] Daniel J. Edwards: *LISP II Garbage Collector*, AI Memmo 19, Artificial Intelligence Projec – RLE and MIT Computation Center, date unknown available at *ftp://publications.ai.mit.edu/ai-publications/0-499/AIM-019.ps*

[EV91] Steven L. Engelstad and James E. Vandendorpe: *Automatic Storage Management for Systems with Real Time Constraints*, OOPSLA, 1991

[FMW96] C. Ferdinand, F. Martin, and R. Wilhelm: *Cache Behavior Predction by Abstract Interpretation*, Science of Computer Programming, 1998. Selected for SAS'96 special issue

[FW97] Christian Ferdinand and Reinhard Wilhelm: *Fast and Efficient Cache Behavior Prediction*, http://www.cs.uni-sb.de/~ferdi/publications.html, 1997

[FY69] Robert R. Fenichel and Jerome C. Yochelson: *A LISP Garbage-Collector for Virtual-Memory Computer Systems*, Communications of the ACM, Volume 12, 11, pp. 611-612, November 1969

[GN94] Hong Gao and Kelvin Nilsen: *Reliable General Purpose Dynamic Memory Management for Real-Time Systems*, TR94-09, Iowa State University of Science and Technology, Department of Computer Science, 1994

[GN97] Alex Garthwaite and Scott Nettles: *Concurrent Collection for the Java Development Kit*, OOPSLA, 1997

[Goldberg91] Benjamin Goldberg: *Tag-Free Garbage Collection for Strongly Typed Programming Languages*, ACM SIGPLAN Conference on Programming Language Design and Implementation (PLDI), 1991

[Harris99] Timothy Harris: *Early storage reclamation in a tracing garbage collector*, SIGPLAN Notices 32, 4, April 1999.

[HD00] Martin Hirzel and Amer Diwan: *On the Type Accuracy of Garbage Collection*, International Symposion on Memory Management (ISMM'00), Minneapolis, 2000

[Hennes93] Wade Hennessey: *Real-Time Garbage Collection in a Multimedia Programming Language*, OOPSLA, 1993

[Henrik97] Roger Henriksson: *Predictable Automatic Memory Management for Embedded Systems*, Presented at OOPSLA'97 Workshop on Garbage Collection and Memory Management, Atlanta, Georgia, USA, October 5, 1997

[Henrik98] Roger Henriksson: *Scheduling Garbage Collection in Embedded Systems*, PhD thesis, Dept. of Computer Science, Lund University, 1998.

[HHMN98] Michael Hicks, Luke Hornof, Jonathan T. Moore, Scott M. Nettles: *A Study of Large Object Spaces*, International Symposion on Memory Management (ISMM'98), Vancouver, 1998

[HKHW96] Steve Hoxey, Faraydon Karim, Bill Hay, Hank Warren: *The PowerPC Compiler Writer's Guide*, IBM Microelectronics Division, New York, 1996

[HM92] Richard L. Hudson and J. Eliot B. Moss: *Incremental Collection of Mature Objects*, IWMM, 1992

[Hölzle93] Urs Hölzle: *A Fast Write Barrier for Generational Garbage Collectors*, OOPSLA, 1993

[Hopp01] Holger Hopp: *Vorhersage des Cache-Verhaltens für optimierende Übersetzer*, Dissertation, Institut für Programmstrukturen und Datenorganisation, Universität Karlsruhe, 2001

[HP96] J. Hennessy and D. Patterson: *Computer Architecture: A Quantitive Approach*, Morgan Kaufmann Publishers, San Mateo, 1996

[HS00] Timothy H. Heil and James E. Smith: *Concurrent Garbage Collection Using Hardware-Assisted Profiling*, International Symposion on Memory Management (ISMM'00), Minneapolis, 2000

[HW98] Lorenz Huelsbergen and Phil Winterbottom: *Very Concurrent Mark-&-Sweep Garbage Collection without Fine-Grain Synchronization*, ISMM, 1998

[Inmos93] *The T9000 Transputer Instruction Set Manual*, INMOS Transputer book series, INMOS Ltd., SGS-Thomson Microelectronics Group, 1993

[JCons00] J-Consortium: Real Time Core Extension for the Java Platform, Draft International J-Consortium Specification, V1.0.14, September 2, 2000

[JH96] R. Jones and R. Lins: *Garbage Collection – Algorithms for Automatic Dynamic Memory Management,* John Wiley & Sons, 1996

[JNI97] *Java Native Interface Specification*, SUN Microsystems Inc., 1997

[Johnstone97] Mark S. Johnstone. *Non-Compacting Memory Allocation and Real-Time Garbage Collection*, PhD thesis, University of Texas at Austin, December 1997

[Johnstone98] Mark S. Johnstone and Paul R. Wilson. *The memory fragmentation problem: Solved?*, International Symposium on Memory Management (ISMM), Vancouver, 1998

[KCKS99] Taehyoun Kim, Naehyuck Chang, Namyun Kim and Heonshik Shin: *Scheduling Garbage Collection for Embedded Real-Time Systems*, LCTES, 1999

[Knuth73] Donald E. Knuth: *The Art of Computer Programming,* Volume 1, 1973

[KS00] Jim-Soo Kim and Yarsun Hsu: *Memory System Behavior of Java Programs: Methodology and Analysis,* Proceedings of ACM SIGMETRICS'2000, Performance Evaluation Review, Vol 28, No. 1, June 2000

[LBJR+94] Sung-Soo Lim, Young Hyun Bae, Gyu Tae Jang, Byung-Do Rhee, Sang Lyul Min, Chang Yun Park, Heonshik Shin, Kunsoo Park and Chong Sang Kim: *An Accurate Worst Case Timing Analysis Technique for RISC Processors*, IEEE Proceedings, Real-Time Systems Symposium, 1994

[LH83] Henry Liebermann and Carl Hewitt: *A Real-Time Garbage Collector Based on the Lifetimes of Objects,* Communications of the ACM, Volume 26, 6, June 1983

[Liu00] Jane W. S. Liu: *Real-Time Systems*, Prentice Hall, Upper Saddle River, New Jersey, 2000

[LL73] C.L. Liu and J.W. Layland: *Scheduling algorithms for multiprogramming in a hard-real-time environment.* Journal of the ACM 20(1), 1973, pp. 44-61.

[LY96] Tim Lindholm, Frank Yellin: *The Java Virtual Machine Specification*, Addison-Wesley, 1996

[KR94] Jens Knoop, Oliver Rüthing: *Optimal Code motion: Theory and Practice*, ACM Transaction on Programming Languages and Systems, Vol. 16, No. 4, July 1994, pp 1117-1155

[McCarthy60] John McCarthy: *Recursive Functions of Symbolic Expressions and Their Computation by Machine*, Part I, Communications of the ACM 3,4 (April 1960), pp. 184-195

[Mehlhorn84] Kurt Mehlhorn: *Data Stuctures and Algorithms 1: Sorting and Searching*, Springer Verlag, Berlin, 1984

[Meyer88] Bertrand Meyer: *Object-oriented Software Construction*, Prentice Hall International (UK) Ltd, Hertfordshire, 1988

[Meyer92] Bertrand Meyer: *Eiffel: The Language*, Prentice Hall International (UK) Ltd, Hertforshire, 1992

[Motorola96] *PowerPC Microprocessore Family: The Programming Environments*, Motorola Inc. and International Business Machines Inc., May 1996

[NG95] K. Nilsen and H. Gao: *The Real-Time Behavior of Dynamic Memory Management in C++*, IEEE Real-Time Technologies and Applications Symposium, Chicago, 1995.

[Nilsen94] Kelvin Nilsen: *Reliable Real-Time Garbage Collection of C++*, Computing Systems, Volume 7, no. 4, 1994

[Nilsen96] Kelvin Nilsen: *Java for Real-Time*, Real-Time Systems, 11, 1996, pp. 197-205.

[NR95] K.D. Nilsen and B. Rygg: *Worst-Case Execution Time Analysis on Modern processors*, ACM SIGPLAN Workshop on Languages, Compilers and Tools for Real-Time Systems, San Diego, 1995

[NT93] Scott Nettles and James O'Toole: *Real-Time Replication Garbage Collection*, ACM SIGPLAN Conference on Programming Language Design and Implementation (PLDI), 1993

[Pendr97] Pendragon Software: *Embedded CaffeineMark 3.0*, available at *http://www.pendragon-software/pendragon/cm3/index.html*

[Persson99] Patrik Persson: *Live Memory Analysis for Garbage Collection in Embedded Systems*, LCTES, 1999

[Pirinen98] Pekka P. Pirinen: *Barrier techniques for Incremental Tracing*, International Symposium on Memory Management, 1998

[QBQ89] Christian Queinnec, Barbara Beaudoing and Jean-Pierre Queille: *Mark DURING Sweep rather than Mark THEN Sweep*, PARLE 1989, LNCS 365, Springer Verlag, 1989.

[Ritzau01] Tobias Ritzau: *Hard Real Time Reference Counting without External Fragmentation*, JOSES workshop, ETAPS, Genova, April 2001

[RMR01] Atanas Rountev, Ana Milanova, Barbara G. Ryder: *Points-to Analysis for Java Using Annotated Constraints*, OOPSLA 2001.

[Rounce91] P. A. Rounce: *A Processor with List Structured Memory*, Proceedings Advanced Computer Technology, Reliable Systems and Applications, 5th Annual European Computer Conference, Bologna, May 1991

[RTJEG00] The Real-Time Java Experts Group: *Real Time Specification for Java*, Addison-Wesley, 2000, http://www.rtj .org

[Siebert97] Fridtjof Siebert: *Implementierung eines Eiffel-Compilers für SUN/SPARC*, Diplomarbeit Nr. 1484, Institut für Informatik, Universität Stuttgart, 1997

[Siebert98] Fridtjof Siebert: *Guaranteeing Non-Disruptiveness and Real-Time Deadlines in an Incremental Garbage Collector (corrected version)*, ISMM, 1998, corrected version available at *http://www.fridi.de*

[Siebert99.1] Fridtjof Siebert: *Real-Time Garbage Collection in Multi-Threaded Systems on a Single Microprocessor*, IEEE Real-Time Systesms Symposium (RTSS'99), Phoenix, 1999

[Siebert99.2] Fridtjof Siebert: *Hard Real-Time Garbage Collection in the Jamaica Virtual Machine*, IEEE Real-Time Computing Systems and Applications (RTCSA'99), Hong Kong, 1999

[Siebert00] Fridtjof Siebert: *Eliminating External Fragmentation in a Non-Moving Garbage Collector for Java*, Compilers, Architectures and Synthesis for Embedded Systems (CASES), San Jose, 2000

[Siebert01] Fridtjof Siebert: *Constant-Time Root Scanning for Deterministic Garbage Collection*, International Conference on Compiler Construction (CC'01), Genova, in Lecture Notes in Computer Science, Springer, April 2001

[Sites92] Richard L. Sites: *Alpha APX Architecture*, Digital Technical Journal Vol. 4 No. 4 Special Issue, 1992

[SMcKM99] Darko Stafanovic', Kathryn S. McKinley and J. Eliot B. Moss: *Age-Based Garbage Collection*, OOPSLA 1999

[SKS00] Ran Shaham, Elliot K. Kolodner and Mooly Sagiv: *On the Effectiveness of GC in Java*, International Symposion on Memory Management (ISMM'00), Minneapolis, 2000

[SLC99] James M. Stichnoth, Guei-Yuan Lueh and Michal Cierniak: *Support for Garbage Collection at Every Instruction in a Java Compiler*, ACM SIGPLAN Conference on Programming Language Design and Implementation (PLDI), 1999

[SPEC98] *SPECjvm98 benchmarks suite*, V1.03, Standard Performance Evaluation Corporation, July 30, 1998

[SS91] Ravi Sharma and Mary Lou Soffa: *Parallel Generational Garbage Collection*, OOPSLA, 1991

[Steele75] G. L. Steele: *Multiprocessing compactifying garbage collection*, Communications of the ACM 18, 9 (Sept. 1975), pp. 495-508

[Strou87] Bjarne Stroustrup: *Multiple Inheritance for C++*, Proceedings of the European Unix Users Group Conference, pp. 189-207, Helsinki, May, 1987

[SUN_JDK] *Java Development Kit 1.1.8_09, 1.2-V* and *1.2.2_05*, SUN Microsystems Inc., 1997-2000

[SUN97] *Java Native Interface Specification*, SUN Microsystems Inc., 1997

[SUN99.1] SUN Microsystems Inc.: Java(TM) 2 Platform, Standard Edition, V1.2.2 API Specification, 1999

[SUN99.2] SUN Microsystems Inc.: *The KJava Virtual Machine*, White Paper, 1999

[SW01] Fridtjof Siebert and Andy Walter: *Deterministic Execution of Java's Primitive Bytecode Operations*, Java Virtual Machine Research and Technology Symposium (JVM'01), Monterey, April 2001

[Tarditi00] David Tarditi: *Compact Garbage Collection Tables*, International Symposion on Memory Management (ISMM'00), Minneapolis, 2000

[WdFD+98] Michael Weiss, François de Ferrière, Bertrand Delsart, Christian Fabre, Frederick Hirsch, E. Andrew Johnson, Vanial Joloboff, Fred Roy, Fridtjof Siebert, and Xavier Spengler: *TurboJ, a Bytecode-to-Native Compiler*, Languages, Compilers, and Tools for Embedded Systems (LCTES'98), Montreal, in Lecture Notes in Computer Science 1474, Springer, June 1998

[Wentw90] E. P. Wentworth: *Pitfalls of Conservative Garbage Collection*, Software – Practice & Experience, Vol 20(7), July 1990, pp. 719-727.

[Wilson92] Paul R. Wilson: *Uniprocessor Garbage Collection Techniques*, International Workshop on Memory Management (IWMM), 1992

[Wilson94] Paul R. Wilson: *Uniprocessor Garbage Collection Techniques*, Technical report, University of Texas, January 1994. Expanded version of the [Wilson92]

[WJ93] Paul R. Wilson and Mark S. Johnstone: *Real-Time Non-Copying Garbage Collection*, OOPSLA, 1993

[WJNB95] Paul R. Wilson, Mark S. Johnstone, Michael Neely and David Boles: *Dynamic Storage Allocation: A Survey and*

Critical Review, International Workshop on Memory Management (IWMM), 1995

[WR93] Malcolm Wallace and Colin Runciman: *An incremental garbage collector for embedded real-time systems.* Proceedings of the Chalmers Winter Meeting, pp. 273-288, Tanum Strand, Sweden, 1993

[WW93] Mario Wolczko and Ifor Williams: *An Alternative Architecture for Objects: Lessons from the MUSHROOM project*, OOPSLA, 1993

[Xanalys01] *The Memory Management Reference*, Harlequin and Xanalys software tools, http://www.xanalys.com/software_tools/mm/

[YLPM+99] Byung-Sun Yang, Junpyo Lee, Jinpyo Park, Soo-Mook Moon, Kemal Ebcioğlu, Erik Altmann: *Lightweight Monitor for Java VM*, ACM Computer Architecture News, Vol 27-1, March 1999

[ZCC97] Olivier Zendra, Dominique Colnet and Suzanne Collin: *Efficient Dynamic Dispatch without Virtual Function Tables*, OOPSLA, 1997

J'ai toujours aimé le désert.
On s'asseoit sur une dune de sable.
On ne voit rien. On n'entend rien.
Et cependant quelque chose rayonne en silence...
– Antoine de Saint-Exupéry

Appendix A: Tables

Chapter 5

Figure 5.8:

Runtime performance for SPECjvm98 benchmarks with and without code for *synchronization points* (minutes:seconds):

Benchmark	**Synchronization Point Frequency**			
	10	**100**	**1000**	**Off**
_201_compress	1:51.8	1:36.3	1:34.1	1:31.6
_202_jess	1:04.0	0:58.4	0:58.0	0:53.0
_209_db	1:32.5	1:22.6	1:21.6	1:23.4
_213_javac	-	1:42.9	1:43.3	1:37.7
_222_mpegaudio	2:05.4	1:53.9	1:49.5	1:44.6
_227_mtrt	1:19.0	0:59.6	0:56.4	0:54.2
_228_jack	0:39.2	0:33.6	0:34.0	0:31.1

Figure 5.9:

File size of executable binary files for SPECjvm98 benchmarks with and without code for *synchronization points* (bytes):

Benchmark	Synchronization Point Frequency			
	10	100	1000	Off
_201_compress	1002952	830440	815752	751496
_202_jess	2127288	1736448	1699968	1580856
_209_db	1144900	940036	923620	852004
_213_javac	-	2752332	2686796	2495340
_222_mpegaudio	1457484	1194188	1170828	1071532
_227_mtrt	1306236	1038076	1008348	926172
_228_jack	1686144	1429856	1402816	1315712

Chapter 6

Figure 6.1:

Number of references saved in root arrays using *late saving*, *early saving* or *mixed* strategies:

Benchmark	Strategy		
	Late Saving	Early Saving	Mixed
_201_compress	398450158	363930826	185934117
_202_jess	267855161	202883345	117570454
_209_db	153055647	161086294	43224532
_213_javac	(*)	210231403	152815067
_222_mpegaudio	184301683	155815253	125232072
_227_mtrt	230442346	108717567	67846163
_228_jack	192074902	101998955	76074333

Figure 6.2:

Runtime performance of the SPECjvm98 benchmarks using Jamaica with *late saving*, *early saving* or *mixed* strategies and JDK 1.1.8, 1.2 and 1.2.2 (minutes:seconds):

Benchmark	Strategy		
	Late Saving	Early Saving	Mixed
_201_compress	1:39.1	1:32.5	1:28.1
_202_jess	0:58.8	0:53.8	0:50.6

_209_db	1:25.9	1:32.4	1:22.9
_213_javac	(*)	1:47.1	1:44.4
_222_mpegaudio	1:49.6	1:47.4	1:44.7
_227_mtrt	1:07.6	0:58.4	0:56.5
_228_jack	0:48.9	0:36.8	0:33.2

Benchmark	**JDK**		
	1.1.8	**1.2**	**1.2.2**
_201_compress	1:13.5	1:21.9	0:48.6
_202_jess	1:01.6	0:55.5	0:22.2
_209_db	2:56.6	2:11.8	1:08.0
_213_javac	1:49.3	1:26.8	0:40.4
_222_mpegaudio	0:58.3	1:16.6	0:38.3
_227_mtrt	0:59.0	0:56.6	0:18.0
_228_jack	1:05.1	0:57.7	0:22.5

Figure 6.3:

File size of executable binary file for application using *late saving*, *early saving* or *mixed* strategies when compiled for SPRAC/Solaris (in bytes):

Benchmark	**Strategy**		
	Late Saving	**Early Saving**	**Mixed**
_201_compress	1171220	822868	828020
_202_jess	2941908	1751220	1755476
_209_db	1496712	946536	952680
_213_javac	(*)	2694580	2699764
_222_mpegaudio	1628476	1192220	1205116
_227_mtrt	1667072	1034048	1038592
_228_jack	2665608	1408624	1432168

Chapter 7

Figure 7.4:

Runtime performance of the SPECjvm98 benchmarks using different block sizes (minutes:seconds):

	_201_compr.	**_202_jess**	**_209_db**	**_213_javac**
16	1:50.4	1:01.9	1:49.5	1:33.3
20	2:20.8	2:15.8	3:09.5	2:29.2
24	2:18.0	1:43.9	2:26.0	2:20.1

28	2:13.9	1:21.7	1:31.1	1:14.8
32	1:35.3	0:53.0	1:31.1	1:14.8
36	2:08.4	1:49.1	2:27.1	2:03.1
40	2:04.6	1:50.7	2:28.5	2:03.7
44	2:08.1	1:51.1	2:14.0	2:04.6
48	2:03.3	1:47.9	2:17.5	2:04.9
56	2:04.8	1:52.4	2:35.1	2:09.2
64	1:30.8	0:53.6	1:35.5	1:15.8
72	1:59.1	1:46.8	2:29.2	2:08.7
80	1:55.7	1:48.2	2:28.1	2:17.2
88	1:59.5	1:55.0	2:45.7	2:28.7
96	1:56.9	1:58.7	2:59.5	2:33.4
112	2:00.1	2:06.1	3:38.3	2:51.0
128	1:26.3	1:02.9	1:53.2	1:52.9
1.1.8	1:21.1	1:02.6	2:56.5	1:31.9
1.2	1:34.6	1:01.1	2:20.8	1:18.4
1.2.2	0:44.7	0:26.4	1:09.7	0:36.3

	_222_mpeg.	**_202_mtrt**	**_209_jack**
16	1:48.8	1:09.5	0:43.9
20	2:12.2	1:28.5	1:04.0
24	2:13.3	1:26.3	1:01.8
28	2:14.0	1:23.3	0:59.1
32	1:53.2	0:56.6	0:37.1
36	2:13.6	1:26.1	0:56.9
40	2:13.1	1:27.1	0:57.9
44	2:12.5	1:31.6	0:57.3
48	2:13.9	1:31.6	0:55.5
56	2:15.5	1:39.2	0:57.1
64	1:50.0	1:04.0	0:36.5
72	2:11.6	1:51.3	0:56.1
80	2:11.0	2:07.0	0:56.5
88	2:11.2	2:18.5	0:57.3
96	2:11.4	2:38.9	0:58.5
112	2:12.2	3:30.7	0:58.4
128	1:54.7	2:40.8	0:39.0
1.1.8	0:59.5	0:57.9	1:06.0
1.2	1:18.5	0:57.5	1:00.9
1.2.2	0:44.2	0:23.3	0:21.5

Figure 7.5:

Minumum heap required for different block sizes (bytes):

	_201_compr.	**_202_jess**	**_209_db**	**_213_javac**
16	39542225	3886206	16650818	19837932
20	47438487	4031236	18142297	22536480
24	54834473	4128155	19251230	22947359
28	62239674	4123709	22110189	23698536
32	30740044	3459648	15472068	18106875
36	34064784	3661647	16606810	29313695
40	37500395	3864441	17280070	21643030
44	40717835	4094175	18702263	23286781
48	44317260	4218582	19962134	36948010
56	50989260	4736411	23313775	42568563
64	27763120	4246550	18464460	39993870
72	30882537	4639521	19134316	35708449
80	34074513	5030581	21149596	48801224
88	37303075	5461959	22851805	53505799
96	40380841	5890982	24997688	57849538
112	47040458	6708252	28813004	66870408
128	26814984	6628504	28757608	70052648
1.1.8	33554432	1484784	12058624	19922944
1.2	35651584	1689256	12582912	24117248
1.2.2	23068672	2457862	12058624	12058624

	_222_mpeg.	**_202_mtrt**	**_209_jack**
16	7210793	15409645	2335217
20	8320813	13004241	2368852
24	9359735	14669372	2291462
28	10533611	15139628	2364604
32	5765226	14932497	2100823
36	6317623	15946384	2193197
40	6828225	17418264	2272320
44	7370009	18630669	2381307
48	7928272	20106638	2524451
56	9031494	22940372	2792335
64	5560310	25058530	2578940
72	6144034	27882353	2807923
80	6729873	30732066	3033469
88	7326639	33592760	3268402

96	7925953	36573549	3512918
112	9100164	42418557	3970866
128	6211664	47468352	4167040
1.1.8	4587520	12582912	1572864
1.2	5505024	12582912	2159616
1.2.2	5376000	8388608	2424832

Figure 7.6:

Amount of memory allocated for contiguous array, tree arrays and objects for different block sizes (MBytes):

_201_compress

blocksize	tree arrays	contig. arrays	objects
16	21.16	130.42	0.026
20	14.62	127.49	0.028
24	10.79	125.64	0.022
28	10.30	122.34	0.025
32	16.67	113.26	0.027
36	19.37	108.54	0.030
40	15.77	110.57	0.034
44	11.70	113.37	0.036
48	12.55	111.49	0.039
56	9.51	112.94	0.046
64	7.32	113.97	0.052
72	13.02	107.37	0.057
80	5.12	114.58	0.061
88	4.91	114.22	0.068
96	8.70	109.95	0.074
112	12.87	105.06	0.086
128	10.58	106.82	0.098

_201_jess

blocksize	tree arrays	contig. arrays	objects
16	0.088	172.14	179.01
20	0.007	179.56	185.98
24	0.014	182.82	223.01
28	0.244	178.39	175.50
32	0.000	153.38	200.56
36	0.000	157.57	225.63

40	0.001	173.08	250.70
44	0.002	184.69	275.77
48	0.000	196.22	242.64
56	0.004	194.95	283.08
64	0.000	173.37	323.52
72	0.000	180.93	363.96
80	0.000	200.81	404.40
88	0.000	220.37	444.84
96	0.001	240.04	485.27
112	0.004	279.64	566.15
128	0.003	319.47	647.03

_201_db

blocksize	**tree arrays**	**contig. arrays**	**objects**
16	1.05	234.54	47.00
20	0.67	184.93	58.75
24	0.96	184.93	70.07
28	0.068	205.99	81.75
32	0.402	226.78	93.43
36	0.328	248.40	105.11
40	0.058	154.85	116.79
44	0.064	170.33	128.47
48	0.763	180.47	140.15
56	0.188	202.05	163.50
64	0.436	223.52	186.86
72	0.309	245.61	210.22
80	0.369	267.62	233.58
88	0.061	289.97	256.93
96	0.366	311.78	280.29
112	0.546	355.97	327.01
128	1.386	399.51	373.72

_201_javac

blocksize	**tree arrays**	**contig. arrays**	**objects**
16	18.488	93.876	91.564
20	15.046	95.066	106.268
24	11.572	101.313	105.495
28	10.629	105.293	98.954
32	11.923	95.303	112.019
36	10.097	103.913	119.780

40	13.795	106.938	130.746
44	14.110	111.390	140.023
48	11.053	111.300	152.810
56	14.488	117.304	177.973
64	12.596	113.762	201.860
72	10.702	126.469	226.861
80	10.835	136.727	252.518
88	12.038	146.795	277.517
96	13.689	145.467	302.513
112	14.511	165.810	353.113
128	8.703	184.283	403.448

_201_mpegaudio

blocksize	**tree arrays**	**contig. arrays**	**objects**
16	0	4.318	0.0295
20	0	4.049	0.0360
24	0	3.888	0.0338
28	0	3.779	0.0387
32	0	3.709	0.0437
36	0	3.656	0.0490
40	0	3.617	0.0545
44	0	3.567	0.0599
48	0	3.539	0.0650
56	0	3.500	0.0745
64	0	3.474	0.0851
72	0	3.446	0.0957
80	0	3.432	0.1063
88	0	3.401	0.1164
96	0	3.393	0.1270
112	0	3.379	0.1480
128	0	3.374	0.1692

_201_mtrt

blocksize	**tree arrays**	**contig. arrays**	**objects**
16	0.264	55.790	160.217
20	6.638	58.872	107.302
24	0.044	46.798	127.514
28	0.134	51.979	142.246
32	0.0278	55.222	161.610
36	0.0184	57.329	181.811

40	0.0306	63.606	202.012
44	0.0003	66.130	222.213
48	0.0000	71.947	242.413
56	0.0000	83.817	282.666
64	0.0000	90.015	323.047
72	0.0089	101.161	363.428
80	0.0254	112.322	403.809
88	0.0363	123.488	444.190
96	0.0346	134.662	484.571
112	0.0385	156.995	565.332
128	0.0000	177.320	646.094

_201_jack

blocksize	tree arrays	contig. arrays	objects
16	0.008	86.829	28.601
20	0.108	88.340	33.071
24	0.282	96.729	27.904
28	0.118	96.051	32.024
32	0.057	85.921	32.802
36	0.000	93.577	36.432
40	1.067	99.570	40.479
44	0.022	107.184	44.527
48	0.198	109.331	48.574
56	0.196	115.855	56.670
64	0.101	109.209	64.763
72	0.000	120.485	72.859
80	0.000	135.554	80.954
88	0.000	141.315	89.049
96	0.004	145.684	97.145
112	0.140	166.336	113.336
128	0.265	187.478	129.526

Figures 7.7 and 7.8:

Total and average number of memory accesses performed for array elements and object fields using different block sizes:

_201_compress

blocksize	arrays total (10^9)	average	objects total (10^9)	average
16	1.777	2.448	3.893	2.195
20	1.733	2.388	3.141	1.771
24	1.625	2.239	2.810	1.584
28	1.725	2.377	2.580	1.454
32	1.647	2.269	2.500	1.409
36	1.684	2.320	2.298	1.295
40	1.644	2.265	2.204	1.242
44	1.651	2.275	2.104	1.186
48	1.576	2.172	2.093	1.180
56	1.569	2.162	2.035	1.147
64	1.524	2.100	1.938	1.093
72	1.542	2.125	1.898	1.070
80	1.181	2.041	1.774	1.000
88	1.496	2.057	1.774	1.000
96	1.515	2.087	1.774	1.000
112	1.573	2.167	1.774	1.000
128	1.503	2.071	1.774	1.000

_201_jess

blocksize	arrays total (10^6)	average	objects total (10^6)	average
16	195.47	2.0001	532.900	1.831
20	194.198	2.000	466.141	1.616
24	194.887	2.007	384.407	1.332
28	195.318	2.012	353.591	1.226
32	194.198	2.000	328.314	1.138
36	194.198	2.000	313.293	1.086
40	194.198	2.000	306.265	1.062
44	194.198	2.000	302.360	1.048
48	194.198	2.000	301.651	1.046
56	194.199	2.000	292.485	1.014
64	194.198	2.000	292.474	1.014

72	194.198	2.000	292.391	1.013
80	194.198	2.000	288.506	1.000
88	194.199	2.000	288.506	1.000
96	194.213	2.0002	288.506	1.000
112	194.223	2.0003	288.506	1.000
128	194.204	2.000	288.506	1.000

_201_db

blocksize	**arrays** **total (10^6)**	**average**	**objects** **total (10^6)**	**average**
16	1147	2.797	343.730	1.4437
20	1002	2.443	298.149	1.2523
24	989.3	2.412	280.960	1.1801
28	973.2	2.373	276.441	1.1611
32	940.1	2.292	263.565	1.1070
36	896.0	2.185	259.160	1.0885
40	844.2	2.059	250.842	1.0536
44	844.5	2.059	250.842	1.0536
48	855.7	2.087	250.842	1.0536
56	844.4	2.059	246.398	1.0349
64	831.4	2.027	246.398	1.0349
72	823.1	2.007	246.397	1.0349
80	834.4	2.035	238.080	1.0000
88	822.8	2.006	238.080	1.0000
96	834.5	2.035	238.080	1.0000
112	839.0	2.046	238.080	1.0000
128	844.5	2.059	238.080	1.0000

_201_javac

blocksize	**arrays** **total (10^6)**	**average**	**objects** **total (10^6)**	**average**
16	379.693	2.918	700.432	2.063
20	349.002	2.682	578.667	1.706
24	336.612	2.587	496.567	1.464
28	329.796	2.536	476.157	1.402
32	312.245	2.402	418.566	1.233
36	304.969	2.345	409.579	1.206
40	309.067	2.375	406.994	1.200
44	312.490	2.402	391.274	1.153
48	303.362	2.333	389.983	1.149

56	312.646	2.403	358.288	1.055
64	297.659	2.287	357.057	1.052
72	293.429	2.256	356.240	1.049
80	291.837	2.245	347.739	1.023
88	290.717	2.237	340.497	1.002
96	293.786	2.260	339.692	1.001
112	295.046	2.269	339.782	1.000
128	280.040	2.154	339.600	1.000

_201_mpegaudio

blocksize	**arrays**		**objects**	
	total (10^6)	**average**	**total (10^6)**	**average**
16	2351	2	974.930	1.7194
20	2351	2	805.400	1.432
24	2351	2	749.141	1.321
28	2351	2	708.180	1.259
32	2351	2	696.572	1.228
36	2351	2	642.050	1.141
40	2351	2	640.177	1.131
44	2351	2	628.149	1.117
48	2351	2	625.745	1.109
56	2351	2	608.032	1.079
64	2351	2	584.227	1.038
72	2351	2	578.085	1.029
80	2351	2	572.963	1.021
88	2351	2	571.263	1.019
96	2351	2	569.576	1.017
112	2351	2	566.202	1.013
128	2351	2	562.828	1.009

_201_mtrt

blocksize	**arrays**		**objects**	
	total (10^6)	**average**	**total (10^6)**	**average**
16	179.680	2.0012	418.385	1.3113
20	181.060	2.0166	353.037	1.1084
24	179.574	2.0001	341.599	1.0727
28	179.569	2.0000	335.500	1.0536
32	179.570	2.0001	329.601	1.0348
36	179.574	2.0000	329.332	1.0339
40	179.575	2.0000	326.100	1.0238

44	179.571	2.0000	324.091	1.0174
48	179.571	2.0000	322.874	1.0136
56	179.571	2.0000	318.937	1.0013
64	179.571	2.0000	318.937	1.0013
72	179.572	2.0000	318.937	1.0013
80	179.574	2.0000	318.517	1.0000
88	179.574	2.0000	318.517	1.0000
96	179.574	2.0000	318.517	1.0000
112	179.575	2.0000	318.517	1.0000
128	179.571	2.0000	318.517	1.0000

_201_jack

blocksize	**arrays** total (10^6)	**average**	**objects** total (10^6)	**average**
16	77.229	2.0004	259.103	2.099
20	77.225	2.0003	215.398	1.744
24	77.236	2.0006	185.591	1.504
28	77.219	2.0001	168.782	1.366
32	77.525	2.008	148.330	1.200
36	77.215	2.000	143.217	1.159
40	77.868	2.017	142.219	1.151
44	77.219	2.0001	138.740	1.123
48	77.222	2.0002	137.649	1.114
56	77.223	2.0002	127.102	1.029
64	77.215	2.000	125.609	1.016
72	77.215	2.000	125.609	1.016
80	77.215	2.000	123.574	1.000
88	77.215	2.000	123.574	1.000
96	77.215	2.000	123.574	1.000
112	77.217	2.000	123.574	1.000
128	77.217	2.000	123.574	1.000

Figure 6.9:

Binary file size (bytes) for compiled benchmarks using different block sizes and arbitrarily lage blocks (∞):

	_201_compr.	**_202_jess**	**_209_db**	**_213_javac**
16	746708	1689076	853516	2705084
20	766404	1754100	878516	2809876
24	765684	1746692	875580	2790692

28	763116	1742532	874084	2760396
32	737444	1662372	842876	2626268
36	762860	1738268	872692	2748060
40	762508	1734660	871692	2746524
44	762428	1734324	872460	2747692
48	762084	1733212	871356	2747676
56	762100	1733956	871020	2742132
64	729964	1643044	834428	2595156
72	757636	1724068	866156	2727108
80	757300	1723684	866044	2726028
88	757556	1723932	866292	2724412
96	757220	1723596	865956	2723700
112	757212	1723556	865948	2723412
128	733244	1650108	837212	2600228
∞	673988	1504708	767348	2381572

	_222_mpeg.	**_202_mtrt**	**_209_jack**
16	1133312	944884	1414616
20	1168448	972660	1442040
24	1165440	970620	1418168
28	1139872	965372	1398872
32	1120320	931964	1354104
36	1161184	965780	1405880
40	1160768	965308	1391736
44	1160352	965100	1405208
48	1159840	964516	1391128
56	1166080	963948	1402360
64	1101344	923092	1322104
72	1145888	959540	1375032
80	1145472	959332	1374840
88	1145440	959596	1375096
96	1145120	959260	1374776
112	1157376	959252	1389720
128	1108832	927548	1331032
∞	965280	853308	1193624

Chapter 9

Figure 9.7:

Runtime performance of SPECjvm98 benchmarks using different heap sizes and running GC in dynamic and static mode (minutes:seconds):

k	_201_compress		_202_jess	
	dynamic	static	dynamic	static
0.289	1:30.9	1:32.7	0:59.2	1:00.0
0.346	1:35.1	1:36.2	1:01.3	1:06.6
0.396	1:32.2	1:32.4	1:03.1	1:06.9
0.439	1:39.2	1:37.4	1:04.6	1:06.7
0.477	1:37.3	1:32.5	1:06.4	1:06.6
0.540	1:33.9	1:37.1	1:08.7	1:12.4
0.589	1:40.2	1:38.5	1:11.7	1:12.4
0.630	1:37.2	1:34.7	1:14.6	1:18.0
0.663	1:36.6	1:38.2	1:17.3	1:18.6
0.691	1:40.8	1:42.2	1:19.6	1:24.0
0.735	1:36.6	1:39.4	1:23.8	1:29.5
0.768	1:35.2	1:45.1	1:27.9	1:35.6
0.793	1:39.2	1:40.6	1:30.7	1:40.2
0.814	1:40.9	1:44.6	1:34.2	1:45.6
0.831	1:45.5	1:54.1	1:38.6	1:52.3
0.857	1:43.2	1:44.5	1:44.1	2:04.5
0.876	1:48.0	1:49.2	1:48.2	2:20.3
0.890	1:50.5	1:51.7	1:52.3	2:31.2
0.925	1:41.4	1:58.6	2:05.4	3:15.9
0.943	1:49.0	2:04.2	2:14.8	4:07.8
0.962	1:49.3	2:22.0	2:25.3	5:40.9
0.971	1:48.5	2:37.5	2:32.5	7:08.4
0.980	1:45.4	3:03.9	2:39.5	10:00.6

k	_209_db		_213_javac	
	dynamic	static	dynamic	static
0.289	1:18.6	1:19.0	1:06.6	1:13.3
0.346	1:19.5	1:22.5	1:06.2	1:15.5
0.396	1:20.3	1:22.4	1:07.9	1:15.6
0.439	1:21.4	1:22.5	1:09.4	1:16.0
0.477	1:22.0	1:22.7	1:10.2	1:15.4
0.540	1:22.9	1:25.8	1:13.1	1:21.7

0.589	1:25.2	1:26.4	1:14.9	1:21.8
0.630	1:25.7	1:29.3	1:16.5	1:25.9
0.663	1:26.7	1:28.8	1:18.0	1:26.2
0.691	1:28.5	1:32.6	1:20.1	1:30.2
0.735	1:30.5	1:35.9	1:23.7	1:36.2
0.768	1:32.9	1:39.5	1:26.2	1:41.1
0.793	1:34.1	1:43.4	1:28.4	1:44.8
0.814	1:35.9	1:46.6	1:30.8	1:49.0
0.831	1:36.3	1:49.7	1:32.3	1:54.8
0.857	1:39.5	1:57.5	1:36.3	2:03.0
0.876	1:41.2	2:07.1	1:39.6	2:18.2
0.890	1:45.1	2:17.2	1:41.4	2:25.9
0.925	1:48.0	2:42.4	1:47.3	3:01.7
0.943	1:50.7	3:12.7	1:54.2	3:40.8
0.962	1:55.3	4:09.3	2:02.0	4:57.0
0.971	1:57.3	5:05.1	2:04.4	6:06.5
0.980	1:58.7	6:49.5	2:11.4	8:21.7

k	**_222_mpegaudio**		**_228_jack**	
	dynamic	**static**	**dynamic**	**static**
0.289	1:51.9	1:52.0	0:37.2	0:37.4
0.346	1:51.9	1:52.1	0:38.3	0:39.5
0.396	1:52.4	1:52.3	0:38.1	0:38.8
0.439	1:52.0	1:52.2	0:39.2	0:39.5
0.477	1:52.3	1:52.4	0:39.4	0:39.3
0.540	1:52.9	1:53.1	0:39.3	0:40.5
0.589	1:53.3	1:53.4	0:40.3	0:40.7
0.630	1:54.0	1:54.1	0:42.2	0:43.2
0.663	1:54.4	1:54.6	0:43.0	0:43.7
0.691	1:51.9	1:52.4	0:43.0	0:44.4
0.735	1:51.9	1:52.1	0:43.6	0:46.0
0.768	1:58.3	1:58.7	0:44.8	0:47.8
0.793	1:52.5	1:52.9	0:45.6	0:48.5
0.814	1:56.7	1:57.2	0:46.5	0:50.4
0.831	1:53.0	1:53.4	0:47.0	0:51.9
0.857	1:52.2	1:52.8	0:47.9	0:54.7
0.876	1:53.3	1:53.8	0:49.1	0:59.3
0.890	1:52.3	1:53.0	0:49.6	1:02.5
0.925	1:52.6	1:53.6	0:51.9	1:13.4
0.943	1:51.5	1:52.8	0:53.6	1:26.3
0.962	1:53.1	1:55.1	0:55.8	1:50.3

0.971	1:52.3	1:55.1	0:57.1	2:12.6
0.980	1:52.9	1:56.7	0:59.3	2:56.5

Figure 9.8:

Worst-case garbage collection overhead on an allocation for different heap sizes and running GC in dynamic and static mode (units of GC work):

k	dynamic	static
0.289	6	3
0.346	7	4
0.396	8	4
0.439	9	4
0.477	10	4
0.540	12	5
0.589	14	5
0.630	16	6
0.663	18	6
0.691	20	7
0.735	24	8
0.768	28	9
0.793	32	10
0.814	36	11
0.831	40	12
0.857	48	14
0.876	56	17
0.890	64	19
0.925	96	27
0.943	128	36
0.962	192	53
0.971	256	69
0.980	384	100

Chapter 10

Figure 10.6:

Runtime performance of the SPECjvm98 benchmarks using Jamaica and JDK 1.18, 1.2 and 1.2.2 (minutes:seconds):

Benchmark	**Jamaica**	**JDK**		
		1.1.8	**1.2**	**1.2.2**
_201_compress	1:28.1	1:13.5	1:21.9	0:48.6
_202_jess	0:50.6	1:01.6	0:55.5	0:22.2
_209_db	1:22.9	2:56.6	2:11.8	1:08.0
_213_javac	1:44.4	1:49.3	1:26.8	0:40.4
_222_mpegaudio	1:44.7	0:58.3	1:16.6	0:38.3
_227_mtrt	0:56.5	0:59.0	0:56.6	0:18.0
_228_jack	0:33.2	1:05.1	0:57.7	0:22.5